KINGS
of the
GRAIL

KINGS
of the
GRAIL

Tracing the Historic Journey of the Cup of Christ
from Jerusalem to Modern-Day Spain

MARGARITA TORRES SEVILLA
and JOSÉ MIGUEL ORTEGA DEL RÍO

Translated from the Spanish by Rosie Marteau

THE OVERLOOK PRESS
NEW YORK, NY

This edition first published in hardcover in the United States in 2015 by

The Overlook Press, Peter Mayer Publishers, Inc.
141 Wooster Street
New York, NY 10012
www.overlookpress.com

For bulk and special sales, please contact sales@overlookny.com,
or write us at the above address.

First published in Spain by Reino de Cordelia, 2014

Cataloging-in-Publication Data is available from the Library of Congress

Manufactured in the United States of America
ISBN 978-1-4683-1135-8
2 4 6 8 10 9 7 5 3 1

Contents

Acknowledgements

We would like to express our public gratitude to the Real Colegiata de San Isidoro in León for the kindness and generosity they showed us throughout the research process, as well as to Toño and Juan V., Maurilio, Dionisio, José María and Jesús for their support and trust. Not forgetting, of course, the Ministry of Culture of the Regional Government of Castilla y León which, in celebration of the 1,100th anniversary of the foundation of the Kingdom of León, gave us direct access to study the Chalice of Doña Urraca while its exhibition replica was being made. Our thanks, too, to the directors of the Monte León Foundation, for having faith in this enterprise and for taking a chance on it. We also wish to express our recognition for the work of Dr Gustavo Turienzo for his translations of the two Arabic parchments used in the book, as well as the other Arabists who helped us along the way. And our families, because without them none of these pages would ever have seen the light. To all of the above, our heartfelt thanks.

Introduction

The Holy Grail, the cup that Jesus Christ used at the Last Supper, has been the subject of intense fascination for nearly two thousand years. Knights, scientists, Templars, fortune seekers and Nazis are among those who have fervently tried to discover its location. Over time, the cup's very existence has been shrouded in mystery, inspiring legends such as those of King Arthur and the Round Table, as well as many volumes of poetry, medieval romance and scholarly research.

Kings of the Grail is not just another book in a succession of thousands. We expect this to be the definitive account and have done since the day when, by chance (if such a thing exists), the medieval Arabist Gustavo Turienzo Veiga led us to certain parchments stored in Cairo. Previously unpublished information from these documents revealed the Grail's whereabouts up until the mid-eleventh century, when it was relocated to Spain. This fortunate and unexpected discovery took place against the backdrop of the popular revolutions in North Africa known internationally as the Arab Spring.

As we began our research, the uprisings reached Egypt. On Tuesday 25 January 2011, known as the 'Day of Rage', President Hosni Mubarak was forced to resign after nearly three decades in power. As these dizzying events unfolded around us, we launched a forensic programme of research in order to demonstrate how Christ's Chalice might have reached Spain. Our aim was to present only that objective information which would support such an extraordinary discovery.

The story begins in Cairo, in the library of Al-Azhar University.

Founded in 975 CE by the Fatimid Dynasty, it was subsequently turned into the centre of Sunni education (specializing in linguistics, law, astronomy and Islamic philosophy) by Saladin, the first Sultan of Egypt and Syria. Under the Mamluk Sultanate (1250–1517), the university became the great pillar of Islamic learning that it remains today.

Muslims from southern Spain and Islamic scholars from every corner of the world flocked to Al-Azhar's doors. During the closing centuries of the Middle Ages, a vast influx of intellectuals catapulted the university to international fame. It retained its reputation for Islamic scholarship and scientific knowledge throughout the Ottoman period and up to the present day. Its library still houses ancient manuscripts with facts that completely alter our understanding of the history of the Holy Grail.

Without wishing to spoil our compelling story, we will only venture to reveal that at some point between 1054 and 1055 the Grail, which had previously been guarded in the Church of the Holy Sepulchre in Jerusalem, was given in friendship and gratitude by the Fatimid Caliph to the Emir of Dénia (a Muslim kingdom in medieval Spain, covering a region of the Valencian mainland, coast and the Balearic Islands), who in turn wished to ingratiate himself with the powerful Christian monarch, Ferdinand I of Spain (1037–67).

Prince of Navarre, and later Count of Castile and León, Ferdinand I went on to govern his kingdom with a firm hand in turbulent times. Two deaths preceded his ascent to the throne: that of his brother-in-law, Bermudo III of Léon, in 1029, and his own brother García, the King of Navarre, who died after their armies crossed swords at the battle of Atapuerca.[1]

The Grail's arrival in Spain marked a new chapter in its history, just as a thousand years later it would change our own lives as experts in Art and Medieval History. Why did destiny bring Egypt and Spain together like this, for a second time? Perhaps everything conspired towards this turn of fate.

Within these pages we will be looking in detail at the land of Jesus, the Judaic religion of his time, what truly took place at the Last Supper, and how the holy relic never left its chapel at the Church of the Holy Sepulchre until it was taken to the Iberian Peninsula (modern Spain, Portugal, Andorra and Gibraltar) in the middle of the eleventh century. Little by little, we decode the revelations of those Egyptian manuscripts and show how historical and archaeological sources support a definitive reading. The 'other grails' do not escape our scrutiny: the reasons behind their being identified as the Cup of Christ will be disproved, if not in some cases their antiquity or prestige, for instance the Valencia Chalice, which has traditional and legendary associations with Saint Peter and the Papacy.

This is a thorough investigation in which we do not claim to convince, dispute, or court confrontation. Do not expect a book on religion or the occult, nor a work of fiction derived from the literary myths of the Grail. Our aim is to present definitive new data arising from scientific and historical research, while encouraging readers to reach their own conclusions.

Here, then, begins the discovery of the Holy Grail, the first step in a journey of two millennia. Let us begin at the beginning.

PART ONE:
A THOUSAND-YEAR
JOURNEY

Jesus Christ, the Last Supper and Passover

The story of the Holy Grail begins in the Levant and in particular in the Middle Eastern kingdom of Judea. Archaeological evidence gives us a reasonably accurate picture of this society at the time of Jesus. It suggests that there was a strong Hellenistic (mid-ancient Greek) influence among the elite, although this did not trickle down to the masses. This was particularly true of Galilee, homeland of the Messiah,[2] which retained a predominantly Judaic culture despite contact with Greco-Roman culture in the nearby Decapolis.[3]

The historical evidence gleaned from excavations and particularly from numismatics (the study of currency), suggests that the Galileans were Jewish descendants.[4] In the Hasmonean period, the ruling dynasty of Judea between *c.*140 BCE and *c.*116 BCE in the area now known as the West Bank of Israel, religious markers and close links with Jerusalem and its monarchy can be deduced from abandoned settlements, coins and annual tax records. These show that, economically and politically, Galilee belonged to territories ruled by the Macabees' royal descendants.

Galilean culture from the Herodian dynasty (*c.*37–4 BCE) reveals significant similarities to that of Judea;[5] above all, in Hebraic religious indicators such as not eating pork,[6] the use of limestone pots and pans[7] and ritual swimming pools,[8] and performing secondary burials in ossuaries in loculi tombs (where the remains of the dead are reburied in containers in separate chambers of a tomb).[9] In settlements traditionally thought of as

Gentile (non-Jewish), such as the Decapolis, the absence of such indicators supports the Gospels' report of respectful coexistence between the two religious practices and ways of life in Judea and Galilee.[10] Capernaum, on the northern shore of the Sea of Galilee, is a good example of such a mutually tolerant community.[11]

These details become important when we consider the close association that Jesus had with Capernaum, as described by Matthew,[12] Mark,[13] Luke[14] and John.[15] The city is widely held to have been Jesus' home, from where he began to teach and which figured in key episodes of his life.[16]

Shared Judaic and Galilean religious practices are representative of a model of behaviour also found in Jerusalem, and Judea as a whole. According to the Jewish historian Titus Flavius Josephus (*d.*100 CE), Judaic life at the time was divided into four great schools of religious doctrine and practice: the Pharisees, Sadducees, Essenes and Zealots.[17]

The Pharisees and Sadducees were the two major groups. The Pharisees showed exemplary piety. They commanded extraordinary respect and their most distinguished teachers were given the title 'Rabbi'. The Pharisees' Hasidic roots and their precise interpretation of tradition and law earned them high esteem among the citizens of Judea.

There was a significant connection between this group and the disciples of Jesus. Indeed, Paul declared himself a Pharisee and a son of Pharisees before the Sanhedrin (a small judiciary appointed in every Judaic city), when defending his belief in the resurrection of the dead, a belief rooted in this sect of Judaism.[18]

The Sadducees were more numerous among the aristocratic elite. They did not refrain from ostentatious displays of luxury goods such as jewels and silverware, which reflected their adoption of certain Hellenistic and subsequently Roman social models. As they did not believe in resurrection, the Sadducees were only concerned with earthly wellbeing and, given their preeminent status, regarded themselves as blessed by God. They were devotees of the Pentateuch, or Torah, and favoured written laws over tradition. The Sadducees also questioned, or even flatly disregarded, other biblical texts, which brought them into direct confrontation with the Pharisees. According to the Acts of the Apostles, the fifth book of the New Testament, the primary opponents to the teachings of Jesus and his followers were Sadducees.[19]

Josephus also tells us that the Essenes[20] can be traced from the second century BCE to the first century CE. Clothed in white habits and strictly disciplined in community life and moral rectitude, they practised purity through ritual baths and celibacy and awaited a priestly Messiah from the House of David. Thanks to the discovery of the Dead Sea Scrolls at Qumran, we know about Essenic practices of solitude, sacrifice and prayer. We also know that John the Baptist's preaching in the desert and even his relationship to Christ were both closely linked to this ascetic sect.

The Zealots[21] came into being at the end of Herod the Great's reign, in 4 BCE. Their spokesman Judas of Gamala, also known as Judas of Galilee, together with the Pharisee Zadok founded a sect based on the staunch defence of freedom and the absolute nature of divine sovereignty. Essentially an Israeli nationalist political movement, they could be considered one of history's first terrorist groups and included a radical splinter group known as the Sicarii (named after the little daggers they carried under their cloaks in order to attack Romans and their sympathizers). Their radical anti-Roman stance would prove a spectacular failure that resulted in the mass suicide of Sicarii at Masada, although the heroic record of their three-year resistance can still be found there.[22]

Jesus' lifetime was turbulent, marked by a latent conflict with Rome that would eventually erupt in open rebellion. This, however, is not the place to reiterate the full story of Christ or his preachings, which are already so well known. Of Christ's final moments, which were destined to change the history of the world, we instead need to focus our attention on the Last Supper, Passion and Resurrection. If the first of these was the foundation upon which the central sacrament of the Christian liturgy, the Eucharist, was built, the latter was a pivotal moment for his followers that would lead to the growth of the faith among Jews and Gentiles alike. Ultimately, this led to Christianity becoming the only official religion of the Roman Empire under the Hispanic Emperor Theodosius I, at the end of the fourth century CE.

A full account of the history of Christianity would detract from our central theme; namely, the Holy Chalice, the cup used by Christ on the day that he brought the Apostles together to dine shortly before being arrested, tried and executed. It is therefore essential to examine this event's links with Hebraic rituals from the time of Jesus, because this will yield vital clues as to how and why Jesus' cup originally took on such holy significance.

A host of questions surround the Last Supper: was it a celebration of Passover according to the Judaic liturgy of the time (that is, a dinner for Christ and his intimate acquaintances, whether or not he knew of his coming end, on an important date for Hebrew people that commemorates the liberation of the people of Israel from Egyptian rule)? Why do the Gospels differ slightly on the timing of the Last Supper? Are they reliable? Was Saint Paul, the only apostle who was absent from the feast, really so central to the Christian conception of the Eucharist? Does the Eucharist hold traces of the influence of Mithraic mysteries? These questions and many others have occupied researchers for centuries, and even today remain controversial.

The First Obstacle: The Date of the Last Supper

Whether or not the Last Supper was a Passover ritual depends on the date it was held. As a Jew, and even more so as a Rabbi, Jesus would have known the Passover ceremony well. A key celebration in the Hebraic calendar, according to Exodus 12[23] and Deuteronomy 16,[24] it symbolized God's restoration of freedom to his people, who had been oppressed by slavery in the land of the pharaohs. The covenant was so meaningful that it had to be remembered every year.

We know of three times that Passover was celebrated during Jesus' public life, as told in the Gospel of John. The first took place when the money-changers were expelled from the Temple of Jerusalem;[25] the second addressed the theme of bread;[26] and the third came after the Messiah's triumphant welcome, which coincides with the date the lambs were chosen, and sets the paschal (Passover- or Easter-related) context for the Passion (the suffering and death of Jesus).[27]

Problems arise when trying to pinpoint the exact date of the Last Supper, and this question is a key factor in determining the nature of the celebration itself. John states that Christ's banquet took place before Passover. He tells us that after Christ was arrested he was taken from Caiaphas's house and brought before Pilate at his palace and that, as it was early morning, the Jews did not enter 'that they might not be defiled; but might eat the Passover.'[28] Before flogging Jesus, the Roman governor, who was aware of these customs, suggested that as it was traditional to grant a prisoner[29] his freedom on that day, the man they called King of the Jews[30] should be the one released.

John's insistence on this date can be explained by his desire to identify Jesus as the new paschal lamb, since, if the Supper was indeed a farewell meal and the arrest preceded the Hebrew feast, Christ's crucifixion must have taken place on the fourteenth evening of the month of Nisan, at the very moment that the lambs' throats would have been slit. So, according to John, a new sacrificial victim of the covenant between God and man would emerge through the blood of Christ.

In opposition to this, in Mark's version of the Passion, the Last Supper coincides with the Passover celebration itself, so that the Eucharist becomes its substitute.[31] His account of the preceding days bears little resemblance to that of John, although they agree on the basics: two days before Passover, members of the Sanhedrin and the Pharisees plotted to have Jesus put to death on a separate day from the festivities, for fear that the people might rise up. As the conspiracy gained pace in Jerusalem, Jesus was in Bethany, at the house of Simon the Leper.[32] Back in Jerusalem for the first day of the Feast of Unleavened Bread 'when the paschal lamb is sacrificed', the apostles suggested that Christ find a suitable place to celebrate Passover according to Judaic liturgy. During the meal, they blessed the bread and wine and sang hymns, before they ascended the Mount of Olives, where Jesus was arrested.[33] For Mark, then, the meal with the disciples is definitively a Passover meal. We find the same idea in Matthew[34] and Luke.[35] Christ eats with his disciples on the day of the sacrifice of the paschal lamb, the fourteenth of Nisan, and is later crucified. This presupposes that the Last Supper corresponds with the Jewish festival.

John's claim that Jesus was executed on the day of the sacrifice of the paschal lamb makes the banquet more of a farewell meal amongst brothers, with customary Hebrew blessings, than an act of religious remembrance, as it occurs before Passover.[36]

However, most scholars believe that the view of Mark, Matthew and Luke, who regard the Last Supper as a true Passover feast, is the more likely explanation.

The Seder Ritual in Judaic Passover
and the Last Supper

Jews celebrate *Pesach*, or Passover, to commemorate the liberation of the Israelites from slavery in Egypt, as told in the book of Exodus. For seven days it was traditionally forbidden to consume fermented foods and derivatives of leaven, which were substituted by *matzo*, unleavened or unfermented bread.[37] Abstinence from leavened food or yeast is thought to originate in the notion that a leavening agent (such as yeast) spreads through food like sin or corruption, or that it takes food away from a natural state, close to God. It may also represent the bread taken by the Israelites as they fled Egypt, which would not have had time to rise. This memory continues to be expressed in the sacred host, or communion wafer, of the Eucharist. It is worth noting here how readily religious beliefs and events were memorialized in ritual and expressed in material, tangible forms.

At the time of Christ, Jewish liturgy precisely specified the materials that could be used to make Passover cups. Porous materials, such as wood or pottery, were expressly forbidden for the ritual. There is a commonly held belief, largely thanks to Hollywood (*Indiana Jones and the Last Crusade*, in particular), that because Christ was a carpenter's son who preached among the poor, he would surely have blessed the Passover meal with his disciples using a cup made of a humble material. Nothing could be further from the truth. Not only did Jesus Christ's followers include both rich and poor, as we are told in the Gospels and the book of Acts, but a wooden or clay cup would have breached Jewish law and Jesus, lest we forget, *was* a Jew. He would never have committed such a transgression.

The central act of Passover is the meal, the *Seder* itself. The house where this takes place has to be cleansed of any grain that might cause fermentation, so the previous day is spent going through every last corner with a fine-toothed comb. The main dish customarily consists of lamb, which had to meet a series of requirements: once acquired at the marketplace of the Temple of Jerusalem it was handed over to the priests for slaughter and its blood collected in a cup that was passed on until it reached the altar, where it was poured as a sacrifice.

The Passover table is prepared and decorated in accordance with tradition. The ritual begins with the blessing of wine and offerings, and the lighting of candles. Thereafter, the celebration follows a ceremonial formula that was only recorded in the eleventh century, which requires that the participants relive, through this meal, the harsh tests that the people of Israel overcame to gain their freedom.

A series of common elements can be traced back as far as Jesus' time. These appear in Deuteronomy 16 and consist of lamb, bitter herbs, flat bread, wine, ceremonial hand-washing, prayers and blessings. But perhaps the most striking aspect is the use of *sacred cups*, each with a unique meaning and purpose.[38] The four cups symbolize liberation from slavery and God's four promises to the Jews: ' . . . and I will bring you out from under the burdens of the Egyptians, and I will rid you out of their bondage, and I will redeem you with an outstretched arm . . . and I will take you to me for a people . . . ' (Exodus, 6:6–7).[39]

In practice, there aren't four different cups used for each of God's promises at the Passover feast. Instead, over the course of the ceremony each Jew has to drink four times from his own cup, which is given a different name each time. If the cup is emptied, it must be refilled so that the ritual can be completed.

The first cup is the Cup of Sanctification, or *Kiddush*, and it reminds us that we must be holy in the likeness of God. In Hebrew, Yahweh is praised with these words: 'Blessed are you Lord, King of the universe, for this wine, fruit of the vine and the work of man.'[40]

The second cup, *Mishpat*, recalls the ten plagues and the suffering of the Egyptians when they dared to contradict the will of God. It implies that a person should not rejoice in the pain of his or her enemies. A drop of wine is spilled for each of the plagues.

The third cup, *Ha-Geulah*, is characterized by giving thanks for redemption. It evokes the spilling of the lambs' blood that marked the doors of the sons of Israel, to protect them from the avenging angel sent against the Egyptians by God. It is used after dinner.

Finally, the fourth cup, the *Hallel* or Passover Cup, is the most significant of all. *Seder* is complete after the hymns and prayers of thanks for God's kindness towards his people have been offered.

The breaking of the bread, the blessing of the wine, the presence of the paschal lamb and the psalms and prayers all show a clear link between the Hebraic liturgical celebration and the Christian Eucharist. But how was it celebrated in the time of the early followers of Jesus?

The Eucharist among the First Christians

The Eucharist, also known as Holy Communion, is the sharing of bread and wine as a re-enactment of the Last Supper (believed by some Christians, especially Catholics, to be transubstantiated into the actual body and blood of Christ). It is one of the most important Christian sacraments, and echoes older Hebraic Passover customs. The primary Christian apologist of the second century CE, Justin the Martyr (*d.*165), reserved the ritual for the baptized and those who pledged allegiance to the Christian faith. He explained the nature of the Eucharist during the earliest Christian period:

> On the day we call the day of the sun, all who live in the
> city or country gather in the same place.
> The memoirs of the apostles and the writings of the
> prophets are read. When the reader has finished, he who
> presides over those gathered speaks to rouse them and
> urges them to imitate these beautiful things. Then we
> all rise together and offer prayers for ourselves . . . and
> for all others, wherever they may be, so that we may be
> found righteous by our life and actions, and faithful to the
> commandments, in order to reach eternal salvation.
> Then someone brings bread and a cup of water and wine
> mixed together. He who presides takes them and offers
> praise and glory to the Father of the universe, through
> the name of the Son and of the Holy Spirit and for a
> considerable time he gives thanks that we have been
> judged worthy of these gifts. When he has given thanks
> and the people have responded by saying Amen, those we
> call deacons distribute the *eucharisted* bread and wine to
> all present.

Justin specifies that these instructions come from the Apostles
and that the Eucharist is a commandment of Christ, as is clear
in the Gospels when Christ takes the chalice between his hands,
gives thanks and says, 'This is my blood', then passes it to his
disciples.[41]

Many other fathers of the Church similarly address these
aspects, but it is Saint Augustine of Hippo who expounded the
glory of the Eucharist with just a few simple words: Jesus Christ
is at once the host, the food and the drink.[42]

The relationship between Christ and the Eucharist derives
from the Gospels and encapsulates Christian doctrine.[43] The
relationship between the Last Supper and the Jewish Passover
feast is also clear, although there has been controversy over its

interpretation: whether as a ritual pioneered by Jewish converts of the apostles to complete the cycle of the Lamb and Sacrifice, altering the old covenant between God and man, or simply as a final supper presided over by Christ, who knew what was to come and wanted to celebrate with his closest allies.[44]

In his first letter to the Corinthians (2:24–26), Paul recounts the institution of the Eucharist. If we set aside John, for whom the celebration of the banquet does not replace the Passover Seder, there are two parallel groups that draw on the accounts of the witnesses and attendees at the banquet. They are the Matthew–Mark school and the so-called Pauline school (Luke–Paul), which is considered the older. Although Paul was not present, his proximity in time to the event and his direct knowledge via the other apostles support his assertions.

In any case, we have few details about the first Christian celebrations of the Eucharist immediately after the death of Christ. They probably did not diverge far from the direct Hebraic inheritance in blessing the bread and wine, but nor did they forget Jesus' sacrifice and its similarity to that of the paschal lamb. Neither did the Hebraic ritual of Passover change substantially over time, especially among the Christian community of Jerusalem.

The few references we have to the Eucharist appear in the writings of Saint Paul. In his first letter to the Corinthians, he seeks to dissuade his small congregation from celebrating sacred feasts for other gods. He recommends that they eat and drink consecrated bread and wine in order to enter into a union with Christ:

> The cup of blessing which we bless, isn't it a sharing of the blood of Christ? The bread which we break, isn't it a sharing of the body of Christ? (1 Corinthians, 10:16)

> You can't both drink the cup of the Lord and the cup of demons (1 Corinthians, 10:21)

Elsewhere, Saint Paul returns to Passover as an example for doctrine:

> Purge out the old yeast, that you may be a new lump, even as you are unleavened. For indeed Christ, our Passover, has been sacrificed in our place. Therefore let us keep the feast, not with old yeast, neither with the yeast of malice and wickedness, but with the unleavened bread of sincerity and truth. (1 Corinthians, 5: 7–8)[45]

Paul thus outlines the key elements of the Eucharist: the bread, the wine and the act of consecration.

Related to these earliest moments of Christianity is a verse in Luke about a stranger appearing before two disciples on the road from Jerusalem to the town of Emmaus,[46] recognizable as the resurrected Jesus only when he breaks bread with them. Other verses in Acts[47] refer to a ceremony based on a meal in which bread is broken, a Jewish custom symbolizing brotherhood and friendship, which involves a set message of thanksgiving.

The book of Acts (20: 7–11) contains more details that are relevant to the Eucharist. One Sunday, the Christians came together to break bread and Paul began to speak to the assembled group. As the celebration went on for a very long time, a young man fell to the ground, overcome by sleep. After proving that he had not died, the apostle carried on with the ritual meal and the breaking of the bread.

Further examples, such as the *Didache* or *The Teaching of the Twelve Apostles*,[48] a Christian treatise from the second half of the first century or possibly second century CE, and the *Letter to Trajan*, by Pliny the Younger from late first-century Syria, also verify that this shared feast was effectively the first step towards the sacrament that Christians know today as the Eucharist.[49]

In the West, the early manifestation of the Eucharist was more conceptual. Not until Justin the Martyr's *Apology*, where we began this section, were its fundamentals secured as a central act in the Christian liturgy, to be celebrated each Sunday.

The Cup of Christ and its First Resting Place: The Christian Community of Jerusalem
(First to Second Centuries CE)

The early days of Christianity were far from easy for its adherents. Following the events that took place after the Last Supper, it is worth studying the first Christians that lived through those uneasy times and who were the recipients of Jesus' teachings and history. Who were they and what were they like? Throughout the early expansion of the faith, internal problems emerged within a context of constant persecution by the Jewish religious authorities and the might of the Roman legions. On top of all this, they had the martyrdom of their rabbi to contend with: their resolve must have been exemplary.

The First Christian Community

The early Christians did not differ much from other Jews. They fasted on the same dates,[50] practised circumcision,[51] respected the purity laws,[52] visited the temples[53] and observed holidays in the Jewish calendar.[54] What set them apart was their belief in Christ's death and resurrection, as well as their incorporation of new ceremonies such as baptism,[55] the breaking of bread,[56] celebrating on Sunday[57] and the communion of goods.[58]

The core group of early Christians soon came under attack by followers of Judaism. Some of them left the Holy City and travelled in different directions, establishing new Christian communities and transmitting the Christian message. From Jerusalem, Christianity rapidly spread through Samaria, the coastal region of Palestine, Asia Minor, Greece and Rome. In 50 CE, just twenty years after Jesus' death, Christianity had already spread throughout the eastern half of the Roman Empire.

Recollections of Jesus' life were preserved and transmitted by these communities. At the birth of Christianity, memory, the spoken word and its repetition were central. We know that a good proportion of Christians came from a social class unfamiliar with reading and writing as a means of storing, conveying and accessing information. As in all oral cultures, words, and in particular teachings, could only be recorded in memory and re-enacted in speech.[59]

Alongside the oral tradition, a correspondence between lived facts and events and the transmitted message has been considered important since the dawn of Christianity. Paul's words on the Last Supper are widely known and studied: 'For I received from the Lord that which also I delivered to you' (1 Corinthians 11:23).[60] His use of the verbs 'receive' and 'deliver' were chosen in the Judaic tradition of rabbinical schools to refer to a faithful rendition of a concrete fact. From this point, we can clearly observe the early Christians' desire to share a true account of events that took place and the fact that these events – the memories of Jesus as a person – were sacred.

It is significant that the growing communities of early Christians followed a very recent oral tradition and were concerned to remain true to the facts, especially when we consider that these people preserved important physical artefacts from the life of Christ.

Various groups branched out from the first community in Jerusalem and started to spread across the Roman Empire.[61] Three of these demand our particular attention. The first was led by Peter, who set out to to take the teachings of Jesus to the twelve tribes of Israel. The second group included the Seven Hellenistic Missionaries, among which were Stephen, Philip and, most importantly, Paul, who wanted to take Christ's message beyond Judea, to the wider world.

Thirdly, the community of Jerusalem was led by James,[62] known as James the Just or the brother of the Lord,[63] and also included other relatives of Christ. They approached Christianity from a strictly Jewish perspective, with a rigorous adherence to law and tradition; it was basically Judaism, but enhanced by the teachings of Christ.

James's Jerusalem group was loyal to the Jewish Temple but saw Jesus as the Messiah that Judea had been waiting for. This group was not subject to Peter's, instead relying on their own experience:[64] they had seen Jesus, expected his return to Jerusalem and felt themselves to be messengers of a mission that bound them to the holy city where, in accordance with the promise, all nations would have to return. Ultimately, though, Peter's vision of Christianity would prevail over that of James.

Expansion beyond the borders of Judea was, above all, the work of the Hellenists, with Paul as their main representative. They did not depend on the Temple or the Law of Moses as strictly as the Hebrew group[65] of James the Just. Most of the Christians led by Peter initially considered themselves closer to the Hebrews than the Hellenists.[66]

Under James's mandate, the community of Jerusalem operated as an autonomous group, albeit one that maintained communion with Peter and even Paul, without separating or forming a sect. Their organization and much of their theology was similar to that of other prophetic or apocalyptic Jewish groups that announced the arrival of God in Jerusalem. But they added a distinguishing factor: the belief that God would come through Jesus, the crucified Messiah, in a blaze of universal glory, to confirm the hope of the Jews and then receive all of the Gentiles. Their location in Jerusalem enabled them to be the first organized community, a congregation of 'the poor',[67] with a bishop (James) at its head and a cohesive group of the faithful at his side. In this, they emulated the organization of other Jewish communities, such as that at Qumran.

The Expansion of Christianity and the Emergence of Tensions

The spread of Christianity beyond the borders of the chosen people started when Peter, who gradually came to believe that Jesus' message should be for all people, not just the Jews, admitted the Roman Centurion Cornelius into the new faith:[68] 'When they heard these things, they held their peace, and glorified God, saying, "Then God has also granted to the Gentiles repentance to life!"' (Acts, 11:18). Thereafter, the first mixed communities to welcome uncircumcised Gentiles were established, such as the one at Antioch in Roman Syria. The community of Jerusalem did not approve of these developments, and 'They sent Barnabas [one of their earliest members] to go as far as Antioch, who, when he had come, and had seen the grace of God, was glad. He exhorted them all, that with purpose of heart they should remain near to the Lord.' (Acts, 11:22–23).[69]

Together, Barnabas, Paul and John Mark (Mark the Evangelist) made the first Christian mission, across the Greco-Roman world.[70] This highly effective journey resulted in the establishment of Christianity in Cyprus, Antioch in Pisidia, Iconium, Lycaonia, Lystra, Derbe and Perga in Pamphylia. On returning to Antioch, the missionaries 'gathered the assembly together, they reported all the things that God had done with them, and that he had opened a door of faith to the nations' (Acts, 14:27).[71] The mixed community of Christians of Antioch rejoiced in the successes achieved, along with their brothers in Phoenicia and Samaria.[72] However, integration of Gentiles into the church without first imposing circumcision and all other prescriptions of the law was eyed with suspicion by many in the Jerusalem group. This escalated, until Paul and Barnabas were obliged to return to the Holy City to address the issue.[73]

The state of affairs in Jerusalem had not improved. In 44 CE King Herod the Great had Saint James the Greater, one of the twelve disciples, assassinated, and arrested Peter, who managed to escape.[74] At this point, the growing thousands of Jewish converts to Christianity in the Holy City were continuing to uphold the Law of Moses.[75]

Around 48 CE, when the Council of Jerusalem was held,[76] the Antioch community was already over ten years old and had admitted many Gentiles without obliging them to observe Jewish law. These Gentiles formed a sub-group with their own identity, so it was in Antioch that the disciples first received the name 'Christians'.[77] The community lived the word of the Gospel, free from Hebraic legal orthodoxy.

The delegates of the Antioch community 'had come to Jerusalem, they were received by the assembly and the apostles and the elders, and they reported all things that God had done with them.' (Acts, 15:4)[78] Although many were delighted to hear the news, others expressed the opposite view. Some converted Pharisees[79] were staunch observers of Judaic law, continuing to circumcise their males: 'The apostles and the elders were gathered together to see about this matter.' (Acts, 15:6).[80] After a long discussion, Peter said to them:

'Brothers, you know that a good while ago God made a choice among you, that by my mouth the nations should hear the word of the Good News, and believe. God, who knows the heart, testified about them, giving them the Holy Spirit, just like he did to us. He made no distinction between us and them, cleansing their hearts by faith. Now therefore why do you tempt God, that you should put a yoke on the neck of the disciples which neither our fathers nor we were able to bear? But we believe that we are saved through the grace of the Lord Jesus Christ, just as they are.'[81]

Peter called on his own experience to justify the actions of the Antioch community. For their part, Barnabas and Paul heralded God's work among the Gentiles: 'All the multitude kept silence, and they listened to Barnabas and Paul reporting what signs and wonders God had done among the nations through them.' (Acts, 15:12).[82]

The last intervention, which brought the debate to a close, was made by James:

'Brothers, listen to me. Simeon has reported how God first visited the nations, to take out of them a people for his name. This agrees with the words of the prophets. As it is written, "After these things I will return. I will again build the tabernacle of David, which has fallen. I will again build its ruins. I will set it up, That the rest of men may seek after the Lord; All the Gentiles who are called by my name, Says the Lord, who does all these things. All his works are known to God from eternity."

'Therefore my judgment is that we don't trouble those from among the Gentiles who turn to God, but that we write to them that they abstain from the pollution of idols, from sexual immorality, from what is strangled, and from blood.'[83]

It was agreed that Judaic law would not be imposed upon Gentile converts, but that they should observe a minimum number of laws.[84] The Council of Jerusalem was the culmination of a process that had begun with the death of Christ. An original cohort of scarcely more than a hundred people[85] had developed into a group of several thousand. From a radical adherence to Judaic law, the community had moved towards a significant relaxation of those precepts and now had a new vision that covered the wider world.

The community of Jerusalem sought to maintain authority over other communities[86] as a source of information and arbitration, and also to preserve the poverty and moral radicalism advocated by James. It was acutely aware of holy and messianic matters, as well as bureaucratic and legal ones. For this community, the authentic interpreter of the gospel was not Peter, but James himself,[87] as the Gospel of Thomas suggests.[88] Later, the writings of Matthew[89] would challenge this idea.

There is no doubt that the nature of the earliest central Christian community is crucial to understanding what became of the Lord's Cup. If it was kept safe, as we will argue in this book, it is more than likely that it would have stayed in the Holy City of Jerusalem, home to the largest and most structured Christian community.[90] Furthermore, preservation of important items was a firmly established Judaic practice; we need only look to the example of the Menorah stored in the Temple. The Cup's intrinsic value was as an object that symbolized one of the fundamental sacraments of the Christian faith: the Eucharist.

Although the community of Jerusalem had already weathered many blows, the death of James came as a traumatic event. In 62 CE, Josephus described his death at the hands of the High Priest Anas ben Anas (Ananias):

Ananias was a heartless Sadducee. Astutely, he chose

a favourable moment to assemble the Sanhedrin. The procurator Festus had died and his successor, Albinus, had not yet taken up the position. He brought James, brother of Jesus, who was called Christ, before the Sanhedrin along with some others to be judged. He accused them of having broken the law and handed them over to be stoned.[91]

Josephus' account is confirmed by Hegesippus, but in his *Ecclesiastical History* Eusebius of Caesarea suggests that before being stoned, Saint James the Just was thrown from a cliff top:

Saint James was called the Just. The people were sure he had never committed a serious sin. He never ate meat, nor took strong drink. He spent so much time praying in the temple that he got callouses on his knees. He would pray for many hours, worshipping God and asking the Lord for forgiveness for the people's sins. The people called him 'he who intercedes for the people'. Many Jews believed in Jesus, moved by James's words and his good example. Because of this, on a day when there was a great crowd, the High Priest Ananus and the leaders of the Jews said to him: 'Since the people feel such great admiration for you, we ask you to present yourself to the crowd and tell them that Jesus is not the Messiah or the Redeemer.' And Saint James stood before the crowd and said: 'Jesus is sent by God for the salvation of all those who wish to be saved. And one day we will see him above the clouds, sat at God's right hand.' On hearing this, the chief priests became furious and said: 'If this man continues to speak, all the Jews will end up as followers of Jesus'. So then they climbed up and threw down the Just man. Then they said to one another, 'Let us stone James the Just' and they began to stone him, for he had not been killed by the fall.

But he, turned and knelt down and said, 'Lord God our
Father, I beg of thee, forgive them, for they know not what
they do.'[92]

The death of James was a major event in its time, and is still
important in the story of the Lord's Cup. The tomb of the 'brother
of the Lord' was erected at the place where he died, beneath the
pinnacle of the Temple outside the city walls, which later became
a site of worship. This place was chosen to be the temporary
home of the Lord's Cup, in circumstances that were particularly
difficult for Jerusalem and its Christian community.

The First Jewish Revolt

A few years after James's death, the situation in Judea worsened.[93]
The powerful Judean monarch, Herod Agrippa I, died in 44
CE, and was succeeded by his seventeen-year-old son Herod
Agrippa II, who was being educated at the court of the Emperor
Claudius. As a result, Judea once again fell under the control of
Roman governors, who so often proved to be inept and corrupt.
The revolt started in 66 CE in Caesarea, the capital of the Roman
province. Like the rest of Judea, the city's population was made
up of a variety of different nationalities and religions. After
winning a legal dispute against the Jews, the Greek community
incited a pogrom in the Jewish quarter and the Roman garrison
failed to intervene. Shortly afterwards, the governor Gessius
Florus confiscated seventeen gold talents from the Jewish Temple
treasury in partial payment of the Roman tax. This enraged
Jewish leaders and led to demonstrations.

To keep the peace, Florus entered Jerusalem with an army,
imposed martial law and ordered the arrest of the rabble-rousers.
Over 3,000 Jews died in the unrest that followed.

Although the governor withdrew to avoid greater disaster in the short term, it became impossible to contain the problem. Later that year a group of Zealots[94] ambushed the Roman garrison at Masada, close to the Dead Sea, and armed themselves with Roman weapons. At the same time, the population of Jerusalem surrounded and laid siege to the Roman soldiers in the towers of Herod's palace. Those soldiers who left unarmed were released, only to be attacked and killed as soon as they left the city limits.

The governor of Syria, Cestius Gallus, assembled an expedition of 30,000 Roman troops to restore order. First he marched on Caesarea, where nearly the entire Jewish community (some 20,000 people) were slaughtered. Then the army moved on towards Jerusalem. Bezetha, the northern part of the city, was set ablaze and the Roman troops reached the Temple walls; however, probably realizing that their position was not sufficiently secure, they withdrew. Their troops were ambushed to the northeast of Jerusalem and a large body of weapons fell into the hands of the rebels. A wider war was now inevitable.

In Rome, the alarm was sounded and Emperor Nero called upon the retired general Titus Flavius Vespasianus, better known as Vespasian. He raised an army of three legions and immediately expanded his troops into Galilee. Moving south and eastwards, he methodically destroyed every town in his path.

Meanwhile, Nero was overthrown and committed suicide. In a short space of time, known as the Year of the Four Emperors, he was succeeded by Galba, Otho and then Vitellius, who was murdered. Thanks to the good reputation Vespasian enjoyed among his troops, he was proclaimed Emperor by the legions of the east. In 69 CE, the Roman Senate confirmed his appointment and he returned to Rome.

Vespasian needed a great victory to secure his position. To this end, he assigned his son Titus to complete the suppression of the Jewish revolt. Although Jerusalem was enclosed, it was not an easy city to take, largely because it was surrounded by deep valleys and fortifications, with the enormous Antonia Fortress as its stronghold. Unable to break the city's defences in a single assault, the army was forced to besiege it, pitching camp on the outskirts. Titus increased the pressure on Jerusalem's diminishing provisions by allowing pilgrims who had come to celebrate Passover into the city, but denying them the right to leave when they were ready.

Under siege, the city was pushed to terrible extremes. Hunger and disease ravaged the population, while anyone suspected of undermining the resistance was hurled from the city walls without a second thought. The Jewish forces numbered around 25,000 combatants, divided into three large groups: the Zealots, who occupied Antonia Fortress, to the north of Temple Mount, and the Temple; the Sicarii, the most radical faction of the Zealots, who controlled the high city; and the Edomites and other parts of the original population.

Titus chose the place to breach the city walls carefully. He positioned the Fifth Legion to the west, on a hillock that overlooked the city. He then turned his attention to Antonia Fortress, but mounting losses inflicted on the Romans by the Zealots temporarily forced them to draw back.

To prevent the besieged from getting help, Titus ordered a wall to be built half a mile from the city. Anyone caught trying to escape or found in no-man's-land would be crucified at the wall. The historian Josephus was involved in several attempts at negotiation with the Romans within the city walls. His account could scarcely be more chilling:

> Seized with bitterness and rage, the soldiers nailed up
> their victims in various positions like a grotesque tableau,
> until the sheer quantity meant there was no more room for
> crosses.[95]

After a series of failed attempts, at the end of August 70 CE the Romans launched a secret nocturnal attack and took control of Antonia Fortress, giving them a strategic position from which to conquer the rest of the city. Next they took the Temple, which was razed to the ground over a matter of days. As the flames spread into the residential area of the city, Jewish resistance rapidly collapsed, although some of the defenders escaped through hidden tunnels. Final resistance in the high part of the city briefly held back Roman troops, but the effort was in vain. By 7 September, Jerusalem was completely under Titus's control.

Josephus tells us that, of the great towers of Herod's palace on the west side of Jerusalem, the Romans left only three standing. The Tenth Legion camped out in the city. Over the course of the rebellion, which had lasted four years,[96] the Romans took approximately 100,000 prisoners. They forced thousands to become gladiators, while others were taken as slave labour to Seleucia (the port town of Antioch), where they were forced to dig a tunnel. The majority were transferred to Rome to work on the Coliseum and the Imperial Temple of Peace.

What was life like for the followers of Jesus, during these four bitterly hard years? Christians saw this period as the fulfilment of one of Christ's prophecies:

> 'But when you see Jerusalem surrounded by armies, then know that its desolation is at hand. Then let those who are in Judea flee to the mountains. Let those who are in the midst of her depart. Let those who are in the country not enter therein.'[97]

As a result of this forecast, the Christian community decided not to take part in the revolt. Many took refuge in Pella, Transjordan, thereby avoiding the direct consequences of the conflict. The remaining Jews regarded this as an act of betrayal and desertion, which became a source of mistrust between the two communities.

The aftermath of the war was disastrous for Judea. Jerusalem was largely destroyed, the land of Israel was under military rule, a new tax, the *fiscus iudaicus*, was imposed on Jews for no reason other than that they were Jewish, the death toll was between 600,000 and 1,300,000 and the country was completely ravaged.

With the Temple destroyed, Judaic worship moved into synagogues. From the original four Jewish schools, only the Pharisees now remained. Once a powerful group, the Sadducees were discredited because of their collaboration with the Roman authorities before the war. They dissipated and were replaced by the Pharisees as spiritual leaders of the Jews. The Essenes were wiped out in the fighting, while the few remaining Zealots who escaped from Jerusalem joined their colleagues at Masada and perished in the mass suicide that followed the Romans' siege of its fortress in 73 CE.

The Pharisees' concept of the Jewish nation categorically excluded Christians, whom they viewed as heretics. Although born Jews, Christians were now regarded as a separate people from the Hebrews. This radical separation is discernible in subsequent events, such as in 100 CE, when the Rabbi Gamaliel II introduced a nineteenth blessing into the *Shemoneh Esrei*,[98] the *Birkat haMinim*, condemning heretics:

> For the apostates let there be no hope and let the reign
> of the arrogant be speedily uprooted in our days. Let
> the Nozerim and the Minim[99] be destroyed in a moment
> and let them be blotted out of the Book of Life and not
> be numbered among the righteous. Blessed art thou, Oh
> Lord, who humblest the arrogant![100]

Those Christians who had still been attending synagogue soon stopped doing so.

The Kitos War and the Bar Kokhba Revolt

From the second century, the Jewish population, which had dispersed throughout the Eastern Mediterranean, agitated against Roman rule once more. The majority of Judea's population was Jewish, but large Jewish minorities were also found in Syria, Cyprus and Egypt. In Alexandria alone, there were 150,000 Jews. The 'rebellion of the diaspora', or the Kitos War, took place between 115 and 117 CE. Led by Lukuas, a self-proclaimed messianic Jew, it started in Cyrenaica (in modern-day Libya), where the Jewish minority lived in a state of friction with the Greek community. Critical lessons had been learned from the revolt in Jerusalem half a century earlier. In a series of heavy surprise strikes, the rebels managed to decimate the Greek areas and destroy many Roman temples and buildings. The result was devastating: the death toll in Cyrenaica alone was reported to have reached 200,000 (although this figure may be exaggerated). Libya was left virtually empty and Rome would be forced to found new colonies in order to repopulate the region.

The rebellion was not limited to the North African diaspora. Success in Cyrenaica and Alexandria emboldened Jews across the entire Mediterranean region. Rhodes, Sicily, Syria, Judea, Mesopotamia and the rest of North Africa witnessed a spectacular uprising which capitalized on the absence of Roman garrisons, which were away fighting the Parthians.

To quell the threat, Trajan sent the Seventh Claudian Legion, under the command of General Lusius Quietus, to wage a merciless campaign of repression. The worst massacre was in Cyprus, where the capital, Salamis, was razed to the ground.[101] Quietus entirely exterminated the island's Jewish population,[102] while troops from Mesopotamia, under Quintus Marcius Turbo, took control of Alexandria. To repair the damage, the Romans confiscated all of the Jews' wealth and property.

The revolt was enormously perilous for the Roman Empire and while the threat had been neutralized, the situation was never fully calmed. From 123 CE onwards, Roman forces were subjected to various raids and terrorist acts until the Jews again rose up in Judea in 132 CE. This time the commander was an astute leader called Bar Kokhba, supported by Rabbi Akiva ben Joseph and the Sanhedrin. The Jewish troops sought to free themselves from Roman control once and for all through focused attacks on their main fortified posts and detachments, and by wiping out any opposition. Their success was such that they were able to set up an independent Jewish state in a large area of Judea.

The Christians had more than enough reason to avoid taking part in these attacks. The leader of the uprising, Bar Kokhba, whose name means 'son of a star',[103] had been recognized as a Jewish messiah, so if they had participated they would have been denying Jesus this status and thus betraying their beliefs. In turn, their refusal to fight the Romans led to persecution of the Christians by the Jewish rebels.

Rarely had Rome faced such dangers within its borders. Hadrian called upon one of his most experienced generals, Sextus Julius Severus,[104] then governor of Britain, and also upon Quintus Lollius Urbicus, a former governor of Germania. In order to suppress the increasingly dangerous Jewish forces, the Romans drew on a great army made up of twelve legions plus auxiliary troops, although their sheer numbers did not spare them significant losses.[105]

The Roman imperial military machine pushed on until 134 CE, and the balance gradually tipped in its favour. The last site of Jewish resistance was the Betar fortress to the southwest of Jerusalem, where Bar Kokhba, the Sanhedrin, thousands of refugees and their most loyal followers were gathered. The Romans, believing in the symbolic power of their actions, attacked the fortress on the anniversary of the fall of the Temple of Jerusalem, and slaughtered everyone inside. Any remaining questions over the Romans' intentions towards the Jewish people disappeared when they forced them to wait six days until they could bury their dead, a direct attack on Jewish funerary rites.

For the Jews, the consequences of this war were horrific. According to Roman historian Cassius Dio, the conflict left 580,000 Jews dead, and 50 Jewish cities and 985 villages completely levelled. Rome had decided to remove the Jewish problem for good, and their wrath would remain implacable until Hadrian's death in 138 CE.[106] Hundreds of thousands of Jews were sold as slaves across the empire. Any sign of independence was quashed, the religion met with reprisals and use of the Jewish calendar was persecuted until it was totally forbidden.[107]

Jerusalem, the centre of Judaism, began to develop into a new city. Romans conducted purification rituals over the largely demolished remains of the former urban centre,[108] while Hadrian ordered statues of Jupiter and himself to be erected on the platform of the Temple for all to behold. He also banned Jews from even entering the city on pain of death.

While the Romans had attacked the very heart of the Hebraic faith, they showed no less animosity towards the Christians. At Golgotha, the hill just outside Jerusalem upon which Christ was crucified, a temple was built to Aphrodite.[109] Although opinions differ, with some authors stating that the emperor had no specific intent, the choice of Aphrodite to displace the Christian cult at this particular site seems more than mere coincidence.

According to Roman mythology, Aphrodite descended to the underworld to take the young Adonis from the land of the dead. When Hadrian, influenced by the Stoics, established a small sacred wood and sanctuary dedicated to Adonis in the Grotto of the Nativity in Bethlehem, it became apparent that he was drawing a parallel between Jesus and Adonis.[110]

Among the coins preserved from the second century, several

show Aphrodite as the protector of Jerusalem, with one foot resting on the hill of Golgotha and her right hand supporting a statue of Adonis. Writing in the fifth century, Theodoret of Cyrus[111] indicated that Christians had always understood the cult to Aphrodite at Golgotha to be simply a pagan reinterpretation of the resurrection of Christ, making the sacrilegious comparison between Aphrodite/Mary and Adonis/Jesus.

By building a temple at Golgotha, Hadrian involuntarily marked the place where Christ was buried. This fact alone is evidence that the Christian community was too numerous for the Roman authorities to ignore. Although they had not participated in the revolt, as far as Rome was concerned they were Jews and, just as they placed statues in the Temple to attest to their power, so they made a concerted effort to occupy Christianity's principal sacred sites.[112]

Eusebius of Caesarea, Saint Jerome and Sozomen all record the empire's resolute desire to cast Golgotha into obscurity and bury it forever:

> (...) they decided to shield this sacred grotto from men's eyes ... They took great pains to transport a large quantity of earth from another area which they used to cover the entire site; afterwards they raised the level of the ground and covered it in stones, thus hiding the holy grotto ... and consecrated a temple to the dissolute divinity Aphrodite.[113]

During the difficult years of the revolts, the Christian community of Jerusalem was governed by a series of bishops, who were successors to Saint James the Just. Many believed that his death in 62 CE had triggered God's wrath, manifested in the city's conquest by Titus. Between then and the time of Hadrian, the fourteen bishops who succeeded him were Jewish in name, according to Eusebius of Caesarea. Following the imperial prohibition which banned the circumcised from entering the Holy City, the Gentiles within the Christian group took over the reins, led by the Bishop Marcus, or Mahalia. Despite persecution, Christianity overcame and survived these complex years in Palestine.[114]

If, despite Rome's efforts to destroy them, it was possible to identify the original sacred Christian sites, what is known about the storage and safekeeping of objects linked to Christ, such as the Cup from the Last Supper?

If we look at events alongside the clues provided by the book of Acts and other key records of these years, a logical sequence can be deduced, which strongly suggests that the Cup was preserved in Jerusalem.

In his first letter to the Corinthians, Paul accurately asserts that the Eucharist was at the heart of emerging Christianity's communal celebrations. Equally, throughout this early period, Jerusalem remained the reference point for the followers of Jesus, initially guided by James the Just, whom Eusebius of Caesarea believed to be the son of Joseph.[115] James's strong personality led him into heated clashes with other high-profile disciples, including Simon Peter, who did not share all of his principles. The highly contested issue of whether Christ's message should be open to all men or should only concern the Jews, as James had maintained, caused Peter's estrangement and departure for Rome.[116]

We might argue that Peter's exile was ultimately favourable for the Christian faith, since his argument proved convincing and his interpretation of Christ's message came to represent its true essence. This does not detract from the fact that, when he left the Holy City, he abandoned the rigid orthodoxy of James the Just, Christ's successor at the head of the nascent Church. A deserter is hardly likely to have taken with him objects that had already become relics of the Lord, such as the Holy Chalice. If the Cup was preserved anywhere during those early apostolic years, it must have been with those who represented the Church of Jerusalem, not those reinterpreting or questioning it, even if only in part. The chalice must have stayed with the Jewish believers in the Holy City.

Furthermore, we must not forget that James, not Peter, was the head of the community. Why would he have entrusted such a symbolic object to someone who would be preaching overseas, in Gentile territory, among obvious dangers? Would it not make more sense for it to remain in Jerusalem, protected by the Christian community there, whose future seemed more certain?

Spreading the 'good news' to all men, not just the Jews, would in hindsight be Peter's real achievement. Nevertheless this first apostolic debate, which turned Christianity into the religion of the West, was a shift away from the essence of the first firmly established and recognized Church of Jerusalem.[117] The accounts of the pilgrims who flocked there during the final phase of the Roman Empire indicate that Jerusalem remained the pillar of Christianity. The relevance of this is demonstrated by the fact that when disputes around doctrine arose, the apostles headed to Jerusalem, rather than Rome, to settle them. Given this, what sense would there have been in the Sacred Cup of Christ leaving the city, this cornerstone of the new faith, to be handed over to the Christian community of Rome, which hadn't yet become fully established? Clearly, the Holy Chalice, central to the Eucharist, which was in turn the essential sacrament of the Christian faith, would have remained in Jerusalem.

The Chalice's Presence in Jerusalem According to Christian Sources
(Third to Eleventh Centuries CE)

Following the Jewish revolt of 132 CE and the overwhelming Roman victory, a new city emerged from the rubble of the old Jerusalem: *Colonia Aelia Capitolina*, or simply *Aelia*, as it would be known. The geographical plan of the city was designed to erase any trace of the period preceding Roman rule. Divided into four parts by two avenue-style axes, the *Cardo Maximus* (running north–south) and the *Decumanus* (east–west), it contained two squares, a theatre, public baths and temples. During the early Roman period, the city was split into two areas: a civic section in the north, and a military encampment in the south.[118]

Even today, there is a clear difference between the street plans of the north and south areas of the Old City. The straight lines and right angles of the north reflect an ordered, geometric layout. In marked contrast, the southern part is a jumble of streets that meet at odd angles. At the end of the third century, the Tenth Legion, which had been assigned to Jerusalem since the Jewish revolt, was sent east, leaving the area unprotected and resulting in indiscriminate and haphazard occupation.

In Rome's redesigned Jerusalem, new sanctuaries were built. As well as the Temple of Aphrodite at Golgotha, the base of the destroyed Temple provided the foundations for the Jupiter

Capitolinus building and, on one of its sides, another site was probably raised to Tyche, the Goddess of Fortune. North of the site, beside the Pool of Bethesda and a stone's throw from the ruins of the former Antonia Fortress, a temple was built to Asclepius. There may also have been temples dedicated to Dionysus and Nemesis. Aelia was, to all intents and purposes, a typical Roman city, and was reduced to the status of a subsidiary regional capital, with Hadrian's appointed governor, Tinneius Rufus, based at Caesarea in Palestine.

The Christians of Aelia Capitolina

What was the Christian community of Roman-conquered Jerusalem, or Aelia Capitolina, like? Its existence is widely documented. There were undoubtedly Christians among the Greek and Syrian migrants to the city, although controversy persists as to exactly where they settled. Tradition states that the community was located on Mount Zion, beyond the city's boundaries, but it seems improbable that settlers would choose to base themselves outside of the city, not least because the only permanent fresh water source, the Gihon spring, was on the east side of the southeast hill. However, over time, it is indeed likely that they would have based themselves in the Mount Zion region. The Tenth Legion's encampment only took up half of the old Jewish city, and Aelia Capitolina had no walls, another sign of its lesser importance and the difficulty of defining the occupied space.

Christianity was still forbidden within the boundaries of the Roman Empire and although periods of brutal persecution did alternate with more permissive times, clandestine practice was the norm. That said, the departure of the Jews and the arrival of the Gentiles did not have a significantly detrimental impact on the conservation of the memories, holy sites and traditions of the previous era.

It is within this context that the first reports of pilgrims arriving in the Holy Land emerge. The Bishop Melito of Sardis[119] visited Aelia in 160 CE and left 'a record of the places where these things were taught and verified'.[120] In 212 Alexander, Bishop of Cappadocia and disciple of Clement of Alexandria, arrived in the city to 'pray and visit the holy sites',[121] provoking such joy within the local Christian community that they refused to let him leave and appointed him Bishop of Jerusalem. Around the same time as Alexander's arrival, the early Christian theologian Origen Adamantius came to the Holy Land in 215 and 230 CE: 'We have visited the (holy) sites to retrace the footsteps left by Jesus, his disciples and the prophets'. He concluded his report with an intriguing reference to the fundamental importance of sites connected to the Messiah for pilgrims who came to the city, by stating that 'visitors from across the world'[122] went to worship at the Grotto of the Nativity.

Although accounts of the time are obviously scarce, we can say with certainty that, over the years, the Christians of Aelia found a way to circumvent difficulties and keep the memory of the most important places in Jesus' life alive. This is a key detail to bear in mind when it comes to sacred objects with symbolic significance, such as the Chalice.

At the beginning of the fourth century there was a significant development across the whole empire that would have a profound impact on the Christian community of Jerusalem: Christianity was recognized as a *religio licita* or 'permitted religion' under the edict of Milan, January 313 CE. In a short space of time, it had progressed from serious persecution under Diocletian (245–311) to a position of prominence under Constantine (306–37), while the relatively new city of Aelia became known as Hierosolyma. Jerusalem took centre stage once more.

The convening of the first Council of Nicaea[123] (now Iznik, in Turkey) in 325 CE was crucial to this process. Bishops from practically every corner of the Christian world[124] came together to try to reach a series of urgent agreements on controversial aspects of doctrine that threatened to destroy the Church, the most important of which was the Arian question that concerned the divine nature of Jesus Christ.

One of the bishops summoned to the Council, Macarius of Jerusalem, sought support from Helena, Constantine's mother. Now eighty years old, Helena's influence over her son's court had grown with age. Macarius described the gradual decline and neglect that the sites of Jesus' birth, crucifixion and resurrection had suffered over the years. Persuaded by his account, the emperor's mother left for Jerusalem with Macarius as her guide, and with the necessary funds to restore sites that were still buried under Roman temples to their former grandeur. Both Eusebius and Saint Jerome give accounts of the rediscovery of the Holy Sepulchre and the later Invention[125] of the True Cross:

> When, layer after layer, the original surface of the ground was revealed, contrary to all expectation, the venerable and hallowed sanctuary of the Lord's resurrection was then discovered, and the cave, which is the holiest place in the entire world, looked just as it had when the Lord returned to life.[126]

On returning to Constantinople, Helena reported to her son Constantine, who gave the orders for Hadrian's pagan temples to be destroyed and Christian monuments to be constructed in their place: in particular, the Church of the Nativity in Bethlehem, the Church of the Holy Sepulchre in Jerusalem and the Church of the Pater Noster (also known as the Sanctuary of the Eleona) on the Mount of Olives.

While other relics were newly discovered in this period, there is no specific mention of the Cup of Christ associated with Helena's visit to Jerusalem. However, presumably, the Cup did not need to re-emerge from beneath the Roman sites – because it had been there all along. Another relevant piece of information supports this conclusion: for the founding Christian community the Eucharist was their cornerstone, as opposed to the Passion, or the preference for miracles in the Hellenistic group's writings. This is logical, given the difficult nature of proselytizing about a religion that lauded the crucifixion of its own Messiah. In the first to second centuries CE, there were still communities that celebrated the Eucharist without making any reference to the Passion whatsoever. Among them is the one that produced the *Didache*, or *The Teaching of the Twelve Apostles*, a work that was revered by the Fathers of the Church and considered canonical in certain areas of the Christian world.[127]

In this ancient text the Eucharist is standardized as a ritual whereby the wine is blessed first, although not as the blood of Christ: 'We thank you, Our Father, for the holy wine of David, which you made known to us through Jesus, your servant'.[128] The bread is then broken and blessed as the bread of thanksgiving, but not as the Body of Christ: 'We thank you, Our Father, for the life and knowledge that you made known to us through Jesus, your servant'.[129] At no point does it mention the commemorative or sacrificial nature of the Eucharist, rather than the link to David. While this area of discussion is beyond the scope of this book, it does demonstrate the vitality of the Eucharist in early Christianity when, in contrast, objects connected to the Passion such as the Cross or the Holy Lance were not attributed the same devotional value. These relics gained greater currency in the early fourth-century era of Constantine and Helena, perhaps because they appealed to pagans with an affinity for Mithraic mystery cults, for whom the life–death–resurrection cycle of the Son of

God would be the crux of the religion destined to become the spiritual lifeblood of the Roman Empire.

We can distinguish between those items and teachings linked to baptism and the Eucharist, such as the Holy Chalice, and those bolstered by the emergence of relics from the Crucifixion, such as the lance or pieces of the cross.[130] Two very different groups formed around these different Biblical objects and events, which, from the fourth century onwards, developed into equally worshipped cults.

Once Rome had chosen Christianity as the imperial religion the celebrated phenomenon of pilgrimage began in earnest, entailing journeys fraught with grave dangers from which many failed to return. Depending on the route, a pilgrimage could take a year or two, excluding the time spent at the destination. The historical data that survives from these pilgrimages is crucial. Interestingly, however, the importance placed on particular locations does not always stay the same, or follow current hierarchies of value. The reader should not be surprised to learn that there are texts which pay more attention to one building than another, which prioritize or leave out one aspect or another. These are merely conceptual differences that change with the times, and should be understood as such.

The Pilgrim of Bordeaux, and Egeria the Galician

The first fourth-century text about the new Christian pilgrimages is the *Itinerarium Burdigalense*. Although its author's identity is unknown, he is believed to have come from Burdigala, present-day Bordeaux (France), because his pilgrimage began there in 333 CE. The dates of his journey coincide with the construction of the first imperial basilicas in Palestine, a detail that renders his eyewitness account particularly interesting:

> On the left-hand side is the mount of Golgotha, where
> the Lord was crucified. A stone's throw away lies a crypt
> where his body was kept, and where he was revived
> on the third day. There (...) by order of the Emperor
> Constantine, a basilica has been built; a church, indeed, of
> outstanding beauty.[131]

As valuable as the narrative of the Bordeaux pilgrim is, an account left by a woman is of even greater importance: that of Egeria, the Spanish pilgrim. A native of Gallaecia, the northwest of the Iberian Peninsula,[132] she was related by marriage to the imperial house of Theodosius I[133] and therefore received protection on her journey to the Holy Land, which was completed between 381 and 384 CE. Her testimony, shared widely across Christendom, reveals a meticulous eye. Egeria's description of the Good Friday celebrations at the Holy Sepulchre is as follows:

> At the sixth hour, they move to stand before the Cross,
> come rain or shine, even though this place is in the open
> air. It is a sort of atrium of ample width and great beauty,
> located between the Cross and the Anastasis.[134]

The Church of the Holy Sepulchre was a complex made up

of various buildings created at Constantine's initiative:[135] the Anastasis (from the Greek ανάστασις, meaning Resurrection), the Rotunda, the Martyrium and the East Atrium. The Anastasis was a rotunda of twelve columns, divided into groups of three and alternated with pairs of pilasters to the north, west and south. The western part of the transept was enclosed by a wide ambulatory, punctuated at three compass points by apses (semi-domed recesses), while fifteen great windows filled the whole complex with light. Contemporary descriptions also tell us that there was a gallery over the ambulatory. The episcopal residence was located to the north of the Anastasis.

Passing through a porticoed courtyard, with the rock of Golgotha to the south, Egeria described reaching the Martyrium, the far chancel end of which gave onto this same open and structured space. The basilica consisted of five naves, separated by rows of columns and the upper gallery. Beneath it was the crypt known as the 'Chapel of the Invention of the True Cross'. Lastly, the East Atrium looked out over the *Cardo Maximus* and deviated from the basilica's main axis to align with the major road.

Work began on the church around 326 CE, and it was consecrated on 17 September 335 CE. Based on all available sources, the Anastasis was not completed until a little before 384, largely due to the laborious task of carving the rock that would house the tomb.

Initially, Calvary was exposed to the open air, but surrounded by a silver balustrade. In the fifth century, Melania the Younger, a Roman travelling to Jerusalem with her husband Pinianus, gave orders for a small chapel to be built on the site of the Crucifixion.

The fifth century brought two significant milestones for Christianity and Jerusalem: the patriarchate, which put the city on the same level as Rome, Constantinople, Alexandria and Antioch; and the presence in the Holy City of the Empress

Licinia Eudoxia, wife of Theodosius II. She first arrived in 438 and settled shortly afterwards in 444, staying until her death in around 460. She was responsible for many religious buildings, as well as the wall along the south of the city, definitively enclosing Mount Zion.

First References to the Cup in Jerusalem

For the most part, the texts from contemporary pilgrims offer few concrete signs of the Lord's Cup.[136] We have to wait until 400 CE to find the first direct reference, which appears in the *Breviarius de Hierosolyma,* the *Jerusalem Breviary,* a sort of pilgrim guidebook to the city. Detailed analysis of this text builds a chronological picture of the years from 400 CE up to the beginning of the sixth century.[137] It includes a description of the complex of the Holy Sepulchre:

> To the west of the site you enter via the Holy Resurrection,
> which contains the Lord's Tomb. From there you go into
> the sanctuary of the Basilica of Saint Constantine. There is
> a chamber there which contains the reed and the sponge,
> and the Cup that the Lord blessed and gave to his disciples
> to drink, saying: 'This is my body and my blood'.[138]

Although it is hard to discern which space is meant by 'the sanctuary of the Basilica', this probably describes the small chapel that opened on to the courtyard of the Rotunda, where we know, thanks to later references, that the sacred cup was stored.

Where had the Holy Chalice been kept prior to this report? If, as it seems, the construction of the covering over Golgotha and the Cup's chapel are intimately linked, then the object was only housed at the Holy Sepulchre from the middle of the fifth century, under the guidance and protection of the Empress Eudoxia. Although the question remains unanswered, in his extraordinary work of translation and compilation about the pre-Crusades pilgrims, *Jerusalem Pilgrimage, 1099–1185* (1988), John Wilkinson refers to the existence of a church called either Saint Theodore or Saint Euphemia, built by an unknown man, 'John', where a festival related to the Chalice was celebrated on 3 July.[139]

In any case, the Cup physically resided in the Holy Sepulchre from the fifth century, where it would remain until the eleventh century. Over the centuries this is mentioned in various sources, providing a record of its preservation at this key Christian site.

Around 570 CE, an anonymous pilgrim from Piacenza,[140] to whom we owe the *Itinerarium Antonini Placentini*, mentions the Chalice's presence. This is one of the accounts considered essential to understanding the sacred sites of Jerusalem because of its sheer quantity of detail.[141]

> In the central courtyard of the Basilica there is a little room where the wood of the Cross is kept . . . In this place there is also the sponge and the reed that are referred to in the Gospel and also the onyx Cup, which was blessed by Him at the Supper.[142]

As well as its physical location, the pilgrim of Piacenza describes the material the cup was made of. The technique of using onyx, a semiprecious stone, is an indication of the object's significant antiquity. In the third century, Urbanus, Bishop of Rome from 222 to 230 CE, determined that chalices should be made of gold and silver, to replace those of wood or glass that were used before this time. In later decrees, the use of these materials was banned and it was ruled that they should be silver-gilt.[143] The fact that such a prized object was not made of precious metal suggests not only its antiquity, but also its quite exceptional nature. This brings us back to the beginnings of the Christian era and very close to the life and the Passion of Christ.

During the Hellenistic period and the first centuries of Roman domination in the East, this type of luxury object took on a heightened value. Some of these objects were of extraordinary quality, just like Christ's Cup, and are still preserved today.

Returning to the history of the time, a significant change had taken place in Jerusalem. In 602 CE Maurice, emperor of the Byzantine Empire that united the lands of the East, was assassinated, sparking civil unrest. Khosrau II, the Sassanid emperor of Persia, took advantage of the ensuing crisis to launch a large-scale assault: he invaded Syria in 604, taking Antioch, Caesarea and Damascus within a few years. Then in 614, Khosrau's son-in-law Shahrbaraz, backed by 26,000 Jews that he had recruited with the promise of returning them to Judea, surrounded and conquered Jerusalem.

According to some sources, up to 90,000 Christians perished in the attack and many of the city's most important buildings suffered considerable damage: a section of the Constantine Basilica burned down, and other churches, such as the one at Zion, were razed to the ground. For the Jews, returning to their city after many centuries, this triumph meant that they could rebuild their Temple, and the relic of the Holy Cross was taken to Persia as a trophy.[144] In this dramatic context, Sophronius of Jerusalem writes his *Anacreontica*, a text that seems to express his desire to return to the Holy City:[145]

And I ascend,
My heart fills with great fear,
And I see the upper chamber,
The reed, the sponge, and the lance.[146]

Considering that Sophronius must have written this around 614 CE, it is curious that he does not mention the Chalice. Had it been hidden to avoid its theft? It does not seem likely that it was taken to Persia as a spoil of war given that shortly afterwards, following the liberation of Jerusalem, its presence in the Basilica of the Holy Sepulchre is casually reported once again. The religious tolerance of Khosrau II[147] is well documented. Concealing the Chalice in a less conspicuous place was perhaps the best way to avoid its loss, at least during the looting period. This is a practice which was documented later, and at various times during the period of Muslim control.[148]

The Persian conquest was nearing its end. In 622 CE, the Byzantine Emperor Heraclius left Constantinople to attack the Persians. The internal dissent and exhaustion caused by fifteen years of war forced the Sassanids to pull back for good. Heraclius' campaign culminated in the Battle of Nineveh in 627. After the victory, he marched eastwards, sacking various strongholds. Khosrau II was deposed and assassinated in 628, the year that peace was agreed. The Sassanid Empire returned the relic of the True Cross and, some months later, Heraclius arrived in Jerusalem in person to venerate the cross and take action against the Jews, reviving Hadrian's old law that forbade them from entering the city.

Restoration of the Constantine Basilica began under Persian rule. Modesto, abbot of the Saint Theodosius Monastery, did what he could to reconstruct the Anastasis, replacing the former cupola with a conical roof. His efforts also led to the erection of a new east-facing apse to house the altar, where the former entrance was located. This building became the main part of the complex as the Martyrium was still in a state of disrepair, except for the crypt housing the Invention of the True Cross. The former splendour that had enthralled pilgrims for centuries now seemed a distant memory.

Details from the *Armenian Guide*,[149] recounting the experiences of a pilgrim who was in Jerusalem in the early part of the seventh century, are illuminating. Written in 625 CE,[150] it contains the last descriptive passage we have from the period immediately before Khosrau II's arrival, and depicts buildings as yet undamaged by the Persian conquest:[151]

> Christ our Saviour's tomb is hewn into the rock, and is the length of a man. It is several yards from the centre of the dome to the Saviour's sacred tomb. And on top of the church's columns a dome has been built, one hundred cubits high and one hundred cubits wide: on each side there are twelve lower columns, and twelve more on the upper level. This gallery contains the lance, the sponge and the gold-covered Cup of Christ.[152]

Based on this description, in the period immediately prior to the Persian conquest, the Chalice was kept in the upper gallery of the Anastasis. This sheds a clearer light on the meaning of Sophronius of Jerusalem writing 'I ascend' to see the relics. On the other hand, this is the first time in which the Chalice is described as 'gold-covered'. As has already been mentioned, it was the norm at various times for all chalices to be either made of, or gilded in, a precious metal. Later descriptions tell us that it was possible to touch and kiss the object, which suggests a need to protect the onyx chalice from damage.[153]

Although the two main relics are the wood of the True Cross and the Holy Chalice, they were always accompanied by other objects which could be described as minor relics. The pieces of the cross were clearly distributed between Jerusalem, Constantinople and Rome, and sources during the late empire period confirm that the cup continued to be stored in Jerusalem. The Lance, Reed and Sponge,[154] however, were reported to have been taken to Constantinople along with the section of the True Cross in the fourth century. This would suggest that these three lesser relics formed a set that was in some way intended to complement the primary relics.

The Pilgrims under Muslim Rule: New Reports

The period of relative tranquillity in Jerusalem's history was never going to last long. In 632 CE, the first deployments of Arab soldiers made incursions into Persian territory. The war years had exhausted the Byzantines and the Sassanids alike. In July 633, the Muslims defeated Heraclius' army at the Battle of Ajnadayn, close to Emesa (now Homs, Syria). A year later they invaded Damascus and the Byzantines were defeated once again at Yarmuk. The Caliph Omar (634–44) set his sights on his next target: the Holy City.

Armed with 5,000 men, Mo'awiya Ibn-Abu-Sufyan failed to take the city by surprise, while Khalid ibn al-Walid[155] continued to lead the main army.[156] In November 636 Jerusalem was surrounded, but its conquest remained a far from easy task. A central garrison defended the city which, thanks to improvements to Byzantine fortifications after the Persian withdrawal, commanded serious defensive might.

The Muslims besieged Jerusalem for four months, cutting off all its supply lines.[157] With no means of receiving aid from Constantinople, resistance was rendered futile. Because of this, the patriarch Sophronius, acting on behalf of the defenders, offered to surrender the city in exchange for payment of a *jizya* (tribute) and a set of conditions that would allow the residents to sustain their churches, sanctuaries and faith, without being forced to adopt Islam. Sophronius also insisted that the Caliph himself ratify the agreement, in person.[158] In April 637 the Umar

Pact was signed. The new Islamic government did not turn the city into the political centre of Palestine, which continued to be Lydda up until 716, and then Ar-Ramla (Ramallah).

Early tolerance enabled Christians to continue their pilgrimages, along with Jews, who were also now permitted to return freely to Jerusalem. As for Muslims, the linking of the Holy City with one of the miracles from the life of Muhammad[159] turned it into the third-most important Islamic pilgrimage site after Mecca and Medina.

We have to wait until the final decades of the seventh century for another text reporting pilgrimages to Jerusalem. In the year 683 an Irish monk, Adomnan, wrote *De locis sanctis* (*On Holy Places*), a treatise on the sites of the Holy Land, based on information provided by the Frankish bishop Arculf. This text is probably the most significant of all those produced by pilgrims, due to its wide distribution throughout Western Christendom. Adomnan describes the complex of the Holy Sepulchre and in particular, the place where the Chalice was kept and displayed:

> There is another chapel between the Church of Calvary and the Basilica of Constantine, in which the Lord's Cup is kept, and the sponge from which he ingested the vinegar, when he was hung in the tree.[160] This is a chapel located between the Church of Golgotha and the Martyrium, and which holds the Lord's Cup, which he blessed and offered with his own hands during the meal that he shared with his disciples on the eve of the Passion. It is a silver cup, which also acts as a sextarius,[161] and is designed with a handle on each side. Inside the cup there is a sponge that his torturers offered to him after soaking it in vinegar on a hyssop branch when they crucified him. It is said that it was from this very chalice that the Lord drank when he ate with his disciples following his resurrection. Saint Arculf saw it,

venerated it and touched it with his own hands through a hole in the carved screen door of the reliquary where it is kept. Every last person in the city makes the pilgrimage to this cup with the greatest of reverence.[162]

The information provided by Adomnan's text is highly significant. Firstly, we learn that having been kept in the upper gallery of the Anastasis, the Chalice was once more to be found in the chapel between both churches. He tells us how it was displayed: it could be seen and even touched, but only through a hole in the meshwork of the reliquary door. This obstacle is presumably the source of the discrepancy between the *Armenian Guide*, which mentions gold, and Adomnan, who refers to its silver coating. Further to this he describes, for the first time, how the Chalice can hold a volume of a sextarius, or 0.546 litres.[163] Finally he tells us that the cup, by this time already famous in the Holy Land and Europe alike, was particularly prized by the Christians of Jerusalem, and pilgrims frequently came to worship it.

Based on Arculf's account, Adomnan's text contains various plans of the Holy Land's churches – unknown until this point – including the Holy Sepulchre. In the main courtyard, between the Anastasis and the Martyrium, we can clearly identify the chapel to which his text refers, marked with the small sketch of a chalice: the 'exedra of Our Lord's Chalice'.[164]

The Holy Grail's location in Jerusalem remained constant throughout the centuries and across various descriptive accounts; both in terms of the nature of the object, and its specific location within the complex made up of the Martyrium and the Anastasis. However, the texts do not always completely agree. A few years later, around 692 CE, the monk Epiphanius wrote *The Holy City and its Sacred Places*, a complex text which has suffered various incorporations and reaches us in copies from the thirteenth and sixteenth centuries. The translator himself, Herbert Donner, questioned its authenticity.[165] Regarding the cup, Epiphanius says:

> And above the door is the sanctuary where the cup from
> which Christ drank of the vinegar and gall is kept. [166]

About ten years later, the Venerable Bede wrote *On the Holy Places*, a review of previous accounts based on the works of Eucherius, Jerome, Hegesippus and, above all, Adomnan.[167] Given that Bede never went to Jerusalem, his account is a direct synthesis of its sources. With relation to the cup, he tells us:

> In the courtyard, which is beyond the Martyrium and
> Golgotha, there is an exedra where the Lord's Chalice is
> placed in a reliquary, and people often come to touch it and
> kiss it through a hole in the door. This silver chalice has two
> handles, one on each side, and can hold a French quart.[168]

The description is similar to that of Adomnan, who wrote his *De locis sanctis* a mere fifteen years earlier.[169] The diffusion of both Bede's and Adomnan's texts would become fundamental to knowledge of the Chalice's existence across all of Europe. We know that Adomnan delivered a copy of his work to the Anglo-Saxon King Aldfrith of Northumbria and that it also enjoyed rapid popular diffusion.[170]

Arculf, through Adomnan's text, showed that Christians did not suffer under Muslim rule. The caliphs of Damascus were tolerant and in some cases Christians even held government posts, for instance John Damascene, who became *protosymbulus*, or chief councillor to the court of Damascus.[171] The period of the Abbasid caliphate of Baghdad was also one of general tolerance towards Jerusalem's Christians and the pilgrims that visited the city. Under the government of Harun al-Rashid, a diplomatic relationship was forged with Charlemagne, as part of which embassies and gifts would be exchanged. Relations between the Muslim and Christian worlds, based on mutual recognition and respect, were certainly more fluid than initial appearances would suggest.

Last Data on the Cup in Jerusalem

In this period of harmony prior to the Fatimid dynasty (909–1171), we encounter the final reference to the Chalice in Christian sources: the *Commemoratium*. This anonymous work clearly and precisely lists the clerics that served in each of Jerusalem's churches:

> Firstly in the Lord's Holy Sepulchre: 9 Priests, 14 Deacons, 6 Subdeacons, 23 Canons, 13 Custodians (called fragelites), 41 Monks, 12 Candlebearers to the Patriarch, 17 Ministers to the Patriarch, two Superiors, two Treasurers, two Notaries, two Guardians. Priests that guarded the Lord's Sepulchre: one for Holy Calvary, two for the Lord's Chalice, two for the Holy Cross and shroud, one Deacon. A Seneschal who, later with the Patriarch, was responsible for all administration, two Cellarers, one Treasurer, one Custodian of the Fountains, 9 Porters. 150 people in all, without counting the three Hospitallers.[172]

The *Commemoratorium* confirms that the Chalice was still to be found at the Holy Sepulchre in the ninth century. The number of religious staff assigned to the various roles is proof that, at the time, the relic's importance was on a par with that of the Holy Cross and generated a similar volume of work. If we look at this alongside the information offered by Arculf, in the words of Adomnan, stating that the Christians of Jerusalem and pilgrims from other lands travelled to see the Cup with the greatest reverence, it is clear that the Chalice was one of Christianity's most highly prized objects, one which required safeguarding and care. Indeed, the fact that two people were specifically assigned to caring for the Chalice is interesting in itself, particularly given that the Islamic sources also refer to 'custodians', as we will reveal in the chapters to come.

After the *Commemoratorium*, Christian sources fall silent about the Cup.

The Path of the Cup of Mystery: The Grail in Islamic Sources

A series of unexpected events in the tenth and eleventh centuries led to an about-turn in the history of the Chalice. We can verify that it was present in Jerusalem from the Roman era up until the brink of the new millennium and, thanks to Christian sources, we know its approximate dimensions and the material it was made of, as well as the fact that it was kept at the Holy Sepulchre. We are also aware of the importance it was afforded in the accounts of pilgrims to the Holy Land, widely distributed across Europe at the time.

Changes to the Muslim government of North Africa and, specifically, the aggressive policies of some Fatimid Caliphs towards Christians, would make it extremely difficult for pilgrims to visit Jerusalem. This led to fewer texts being written about the Holy City, and new information became extremely hard to come by. Therefore, older descriptions continued to be used and recycled in sources across Europe.

When the crusades reached Jerusalem towards the end of the eleventh century, the crusaders encountered a serious problem: the Holy Chalice was no longer there. Reports are vague, and although the city's Christian community reported that that it was traditionally held to have been present some decades earlier, the reality was that the relic had disappeared from Jerusalem. This is where the myriad legends surrounding the Chalice began, best exemplified by the poems and stories about the Holy Grail that were so popular in the European chivalric tradition of the Middle Ages.

What happened? In the tenth century, the Fatimids had taken power in North Africa, from Tunisia to Syria. This royal line of thirteen Caliphs began with Abdullah al-Mahdi Billah (909–34), founder of the dynasty descended from Fatima, the Prophet Muhammad's daughter, and remained in power until the time of the famous Saladin at the end of the twelfth century, ending with the last ruler al-Adid (1160–71).[173]

Life for Jerusalem's Christian community, much like that in the other territories under Muslim rule, was marked by highs and lows. Periods of relative calm gave way to spells of persecution, although Christians were generally treated with respect. Something changed, however, under the sixth Fatimid caliphate.

Under the Government of Al-Hakim bi Amr Allāh

Al-Hakim bi Amr Allāh held the caliphate between 996 and 1021. His eccentricities made him one of the most remarkable leaders in this period of history. Although they led to serious dissent within his army, he put into practice policies such as killing every dog in Egypt, banning women from going out into the street, preventing people from playing chess and forcing Cairo residents to work at night and sleep by day.[174] Given that he was such a strange character, it is unsurprising that he also behaved aggressively towards the Christian community.

In his *al-Jitad*, Taqi al-Din Abu al-Abbas Ahmad ibn 'Ali ibn 'Abd al-Qadir ibn Muhammad al-Maqrizi, a well respected Arab historian more commonly known as al-Maqrizi,[175] describes what happened to the Christians under al-Hakim:

Year 398 (of the Hijra)[176]

During this year, the Nile flooded, putting the population in grave danger. Women and children were perishing everywhere, and it overflowed the riverbed farms, flooding and ruining the harvests, which were deluged with water. It was impossible for anyone to harvest until (the waters) drew back, and the price of rice increased inordinately.

As custom dictated, al-Hakim called the obligatory prayer procession and sermon on the almozala[177] and at the designated Meeting Place. (. . .)

Throughout (the year), Egyptian Christians travelled in huge, coordinated groups from Egypt to Jerusalem, in order to celebrate the Resurrection[178] with great pomp and circumstance. (This procession was held) regularly every year, with great respect and reverence, in a very similar way to Muslims undertaking the Hajj.

Al-Hakim asked Jatkin al-Ddayf al-Adadi and some of his qa'ids[179] what this matter of the Resurrection was all about and urged them to send him any information they could find out about the event. He was told that all Christians, whatever their country of origin, celebrated this festival with great solemnity and travelled (to Jerusalem) abundantly to celebrate it in great numbers, among them even powerful men and kings. They all arrived equipped with considerable wealth, clothes of fine quality, tapestries, candles and crosses adorned in gold and silver, showing great devotion and firm belief in the event. (They told him) how honestly the Christians honoured this date, since they always came together in great numbers to celebrate the anniversary of the Resurrection, displaying their crosses with pride and carrying over-spilling candles in their hands (al-za ibaq),[180] whose wicks had been impregnated with oil in remembrance of the Passion, lighting up the rooftops such that the streets were so well lit it was if the sky was ablaze.

Al-Hakim was profoundly displeased to learn this and ordered his scribe, Basir ibn Surin, to write to the emissary Ahmad ibn Ya qub, to order him to head to Jerusalem to sack and raze the (Church of the) Resurrection to the ground, and cast the people into abject shame.[181] As it was ordered, so it was done. Afterwards he decreed that the same should be done to every church within his lands, but the Muslims, afraid that Christians would take the same measures towards the mosques that had been built in their countries, stopped him from acting on this threat.[182]

As this account relates, some months before 1009, al-Hakim made his first attempt to attack the Church of the Holy Sepulchre. The Holy Week festivities, celebrated with such pomp in Jerusalem, lay at the roots of his hostility. This must have been when the Holy Chalice moved from the place where it had been for six centuries to another, less conspicuous, location.

The historian goes on to describe events over the following years:

Year 400 (of the Hijra)[183]

Ibn Surin, his scribe, investigated the actions that had been carried out with regard to the Church of the Resurrection in Jerusalem. (. . .) And both Jews and Christians alike were firmly ordered to dress in specific clothes that would clearly distinguish them from (Muslims).[184]

The slightly cryptic tone of this quotation suggests that the Fatimid ruler's order may not have been obeyed as strictly as he had demanded. According to recent research, a large part of the church was destroyed, and the Holy Sepulchre was even attacked with hammers and picks. However, despite building a huge pyre on top of it, al-Hakim's men did not succeed in destroying the funeral chamber.

Restoration work began in 1012, driven by pilgrim donations with significant aid from the Byzantine Emperor Michael IV the Paphlagonian (1034–41). There were not enough funds, however, to finish the repairs, and a large section of the original building had to be abandoned – the atrium and the basilica were lost and only the courtyard and the rotunda survived.[185]

Al-Hakim's hostility towards non-Muslims did not stop there:

Year 403 (of the Hijra)[186]

(Al-Hakim) forced the Christians to carry a cross weighing 20 pounds and as long as their arms,[187] hanging it from their bodies in such a way that it was always clearly visible. Many Christians chose to convert to Islam, while others set off on pilgrimages to churches, the building of which within the community's territory was strictly forbidden, while existing churches were being converted into mosques from which the (Muslim) call to prayer was heard.[188]

Right up until his death, the Caliph al-Hakim remained a sworn enemy of Christians and Jews, for whom life only became worse. Despite being repaired on various occasions, the Church of the Holy Sepulchre was serially sacked and suffered numerous attempts at destruction.

At the beginning of Ramadan in the very year he died, al-Hakim announced that he would travel to the Great Mosque, taking with him the appropriate foods for breaking his fast. He issued a decree to make it known that anyone who did not accompany him would die. His heralds cried out things like: 'Peace be with you, oh Unique and Special One!'[189] and went on in this fashion, spouting ever more astounding and ridiculous nonsense, which not only likened (al-Hakim) to Allah, but also gave him the title of Commander of the Muslims.

The Caliph became increasingly unpredictable. He was even known as Bi Amr Allāh, 'he who governs by God's mandate', and was an unstable visionary who regarded Christianity as his main opponent.

When al-Hakim had seized control of the holy sites, the Alawites offered the people of Medina many assurances about taking possession of Ya'far Ibn Muhammad al-Sadiq's residence.[190] Once he had become master of that place, he found within it a hard and polished chalice,[191] a copy of the Qur'an, a bed of plaited palm leaves and a throne.[192] The house had never been opened before. Al-Hakim saw that the following inscription had been written over the throne:[193] 'He vanquished his enemies and destroyed the Church of the Resurrection in the year 338'.[194] He charged a servant with writing up a report to be sent to the Grand Vizier (as follows): 'Your Excellency, the Great Imam, has ordained that the Church of the Resurrection must immediately be destroyed, entirely, until no trace of it remains. Every last inch of it must be levelled, from top to bottom, from its highest pinnacle to its very foundations.'[195]

Only al-Hakim's death in 1021 prevented him from carrying out his intentions. This had been the worst period for Christians under Muslim rule, due to the arbitrary nature of the Caliph's actions. However, al-Hakim's departure did not spell the end of their hardships; over the following decades, there were alternating periods of tension and calm – albeit in response to the geopolitical situation of lands in conflict, rather than the whim of a head of state.

'Alī az-Zāhir, Internal Problems in Egypt and Help from Dénia

'Alī az-Zāhir succeeded his father al-Hakim as the head of the caliphate at a turbulent time, marked by plagues and widespread famine across North Africa. Despite maintaining reasonably good relations with the Byzantine Empire, there remained moments of heightened tension.

Year 418 (of the Hijra)[196]

Over the course of the year the situation in the convents of Egypt and Syria went into a significant and perceptible decline, and written correspondence between them became very intense. Sermons given by the Rumis[197] used the bleakest of terms to describe these events, and they were overcome by the deepest affliction. (In response, the Christians) launched an attack on the mosque of Constantinople and laid siege to it for some time. The news spread quickly and al-Tahir wasted no time[198] in entering the Church of the Resurrection in Jerusalem, seizing the riches and pearls that the Christian kings had amassed there. A deep hostility towards the Christian religion, the like of which had not been seen since the days of al-Hakim bi-Amr Allah, spread throughout the Muslim world.[199]

'Alī az-Zāhir's government (1021–36) was committed to

solving domestic issues, such as the Bedouin rebellion, which briefly established a rival caliphate in Palestine between 1024 and 1029. Ali Ibn Ahmad al-Jarjarai played an important role in the relationship with Byzantium. He became vizier in 1028 and remained in the role under az-Zāhir's son, Abū Tamīm Ma'add al-Mustanṣir bi-llāh, known as al-Mustanṣir, until 1045. It is often wrongly believed that permission was granted to restore the Church of the Holy Sepulchre under 'Alī az-Zāhir's government,[200] but it was in fact under al-Mustanṣir's caliphate, following negotiations with the Byzantine Empire, in 1037–8.

Year 429 (of the Hijra)[201]

> Over the course (of this year), al-Mustanṣir signed a peace treaty with the King of the Rumis, whereby the latter agreed to send back 5,000 prisoners in return for al-Mustanṣir rebuilding the masonry work of the (Church of the) Resurrection, previously destroyed by al-Hakim. He sent the necessary workers and rebuilt the structure of the (Church of the) Resurrection, and also sent funds intended to help it regain its (former) glory.

The restoration work on the Church of the Holy Sepulchre, which had begun in 1012, was now resumed. A large section of the old basilica could not be salvaged, so the imperial architects, sent by Constantine IX Monomachos, decided to acknowledge the importance of the part that had been preserved and thus covered the former Anastasis in mosaic work. The loss of natural light caused by the restoration was partially compensated for by the splendour of the mosaics by candlelight.

Al-Mustanṣir was only seven years old when he succeeded his father as Caliph. His mother and the aforementioned Vizier Ali Ibn Ahmad al-Jarjarai were fundamental to his rule in these early years, especially in the treaty with the Byzantine Empire. He went on to become the longest-standing governor of all the Islamic states, holding power for sixty years, through a period marked by climate change, economic difficulties and famine.[202] It is this disastrous context that created the necessary conditions for the arrival of aid from Dénia (in Spain) and the subsequent removal of the Lord's Cup to the Iberian Peninsula.

During the Islamic conquest of 711–88, Moorish armies had invaded most of southern and central Spain, calling the conquered territory Al-Andalus. Over time, Al-Andalus split up into several Islamic-ruled fiefdoms or principalities, known as *taifas*, which were at first loosely allied under the Caliphate of Córdoba.

Following the dissolution of the Caliphate of Cordoba at the beginning of the eleventh century, Dénia's territories, governed by Muyahid al-Muwaffaq and his son Ali Iqbal al-Dawla, enjoyed a period of independence from 1010 until they were conquered in 1076 by Zaragoza, their powerful neighbour from the Ebro region.

Although small, Dénia had a specific advantage that allowed it to generate wealth: its mighty fleet. This asset enabled it to trade across the entire Mediterranean,[203] as well as to conquer the Balearics and Sardinia. Dénia's Emir, Ali Iqbal al-Dawla, was a proactive character, who kept up regular trade with Egypt and looted Christian coastal areas. Cinnabar[204] (the common ore of mercury, essential to the process of purifying gold) was one of Dénia's key commercial exports. This mineral was a basic resource for the Fatimid state, and it levied taxes on its consumption. So this relatively small *taifa* did not escape the attention of the Fatimid authorities – they noticed that Dénia was valuable because of its cinnabar trade.

The Emir had the additional peculiarity of having been born to a Christian mother, which would at various times provoke mistrust from the rest of the Muslim community.

There were further developments in the story of the Lord's

Cup around the middle of the eleventh century. The Byzantine authorities refused to allow al-Mustanṣir's name to be mentioned during the invocation and sermon given in the Constantinople Mosque, and this insult led him to direct his sense of grievance towards the Christian community in his own territories, which created tension in Jerusalem. Added to this, the distressing economic situation and constant famines forced al-Mustanṣir to petition the wider Muslim community for aid. All we know is that help was sent to Egypt almost immediately by the Emir of Dénia, Ali Iqbal al-Dawla, and that he was rewarded for his generosity: facts which may at first seem unconnected, but will prove to be directly related to our story.

Year 447 (of the Hijra)[205]

During his journey, al-Mustanṣir headed for Jerusalem's Church of the Resurrection, taking possession of anything and everything he could find within.

This happened as a result of the failure of the diplomatic mission of the Qadi[206] Aba'Abd-Allah al-Qida'ī. He had been sent by the Caliph to the Queen of Rūm[207] with a missive and petition – addressed to Queen Theodora[208] –, requesting that the invocation and sermon given in the Constantinople mosque be carried out in the name of al-Mustanṣir. Al-Qida's request was flatly refused and he returned (to the capital) disappointed, having been overlooked in Constantinople in favour of an ambassador of Sultan Tughril Beg of Seljuq, who succeeded in securing the invocation of the Caliph al-Q'im bi-amr-Allah al-'Abbasi (at Constantinople) from then on.

Al-Qida'ī returned to face al-Mustanṣir and informed him of the (pitiful) outcome of his mission. Provoked by this, he seized everything he could from the (Church of

the) Resurrection in Jerusalem, until there was nothing
left. He (also) banished the Patriarch to the Isolated House
(Dūr al-Mufradata), barred the doors of every church in
Egypt and Syria and ordered Christians and monks to pay
four years' worth of the per capita tax (jizya). These events
changed the ties that bound the Egyptians (al- miṣriyyīn)
and the Byzantines (al-rūm).[209]

In this passage, we learn when and why the Holy Sepulchre
and other churches were attacked, something we will return to
later.[210] The attack happened at almost the same time as supplies
were being sent to Egypt[211] from Dénia. The following missive
was sent by the Emir of Dénia:

It has been a year of such terrible and tremendous lack (in
Egypt), the like of which has never before been seen or
heard. As we have learnt, in an astoundingly short space
of time the very last blade of grass has withered, leaving
nothing left, and the whole population is imprisoned by
a terrifying hunger, suffering from an unbearable and
devastating need; may Allah take pity on them and answer
their prayers.

The Qadis have documented these tragic events and
alongside the Alfaqis[212] have declared their shared view that
this terrible incident is unprecedented, in both duration and
intensity. It is imperative then that this situation is resolved
quickly, and its damaging results alleviated as far as possible,
for it is inexcusable not to bring comfort to the needy. With
this aim, they support the collection of as many fruits (and
other foods) as is necessary, to be sent over the seas, for in
so doing we will not only serve the dynasty – honouring it
as it is due –, but we will also go some way to fulfilling our
responsibilities in this matter, since alleviating the needs of

Muslims is not simply about seeking divine blessings, but is instead an essential duty for any servant (of the Divine), by his very nature, and his inherent status as a Muslim. No effort must be spared in pursuit of this endeavour, for if an act worthy of reproach is thus avoided, the Emir of the Muslims will certainly therefore be praised, by being moved to act to the greater glory of Allah.[213]

The fact that supplies were sent from Dénia in 1055[214] is confirmed in Hispano-Muslim sources.[215] The Egyptian Caliph's response came quickly. A few months later, a boat loaded with gifts set sail for the Spanish coasts as a sign of gratitude. But what were these gifts?

The Cup's Transfer from Jerusalem to Dénia, with León as its Final Destination

The remarkable final clues are to be found in an extraordinary anonymous text that has remained unpublished until now. The text in question recently came to light in the Al-Azhar Library in Cairo and refers to a piece of writing by Abu-l-Hasan Ali ibn Yusuf ibn al-Qifti (568–646 Hijra / 1172–1248 CE), a Muslim writer famed for his biographies of learned men.

(Note that in the original manuscript there are a series of stains which make it impossible to read some words. In this translation these are marked with the word '[stain]' in square brackets.)

Al-Qifti tells us that the cup that the Christians call the Cup of the Messiah – peace be upon him –, used during the celebration with his disciples – may God have mercy on them –, was found in one [stain] of the small churches that are in the outskirts of Jerusalem – may Allah return

The Fatimid Dynasty
(Tenth – Twelfth Centuries)

Abdullah al-Mahdi Billah
(909–934)
↓
Muhammad al-Qa'im Bi-Amrillah
(934–946)
↓
Isma'il al-Mansur Bi-Nasrillah
(946–952)
↓
Ma'ad al-Muizz Li-Dinillah
(952–975)
↓
Abu Mansur Nizar al-Aziz Billah
(975–996)
↓
Huséin al-Hakim Bi-Amrillah
(996–1021)
↓
Ali az-Zahir
(1021–1035)
↓
Ma'ad al-Mustansir Billah
(1035–1094)
↓
Al-Musta'li
(1094–1101)
↓
Al-Amir Bi-Ahkamillah
(1101–1130)
↓
Al-Hafiz
(1130–1149)
↓
Az-Zafir
(1149–1154)
↓
Al-Faiz
(1154–1160)
↓
Al-Adid
(1160–1171)

it to the nation of Islam –. This church is famous because
of the presence of relics of the Bishop Jacob [stain], the
Messiah's true disciple – peace be upon him –. And there
the cup was found, under the protection of some brave
Rumis, who had sworn an oath to protect it, hidden
behind a pair of small curtains, in a niche between the
walls, far from view. The Christians insist that this cup
has extraordinary medicinal powers [stain], a rumour that
is revealed [stain] by the tongues of both Christians and
Muslims, heightening the cup's fame and popularity. But it
is disregarded by men of science and doctrine, and certain
Muslims even strongly reject the claim that any such
church exists [stain] healing.

In the year of the great famine (447), Ali bnu Muyahid
ad-Danii sent a boat with a great supply of provisions
to the country of Egypt. And as he had already heard
something of the power of the Cup, he asked the High
Imam al-Mustanṣir for it, in exchange for whatever was
necessary to offer him for handing it over [stain] since his
intention was to send it to the King of León, Ferdinand
al-Kabir, [stain] king of this land, in the year 429, to
strengthen their alliance. This king already suffered
gravely with the disease of the stones, which would cause
him to die a painful death.

There are others, however, who say that Ali was really a
Christian and his mother was still living in Christian lands,
but that he had not been able to accompany her.

The infidel (in terms of their religion: Christians)
guardians feared that the Cup might fall into Muslim
hands during its movement from one place to another.
Knowing the antipathy that the Jews and the men of
science and doctrine felt towards the cup and [stain] the
act of pilgrimage [stain], they entrusted it to a Frankish

bishop from Al-Yalaliqa, who al-Masûdi mentions in
his book, was in Jerusalem at the time on pilgrimage.
Accompanied by some of the custodians of the Cup, and
his own men, the bishop [stain] gathered up what was
necessary for the journey, and quickly set forth [stain].
And it is known that during the journey [stain]...[216]

After nearly 1,000 years, the voyage undertaken by the Cup
of Christ is finally becoming clear. It was a journey that ended
in the north of the Iberian Peninsula, thanks to the generosity of
Dénia and the power of a monarch destined to change history:
Ferdinand I, King of León.

Information from other sources only serves to corroborate this
extraordinary piece of writing. James the Just, the first bishop of
Jerusalem (also known as the Lord's brother), was buried to the
east of Jerusalem under the pinnacle of the Temple, close to where
he died. This fact is recorded by Hegesippus, Eusebius and Jerome,
all of whom saw the tomb over the first centuries of the era. Over
the years, it seems that a church was built on top of the burial site,
as was customary. Evidently, given the frequent Muslim raids on
the Church of the Holy Sepulchre, it became necessary to move
the relic to a less conspicuous and dangerous place and so it was
brought to this smaller church, the resting place of James the Just.

When we bring the various Christian sources previously
discussed into play, several key points of consensus emerge.
We can see that the employees named in the *Commemoratium*,
the 'two for the Lord's Chalice' whose job it was to care for and
safeguard the Lord's Cup, become in the Muslim writer's words
'some brave Rumis, who had sworn an oath to protect it'. It is also
interesting that the specific way that the Chalice was exhibited in
the Constantine Basilica 'in a reliquary, and people often come
to touch it and kiss it through a hole' (according to Bede), was
translated into a similar arrangement, 'in a niche between the

walls, far from view', in the church which housed the remains of James the Just.

Our sources are a reminder of the terrible challenges that Christians faced during the early part of the eleventh century. Moving as precious a relic as the Lord's Cup from the Church of the Holy Sepulchre to another location cannot have been an easy decision to make after five hundred years. Even more so to have given consent, albeit under duress, to the Cup making a one-way trip to the Iberian Peninsula, leaving the place where it had been stored, in spite of the many tremendous problems it had endured, since the time of the Messiah. Al-Qifti's text suggests that the Chalice's guardians were aware of what was happening, which explains the involvement of the Frankish bishop who was, as they saw it, the only thing preventing this highly sacred relic from being desecrated during its long journey towards Dénia and later, León.

We also have evidence of journeys made by Frankish bishops around the same time, which suggests that it was not unusual to see Gallic and Hispanic prelates in the Holy Land.

In 1054, Saint Lietbertus, bishop of Cambrai, began the pilgrimage to Jerusalem, accompanied by 'part of his flock'. After suffering great hardships while travelling through Bulgaria, Dalmatia, Isauria and Corinth, he ended up in Cyprus. There, deceived by sailors who had decided not to continue to Jerusalem in order to avoid ambushes, Lietbertus reluctantly decided not to tempt fate and chose to return without completing his journey.

While the life of Lietbertus is interesting, his return voyage is even more so. He describes returning in 1056 'with the bishop of Laon, Elinand',[217] who had managed to reach the Holy City. This is worthy of note because in Elinand's biographies there is no mention of him ever having visited Jerusalem.[218] The bishop of Laon (a diocese in modern-day Picardy, France) was an intriguing character who collaborated with the King of France on various complex diplomatic missions. Could this journey have involved the transfer of the Holy Chalice, a duty so important and mysterious that he preferred to keep it a secret? There is little doubt that taking the Grail from Jerusalem to a Muslim taifa in Iberia was likely to have been interpreted very unfavourably by many Christians, even if it could be seen as the lesser of two evils, and a necessary way to protect one of the faith's most valuable relics.

When it came to classifying Christians, the Muslims made a geographical distinction between those that came from the Byzantine Empire, who they called '*Rumis*' (Romans), and those who came from western lands, or 'Franks'. To refer to someone of Western European origin, the Muslims used 'Frank', regardless of whether they were, in current terms, English, French, Italian, Spanish or Portuguese. For them, any Western European was a Frank.

When describing exactly where the Frankish bishop who guarded the Holy Chalice on its journey to Dénia came from, al-Qifti tells us he is from Yalaliqa. This information is key, because Muslim geographers only identified the territories of the northeast of the Iberian Peninsula, i.e. those that belonged to the medieval kingdom of León, as Yalaliqa.

A further piece of information clarifies the context. As well as the pilgrimage made by the Bishop of Laon (in France) to the Holy Lands, which illustrates that there were western priests present in Palestine over the period, we also know that Christians from other parts of Europe headed East, so it is not surprising that someone from Yalaliqa would have been there. In fact, there is a report of a pilgrimage to Jerusalem by a monk called Jacinto (Hyacinth, to give his Anglicized name), around the same dates as the events we describe. The Leonese cleric Jacinto's eyewitness account and description of the holy sites remains unpublished to this day, in the archives of Léon Cathedral.[219]

There is a further allusion to the Lord's Cup in another Islamic source. Ali Iqbal al-Dawla, whose Muslim faith was occasionally called into question, thanked the Caliph for the gifts he had received:

> And you, Oh Lord of Egypt! You have been no less gracious
> than is to be expected of a generous and noble soul in receipt
> of kindness at a time of need, pouring a cascade of gifts that
> are not only coveted by Humanity, but are also the ones you
> value the highest. You have more than returned the favour
> of those who have offered their gifts as generous servants
> of the Lord and have taken pity on those who suffer for His
> will: this letter is a show of respect for your magnanimous
> gesture; may His message come to pass in you (. . .). There
> will be no tongue that will not praise you, no joyous heart that
> will not sing your praises. On receiving your gifts, not one of
> the needy will pray without calling upon you the blessings
> of the Almighty, because neither efforts in the service of
> Allah nor any other religious merit can compare to your
> benevolence (. . .).
>
> Among all the highly prized gifts sent in proof of your
> generosity, the merits of one gift stand out above all
> others: the Destiny of Destinies, the Cup brimming with
> mystery (. . .).
>
> The gift offered up its wonders in abundance until it
> reached your hands and – oh mystery of mysteries, oh the
> heart's untold joy! – each of them, marvellous, was bettered
> by the next miracle. Can there be any ineffable mystery
> greater than such an extraordinary relic? Did it not become
> a beaming lighthouse during the ship-wreck weather of the
> crossing? And did it not settle the sailors' fearful minds and
> calm the seas when they threatened to engulf the ship? When
> it reached us, its reputation was already long established,
> and it was guarded warily by some devoted custodians, for
> traps set by its enemies had prepared them to expect acts of
> wickedness, and the imams kept watch over it too, eager to

benefit from its virtues (. . .).

And so, as it reaches you, oh Iqbal, crowning glory of magnanimity, it will show you the way of peace and spread happiness across every land, just as it did before. How can the most sumptuous gifts, wealth and jewels compare to it? They cannot. Although the boat was filled to the gunwales with the most outlandish gifts, all these were mere bagatelles (. . .). What are earthly gifts before the unfathomable mystery of Eternity?

(. . .) It calms the spirits and eases hardships; it is a tonic for tortured souls and a gift for sick bodies. (. . .) Every land will benefit from its influence, and it will not only allow you to allay the ill fortunes afflicting your land, but it will also protect your borders, providing you with the most powerful of allies: so it shall be, because this strange marvel that has landed here in the West is the most prodigious wonder. And a magnificent stone case shall be built to house such a valuable gift.[220]

Despite its hyperbolic tone we can extract some useful details from this text, which leaves no question that the Chalice's appearance in Dénia was enormously significant for Ali Iqbal al-Dawla. 'Destiny of destinies, the Cup brimming with mystery' implies that receipt of the cup represented a highly significant turning point for the Emir. Firstly, this is because the Chalice's status promised him a certain preferential position in future commercial dealings with Egypt. Secondly, it is because by giving it to Ferdinand I, King of León (*amir de Liyūn*), he would be able to secure his support within the turbulent Iberian Peninsula.[221] For a small taifa like Dénia, potential allies such as these were vital, not least because the threat of Zaragoza and the highly dangerous proximity of Valencia made for routine instability. In fact, around that same time, Ferdinand I showed no hesitation in taking on the eastern provinces, and even managed to lay siege to Valencia.

The text also emphasizes the miraculous nature of the Chalice. As well as its 'extraordinary medicinal powers', something must have happened during the sea crossing that heightened the relic's fame:[222] this 'most prodigious wonder' far exceeded all the other gifts, riches and offerings that came with it.

Furthermore, as if we were picking up where a plot line left off, the Chalice's escorts make an appearance again, both the 'devoted custodians', who are none other than those 'brave Rumis' or Christians dedicated to guarding and protecting it, as referred to in the *Commemoratium*, and the 'enemies' who are a shadowy, yet constant presence in any references to the Chalice, a presence that was also felt in Dénia.

The texts suggest that the Emir spent some time enjoying his possession of the Chalice until, under pressure, he decided to send it on to the person for whom it was ultimately intended, Ferdinand I, who was constructing a magnificent stone 'case' in which to house it. It is around this time that the construction of the Basilica of San Isidoro in León is documented – this is where the Chalice would finally come to rest.[223]

The Cup of Christ's presence in Dénia was a problem. The Muslims recognized its quality, and also held Jesus in high regard as a prophet, but it was not considered appropriate for a Christian relic to remain in the Islamic kingdom for any longer than a brief period before continuing its journey to the border.

The historian al-Maqqari describes a letter addressed to the Emir of Dénia from the Qadi Ibn al-Salim in which he expounds the Cup's virtues in verse, from which we can deduce the inherent danger for a Muslim in possessing it:

> Neither magi nor sorcerers, exploiting their many arts, would succeed in expressing, in any tongue, our gratitude for all the gifts and presents that you have granted us, far surpassing our most excessive hopes.

For not only have you bestowed blessings upon us by
sending us such a vast and varied array of your most sublime
possessions, the largest and most glorious of gems, whose
radiance dazzles us, but in your boundless excellence oh,
great lord, you have openly and honestly shown us the Cup,
and lavishly poured its fascinating contents upon us.
And so splendid are your treasures, that there can be none
greater than the hope, already fulfilled, of having laid eyes
upon this peerless trove.[224]

We do not know how the Cup reached León, but we have
found evidence that it did so, in the form of none other than the
Chalice of Doña Urraca, Lady of Zamora. It formed the upper
agate cup, joined to another cup, one turned upwards, the other
down, and mounted with gold and the princess's personal jewels.
Also preserved within the treasury of the Royal Pantheon at the
San Isidoro Basilica in León is a small chest in niello silver that
accompanied the Cup. It is dedicated to Sadaqa, (Yūsūf al-Ṣadiqī),
an Egyptian vizier who was executed by al-Mustanṣir, the very
same Fatimid Caliph who had offered the Cup of Christ to the
Emir of Dénia. It is one of several luxury items that are also Fatimid
in provenance, all dateable to the same period: the middle of the
eleventh century, when they left Dénia for the capital of the most
powerful Spanish Christian kingdom of the time, León. This
particular piece, like others in the San Isidoro collection of the
same date and origin, undoubtedly arrived in the same cargo as
the Holy Chalice, and further substantiates its presence.

The journey taken across the Iberian Peninsula would probably
have followed the most direct route to León. Steering clear of
conflict zones, such as Valencia and its powerful ally Zaragoza,
it would have been possible for a small, heavily armed group to
keep a low profile by avoiding large population centres, and to
reach the south of Castile by crossing Toledo.

Saladin Confirms the Cup's Journey

These two extraordinary texts are complemented by a third, which, thanks to its provenance, is hugely valuable and offers further proof of the Chalice's arrival in León. The names associated with the previous writings were important in their own age, but the passage of time has relegated them to the domain of academics and specialists.

If we were to describe the protagonist of the next text as the Kurd al-Nāsir Salāh ad-Dīn Yūsūf ibn Ayyūb, the same thing might be presumed to have happened. However, given the title by which he is better known to the Western world, Saladin, it is a rather different story.

Saladin (1138–93 CE) was one of the greatest Muslim rulers of any age. Defender of the Sunni orthodoxy, he unified the Near East and symbolized the epitome of the Muslim nobleman in the Middle Ages. His great victory over the crusaders at the battle of Hattin opened up the gates of Jerusalem and the Holy Land. The relevant document, which is previously unpublished, contains the following report concerning his daughter:

> Given the state of our daughter's health, who as you
> know suffers from diseased blood flow and the sickness
> of the stone, and having previously taken advice from the
> physicians and mufti of Jerusalem, we ordered a piece of
> the holy stone to be sent, which had been cut from it with
> a kommeyya [a curved blade used by the Moors, literally
> meaning 'of the sleeve', because it could be hidden within
> one][225] by the leader of Banī-l-Aswad's men in the year
> 447, when the wicked al-Mustansir named him head of the
> expedition to Dénia in the far West [stain]. And it is known
> how doing so darkened his face and hands [stain].
> The shard taken from the Cup was sent to Salah ad-din,

may God have pity on him, and after his daughter was
healed by the piece of stone placed upon her body, he
ordered for it to be kept in a cabinet in the House of Wealth
[the Islamic public treasury].[226]

This passage describes events of little more than a century
after the Chalice was moved, and contains information that
corroborates our previous assertion. Saladin refers to a daughter
of his; the only daughter that we know of married Malik Shah II
Qutb ud-Din, son of Kilij Arsalan II, Seljuk Turks and Sultans from
Konya or Rum.[227] This document also confirms the date that the
Holy Chalice was moved to 'Daniyya' (Dénia) as the year 447 of
the Hijra (1055–6 CE).[228]

Saladin's text also reveals new information about the journey.
First of all, apart from the Frankish bishop, al-Mustanṣir also
commissioned a member of the Banī-l-Aswad family to supervise
the mission, and secondly, it refers to the fact that the Holy Chalice
had been chipped – in Dénia, around a century before Saladin
ordered the shard to be sent – using a kommeyya. The fact that
al-Mustanṣir is described as 'wicked' should not come as a surprise,
given that from the outset Saladin took every opportunity he
could to criticize the Fatimid dynasty, until its destruction was
complete. Nor is it unusual that the leadership of the expedition
should have fallen to someone he trusted, in light of the wealth of
gifts that accompanied the Chalice. The really notable thing is the
description of the fine shard, the 'piece of the holy stone', taken
from the Chalice by the member of the 'Banī-l-Aswad' family
using a double-edged kommeyya. This is extraordinary because
the Cup at San Isidoro is clearly damaged on the upper edge, with
a missing piece around three centimetres long, made with a linear
object, such as a kommeyya.[229] The upper part of the Chalice of
Doña Urraca, kept at the Basilica of San Isidoro in León, must
therefore be the very same cup that was brought from Jerusalem

in the middle of the eleventh century.

There are two final aspects to consider: firstly, the miraculous or healing properties of the Chalice, reiterated various times and by several different sources. It is significant that Saladin, having 'previously taken advice from the physicians and mufti of Jerusalem', would choose to ask for the piece of the Cup kept in Cairo. This is also unexpected, given that 'men of science and doctrine' had expressed misgivings, if not outright hostility, about the Chalice. Secondly, there is the intrinsic value of the shard, which was kept in the House of Wealth, the Islamic public treasury: probably the most secure location in the whole of North Africa.

Before we move on to look at the next period in the history of the Grail, let's summarize what we have learned thus far. In light of the information from the Egyptian manuscripts which had lain undiscovered for a millennium, we are convinced that the Holy Cup that was once kept in Jerusalem is encased within the upper part of the Chalice of Doña Urraca, stored in San Isidoro Basilica in León. Jerusalem's Christian community suffered numerous attacks in the first part of the eleventh century, centred on the Church of the Holy Sepulchre, and it seems that these attacks led to the decision to move the Cup to the outskirts of Jerusalem, to a small church housing the remains of the city's first bishop, Saint James the Just. We have also learned that the Muslims located it there in 1055 and gave it as a gift to the Emir of Dénia; that it was accompanied on its journey by a dedicated custodian of the Chalice, a Frankish bishop and a member of the Banī-l-Aswad family, whose role was to supervise the expedition, and who broke off a piece that was stored in the public treasury of Cairo.

Together with the details contained in other texts that were only previously known out of context, there can be no doubt that these insights provide an answer to one of the greatest questions of all time. They reveal the real and final resting place of Christ's Chalice: León, political arbiter of Iberia and capital of the most important Christian kingdom of its time.

PART TWO:
THE CHALICE
IN LEÓN

Ferdinand Al-Kabir, Emir de Liyun, First Guardian of the Cup of Christ

Following the Islamic conquest of 711–88 CE, Asturias, a small Christian kingdom in the northwest of Spain, became the launching point of the *Reconquista,* the Christian fight to reconquer the Islamic territories of Iberia. Over subsequent centuries, the Christian kingdoms of the north and west, including Galicia, Portugal, Navarre and Aragón, gradually expanded by repopulating territory that had been abandoned by the Moors. The Reconquista would not be complete until the fall of Granada in 1492, at which point the whole of the Iberian peninsula was finally returned to Christian rule.

As we have concluded, the chipped Holy Cup travelled from Jersusalem to Dénia as a gift to its Emir, granted by the Caliph in recognition of the aid that Dénia had provided during the Egyptian famine. The Emir then gave this most important of Christian relics to King Ferdinand I of León, in northwest Spain. By donating the Chalice, the Emir meant to bolster Ferdinand's burgeoning religious authority and thus gain for Dénia his protection during a period of intense political instability throughout the Iberian Peninsula.

León's eponymous capital was based at the confluence of the Bernesga and Torío rivers, a position with a commanding vantage point. It had been founded by the Roman Sixth Victorious Legion (*Legio VI Victrix*) around 29 BCE during the Cantabrian Wars that secured the conquest of Hispania during the reign of Octavius Augustus. The settlement then became the peninsula's military headquarters under the Seventh Twin Legion (*Legio VII Gemina*), created by the Emperor Galba in 68 CE.[230]

For most of its existence, the focus of the Seventh Twin Legion was to oversee the exploitation of gold, at sites such as Las Médulas in the northeast, and to ensure stability in Hispania, although one or two of its detachments would still participate in campaigns at the Empire's borders. At the beginning of the fifth century, Suebi, Vandal and Alan invasions of Iberia took the focus away from León, leaving it open to invasion by both Moorish and Visigothic forces over the following centuries. Eventually, after becoming part of the Kingdom of Asturias in 742, it would go on to play a prominent role in the Reconquista.[231]

Alfonso III, the last king of Asturias, died in 910, at which point the seat of the Iberian Christian kingdom shifted from Oviedo to León, which was now a separate kingdom. By the early eleventh century, the Christian Spanish territories occupied approximately a third of the Iberian peninsula, bounded by the Atlantic to the west, Navarre to the east, the Atlantic coast to the north and the river Douro to the south. León was both a conflict zone exposed to Muslim invasions and a meeting place for Islam and Christianity's different worlds.

Founders of the kingdoms of Castile (1065) and Portugal (1139), conquerors of Toledo (1085) and originators of the first European courts attended by the popular classes (1188), the monarchs of León took the title of *Imperator Totius Hispaniae* (Emperor of All Spain). This office was first held by Ferdinand I, the next recipient of Christ's Chalice.

The Early Years: Prince of Navarre, Count of Castile

The great monarch Ferdinand I, born c.1015, was the second son of the sovereign Sancho III Garcés of Navarre and the noblewoman Muniadomna Sánchez, daughter of Count Sancho García of Castile. The royal blood of León and Pamplona as well as the noble lineages of the Pyrenees, Castile and Saldaña ran through his veins. Genetically, the prince was, like his father, more Leonese than Navarran.[232]

Sancho III had married his wife in around the year 1010. At the time, her family was at the zenith of its power and influence. The Counts of both Castile and Saldaña were politically active north and south of the border, and their famed military campaigns even went as far as the capital of the Al-Andalus caliphate (the Islamic Iberian territories), Córdoba, in southern Spain.[233]

This marriage met with widespread approval. The couple collected artefacts from Christian raids in Muslim lands, such as the Leire ivory casket. Carved from the finest elephant tusk by the artisan Faray (1005) for the heir of the Islamic ruler Almanzor, Abd al-Malik al-Muzzaffar, the casket was considered one of the most exceptional works of Andalusian art.[234]

The Christian kings and noblemen of León and Navarre had always been interested in the products of Moorish artisans. Numerous accounts refer to Islamic tapestries and other rich Córdoban or Fatimid gifts offered by the emirs and caliphs to the powerful nobles of the north as a way of sealing treaties.[235] It is not surprising, therefore, that the Leire ivory casket and other such luxury goods were to be found throughout Pamplona, Burgos and León in the eleventh century.

As second in line, the order of succession ought to have relegated Ferdinand to a lesser destiny. However, his fortune changed due to a series of deaths and the ambitions of his father, Sancho III, whose opportunistic drive to increase his territory overrode any regard for ethics or tradition. In 1028, the death of Alfonso V of León gave the young Bermudo III[236] the throne, opening up access to a territory in which Doña Urraca of Navarre, the king's widow and Sancho III's sister, would play a key role.[237] The following year, Prince Don García, the Count of Castile in León, was assassinated and the Counts of Saldaña, Carrión and Cea 'disappeared'. This left Muniadomna Sánchez of Castile, Queen of Navarre, with an inheritance that she promptly claimed in the name of her husband, Sancho III. Sancho wasted no time in expanding his estate,[238] becoming the Pyrenean Count of Ribagorza.

In 1034, Sancho III seized control of Astorga and León and proclaimed himself imperator, appropriating a title that had previously been tied to the monarchy of León, still held at that time by Bermudo III.[239] To reinforce his grip upon what was then the most powerful kingdom of Christian Iberia, Sancho married two of his children to León's monarch and his only sister. This double marriage left the throne to Bermudo and his wife, Jimena of Navarre, and the county of Castile plus the territories up to the river Cea to Prince Ferdinand and his spouse Sancha de León. Thus began the separation of the kingdoms of Castile and León.[240]

In 1035, at the height of his power, Sancho III died. By then, he had already written his will and divided up his estate. To his first-born son, García, he left Navarre, some areas of Aragón and a part of the old county of Castile: principally La Bureba, Álava, Montes de Oca, Trasmiera and Encartaciones. The remaining Castilian territory from Burgos to Cea went to Ferdinand, who had governed Castile in its entirety since 1029, prior to his father's death. Surprisingly, the remaining inheritance was shared between Sancho's last rightful male heir, Gonzalo, who received Sobrarbe and Ribagorza, and his illegitimate son Ramiro, to whom he granted Aragón. Both Gonzalo and Ramiro became vassals of the Kingdom of Pamplona, but as Count of

Castile, Ferdinand remained beholden to the King of León, Bermudo III.[241]

Thus, tensions arose between Sancho III's heirs as soon as the king died. Ferdinand found himself with a substantially reduced inheritance, which he deemed a provocation and impingement of his rights. He wouldn't express his resentment, however, until after he had become the sovereign ruler of León.[242]

From Count of Castile to King of León (1037–8)

With Sancho III gone and his territories carved up among his four sons, Bermudo III could rest easy in the short term, without the threat of imminent attack from the Pyrenees. He immediately reasserted his power. Documentary evidence from the period allows us to reconstruct his actions.

In February 1035, along with his spouse Jimena, Queen of Navarre, Bermudo granted a series of privileges to the bishopric of Palencia. Surprisingly, the record of this act makes no mention of his sister, Princess Sancha of León, or his brother-in-law the Count-Prince Ferdinand,[243] both of whom were undoubtedly more involved in the affairs of a diminished Castile, and still under the watchful eye of Navarre.[244]

A year later, in January 1036, we find a reference to Princess Sancha, who is confirmed as '*Sancia, prolis Adefonsi principis*' in a document linked to Sahagún monastery, situated in Cea, a region disputed since Sancho III's unfortunate intervention in León.[245] This is particularly intriguing, because, as Count of Castile, these lands were part of Ferdinand's wife's dowry, while as far as Bermudo III was concerned, they were strictly part of León. Sancha's presence, therefore, provided political security for the brothers-in-law, who were now destined to come into conflict over Cea-Pisuerga.

In June 1037, we find the very last example of Bermudo III's name, alongside his wife's,[246] ratifying a legal act. In late August or early September, he confronted his brother-in-law and vassal the Count of Castile at the battlefield of Tamarón in Tierra de Campos. Ferdinand's troops, bolstered by an alliance with the new King of Navarre, defeated and killed the rightful monarch of León.[247] The *Historia silense,* a medieval Latin chronicle of the Iberian Peninsula, describes the battle:

> The two armies had locked eyes, challenging one another,
> their weapons glinting, when Bermudo, emboldened and
> full of daring, digs his spurs into his famous steed Pelagiolo
> and, battle hungry, surges forth, his spear aloft betwixt
> the tight ranks of the enemy; but bitter Death, whom
> no mortal can defeat, throws him to the ground in this
> tempestuous gallop, while brutal García and Ferdinand
> fought ever more fiercely, setting seven of their strongest
> warriors upon him in turn.[248]

The same source describes the numerous difficulties facing Ferdinand after he became king, thanks to his marriage to the Princess Sancha, who was sole heir to the throne since Bermudo III had died childless. Firstly, he was forced to lay siege to the kingdom's capital, which had refused to recognize him. The baron who defended it, Count Fernando Fláiniz, came from a powerful bloodline, closely linked to the throne. For months, Ferdinand I was unable to secure the legitimacy that would come from ruling the city. The siege lasted until 1038 when, surrounded by noblemen of León and Castile, he finally succeeded, as confirmed in a contemporary account:

> I, King Ferdinand, entered León and received its
> recognition, endorsed and confirmed by every Castilian and

The Royal Dynasty of Léon and the Main Dominas of the Royal Infantado of San Isidoro

FAMILY TREE OF THE NAVARRAN DYNASTY

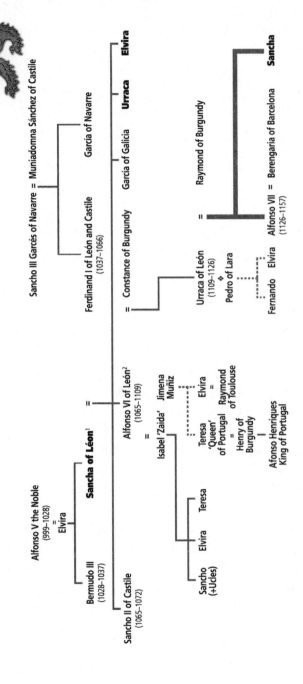

1 In bold are those queens and princesses who were dominas of the infantado during the eleventh and twelfth centuries.
2 We have included the two marriages that led to proven succession.

103

Leonese here present, as if they were but one man . . . [249]

The *Historia silense* also describes the coronation at León Cathedral, overseen by Bishop Servando. Ferdinand's wife Sancha was now his sole source of legitimacy to the throne, his own claim having been tarnished by the battle of Tamarón.[250] Ferdinand presided over a new era and a dynastic change that would last until the death of his granddaughter, Urraca, in 1126.

Until he was genuinely accepted by the Leonese aristocracy, the new sovereign chose to focus on addressing immediate domestic issues, firefighting among the nobility and, above all, trying to resolve the border problems caused by the division of his father's legacy.

Ferdinand I the Great, King of León (1038–65)

At first, Ferdinand accepted the territorial losses in the will that gave Castilian lands over to Navarre. However, as monarch of León he could no longer allow such illegitimate borders to stand, meaning that war with Navarre was inevitable. Ferdinand's reputation amongst his Leonese peers was at stake. For Ferdinand's few sympathetic barons, the definitive proof of his *Leonese-ness* would be to confront his own brother, García.

Ferdinand I initially tried to use diplomacy to demand that the old borders between Castile and Navarre be restored to their pre-1035 position. Faced with the sheer impossibility of coming to an agreement with his broken family, he wasted no time in raising an army by calling up every nobleman from Galicia to Castile. Ultimately, however, this was not the only reason for the battle. Besides the border skirmishes, there were further problems between the brothers; when Ferdinand visited Nájera in Navarre, seeking treatment for his illness, he had been gravely offended by King García. A repentant García tried to make peace with his Leonese brother, but the disharmony was palpable.

The *Historia silense* provides a more detailed account of these events:

> King Ferdinand raised a great army all the way from the farthest reaches of Galicia, and set forth to avenge the insult. But first he sent ambassadors to García suggesting that they should each go on living peacefully in their kingdoms without resorting to arms to resolve the dispute, for they were both brothers and should be at ease in their homes. But he also warned García that he would not be able to withstand the many men he had at the ready.

García rejected his brother's olive branch, and the monarchs resolved to meet on the battlefield at Atapuerca in 1054:

> García of Navarre had already set up his encampment in the middle of the Atapuerca valley, but that night Ferdinand's soldiers occupied the hill next to it. These fighters were related to King Bermudo and knew full well that Ferdinand wanted his brother (García) to be captured alive, at Queen Sancha's request. But (these men) wanted to avenge the blood of their kin.

This is the background to the fratricidal clash as well as the territorial claim: win the battle, and Ferdinand would earn his vassals' lifelong and unshakable loyalty.

> As soon as Titan (the sun) rose the next day, ordered formations (of soldiers) from both sides advanced amid the heavenly rays, to the sound of loud cries. They fired their arrows from distance, brandishing their deadly swords

as they collided, and the aforementioned group of strong fighters made a frenzied charge down from on high and, carving their way through the enemy at great speed, all headed to converge on King García, who fell from his horse, lifeless, run through by their pointed spears. The Moors who had been brought to the battle tried to flee, but most of them were captured. They gave the mortal remains of the king a burial in the church of Santa María de Nájera that he himself had built with such great devotion.[251]

The battle resulted in the kingdom of Navarre being inherited by a child, Sancho IV Garcés of Peñalén.[252]

These events occurred shortly before the Chalice's arrival in León, and there is no doubt that they caused Ferdinand I profound unease. In just a few years, not only had he reshaped his father's legacy, but he had also altered fate. Perhaps he felt that God had chosen to elevate him above his brothers and his Muslim neighbours in the peninsula. A heavy burden rested on his shoulders, but he felt he could count on divine protection.

When Ferdinand I took possession of the Chalice, it validated his status as the defender of the Christian faith, acting as the spur that would shape his future government. It would also be written into the royal dedications of manuscripts: *Rex Fredenandus* gave way to *imperator* – a very significant change indeed.[253]

Later, in 1063, the disputes with Navarre that had been settled in Ferdinand's favour came full circle, in the form of an armed confrontation with his other brother, Ramiro of Aragón, a conflict that Ferdinand undertook to defend the interests of the Muslim Emir of Zaragoza.[254] In retaliation for Ramiro's attack on the fortress at Graus, Ferdinand I sent troops to support his ally al-Muqtadir. Ramiro died in battle and was succeeded by his son, Sancho Ramírez.[255] Only the removal of his brothers from the Iberian political scene granted the Leonese king a brief respite from familial conflict.

Overcoming the delicate balance of kinship and politics that came from being involved in neighbouring – but not always allied – kingdoms, Ferdinand consolidated his fame and glory and established his authority within Iberian Christianity, just as he had done with the Andalusian Muslims when the fall of the caliphate of Córdoba in 1031 saw them fragment into different taifas.[256]

A shrewd strategist, Ferdinand I knew that such relationships offered opportunities to expand his territories and demand protection payments or tributes, known as *parias*, in exchange for signing alliances or peace treaties.[257]

His first intervention came in 1043 when Yahya ibn Ismail al-Mamun of Toledo appealed to the monarch for help against the Emir of Zaragoza. This aid provided Ferdinand I with an extra source of income for the royal treasury: his ally paid him an annual duty.[258] From this moment on, Christian state intervention in internal Muslim affairs became the norm.

In 1055, with the approval of the members of his palatium, Ferdinand I entered the taifa of Badajoz and laid siege to the city of Seia, launching a series of military campaigns in Portugal that culminated in the taking of Lamego (1057) and Viseo (1058), where his father-in-law Alfonso V had met his end some thirty years earlier.[259]

Based on the recently discovered manuscripts – coupled with our prior knowledge of the relations between the Emir of Dénia and the King of León – it would have been the late 1050s when the Chalice reached the north-eastern capital at the end of its journey from Jerusalem.[260] This most valuable of gifts was a clear endorsement for a monarch who had by then established himself as the leading Iberian Christian, blessed by God: according to the religious mentality of the time, a new David. Around the same time, being buried in León began to carry great esteem, and the dynasty founded its royal vaults.

In 1060 Ferdinand turned his attentions to Zaragoza,[261] conquering the fortresses of Gormaz, Berlanga and Aguilera and making a vassal of his former ally the Emir al-Muqtadir. In 1062 it was Toledo's turn, when its ruler al-Mamun failed to pay him the agreed duty.[262]

In 1063 Ferdinand's intimidation campaigns secured him protection payments from Seville, Badajoz, Toledo and Zaragoza.[263] This also enabled the Leonese king to ask al-Mutadid, the ruler of Seville, for the body of Saint Justa. His ambassadors, the bishops Alvito of León and Ordoño of Astorga, travelled on the mission to Seville along with the count Munio Muñoz and a substantial group of knights. However, they returned with the remains of Saint Isidore of Seville (San Isidoro) instead. The Leonese prelate claimed that he had been visited by a vision of Saint Isidore, who told him that it was God's will for his body to be worshipped, rather than Saint Justa. A week later the bishop died, just as the Sevillian saint had foretold.[264]

At this point, you may have noticed that not one of the great Leonese king's threatening campaigns or conquests was directed at Dénia. This is a significant fact, not least because trade made Dénia a particularly wealthy territory, and tributes from other Muslim kingdoms contributed so significantly to Ferdinand I's state coffers. His latest southerly raids had targeted the large taifas, and especially those which in one way or another represented a threat to Dénia, such as Zaragoza or Valencia. This favour can be explained by the special bond formed between León and Dénia as a result of the gift of Christ's Chalice.

In the same year as Saint Isidore's remains reached his kingdom, Ferdinand I summoned his barons to announce the division of his lands. His first-born son, Sancho, would receive Castile and the tributes from Zaragoza; Alfonso received León and the Toledo tributes; while the youngest of his male children, García, received Galicia and the tributes from Badajoz and Sevilla. His daughters Urraca and Elvira would inherit the *infantado*, or the right to the principality, an institution that would boost San Isidoro's status as home of the royal bloodline.[265]

It is traditionally thought that the reasons for such an unusual decision lay in the monarch's desire to reinstate the Navarran hereditary models used by his father, Sancho III, and distribute territories between his different sons.

We do not wish to entirely discard the conventional historical view. However, Ferdinand I's exceptional political vision, which led him to conduct effective and assertive strikes on the taifas without excessive harm, and his understanding of the Hispanic Muslims' weaknesses, might also suggest that he was trying to decide the territorial future of the peninsula by moving his pawns on the geopolitical chessboard.

Perhaps he was trying to replicate the former division of the Islamic border regions during the caliphate – which he would have remembered from his youth – into three separate zones or sectors: the upper region, led by Zaragoza, the middle, centred on Toledo, and the lower area around Mérida. Incidentally, each of the kingdoms that he entrusted to his sons came with its taifa counterpart, as if, as well as distributing the tributes, he also wanted to mark out an area of potential expansion under the Reconquista.

As an intriguing strategic panorama opened up, there were clear reasons to intensify Christian efforts in the border region: by taking on the area around Zaragoza, Ferdinand's Castile, to which he joined Navarre, could curtail expansion by the recently founded kingdom of Aragón. His Castile would reach right across the Ebro valley, to the Mediterranean coast.

León, with its special relationship with Toledo, would extend as far as the Sierra Morena mountains, opening up many opportunities over the border into the Guadalquivir valley. This is somewhat comparable to the conquest proposed by Alfonso VIII of Castile and Ferdinand III in the thirteenth century.

Like Castile, the kingdom of Galicia was created in 1065 and was shaped by the backbone of the Atlantic coast. More than a century later, Algarve was taken, completing the Portuguese part of the Reconquista, and a section of Galicia was added to the independent kingdom of Portugal, while the Christian neighbours disputed sovereignty of the Extremadura region.

Ferdinand's dream was to dominate the Islamic peninsular territories through his sons, to solidify their role as Christian governors, and to cut off any routes to expansion for the Navarrans, Aragonese and Catalans. A set of kingdoms in the hands of one dynasty, then, and one dynasty alone: his own.

Once the division had been made official, Ferdinand launched his next campaigns: the first against Coimbra in Portugal (1064),[266] which he managed to conquer after a long siege, thereby extending the Leonese borders as far as the river Mondego. In 1065 he took on Zaragoza, which had once again refused to pay the agreed tribute. On this occasion Ferdinand went as far as the city walls of Valencia (1065), which he besieged. However, he was then forced to back out, tormented by the serious illness that would lead to his death on 27 December 1065.[267]

According to the *Historia silense*, Ferdinand's death throes lasted for several days until, on Monday 26 December, he asked to be dressed with all the royal attributes such as his robe and crown of gold and, accompanied arm-in-arm by noblemen and priests, prostrated himself at the altars blessed by the bodies of the saints. There, still clear of voice, he relinquished the ornaments of power in an act of public penance that, in Visigothic fashion, climaxed with his tonsure; the religious act of his head being sheared. From that moment, Ferdinand was effectively considered to have died, withdrawn from public life, from the throne and from power. With great humility and extraordinary faith, thus departed the Navarran prince who had gone on to become the Count of Castile, King of León and the most significant figure of the Iberian political world of his era. He was, undoubtedly, one of the greatest and most clear-sighted monarchs of medieval Spain.

The Consolidation of a New Dynasty and the Construction of San Isidoro in León

The Leonese kings before Ferdinand I had chosen various different burial sites. Most were buried at Oviedo, the Cathedral of León, or the palace and monastery complex at San Salvador de Palat de Rey.[268] Alfonso V (999–1028) decided to create a new site,[269] the Church of San Juan Bautista,[270] to house all the royal remains that were spread across the capital and beyond. San Juan Bautista would become the basis for the future royal complex of San Isidoro of León. From the tenth century, this precinct housed the San Pelayo convent, where the new Leonese episcopal tomb was built.[271]

The main reason that Ferdinand I chose to be buried in San Isidoro was the influence of his Leonese wife, Sancha. Their strong union superseded his original decision to be buried in Oña or Arlanza, locations that were linked to the Counts of Castile, the title he had held before the battle of Tamarón. Acceptance of his wife's suggestion effectively created a definitive bond in death, granting dynastic legitimacy to Ferdinand and his descendants, and rooting his legacy within the old Asturian monarchy.[272]

Having settled on this course of action, Ferdinand and Sancha constructed the temple, which was consecrated on 21 December 1063, in the presence of the king himself. Both he and his wife would find their final resting place under its protective mantle. It was in this year that, after his triumphant campaign against Mérida and while he was in the former Roman city, Ferdinand sent the bishops Ordoño of Astorga and Alvito of León to Seville, to collect the remains of Saint Justa. He wanted to sanctify his temple with the relics, although, as we have seen, it would instead be Saint Isidore who was eventually brought back to León.[273]

A day later, on 22 December, accompanied by their children Sancho, García, Alfonso, Elvira and Urraca, together with other close family members, Ferdinand and Sancha lavishly decorated the church and convent with ornaments and jewels. Those mentioned in the document signed by the monarchs are of particular note.[274]

Ferdinand's death in 1065, and that of his wife two years later, ended the period of tense calm that followed the division of his lands decreed by his will. As soon as Doña Sancha died, war broke out between the sons. The confrontation was initiated by Sancho who, as first-born son, felt aggrieved by his inheritance. After various clashes, García was imprisoned and Alfonso left for exile in Toledo. However, as we shall see, Sancho went on to perish in 1072 in the siege of Zamora, a city ruled by Urraca, at which point Alfonso regained his territories, as well as Castile and Galicia. Seven years after Ferdinand's death, Alfonso ruled all the lands once governed by his father.

Little is known about the royal vaults at San Isidoro during those seven years. From 1072 onwards, Urraca, as custodian of the memory of her parents and forefathers and as guardian of the remains of San Isidoro and other treasures, gave the Sevillian saint an elevated status, being symbolic of the entire territory. The remains were now assumed to grant protection not only to the deceased monarchs, but also to the kingdom and, therefore, to whoever governed the destiny of its female guardianship: the *infantado*. A woman, echoing the oldest Grail poems, fulfilled the leading role in the temple of the Chalice.

Thanks to Urraca, the Isidorian vaults became a monumental space, housing a growing number of treasures. Standing out among them is the Chalice which took her name[275] and whose construction encased one of Christianity's most valuable artefacts, the Cup of Christ, which had arrived a few years earlier from Dénia, and on the node of which can still be read: IN NOMINE D(OMINI) VRRACA FREDINA(N)DI.

San Isidoro helped to construct and legitimize the monarchy, and Urraca's role was fundamental. She oversaw the building of the vaults themselves, and exercised significant influence over the architectural design, planning and development of the temple and its precinct. She was undoubtedly the dynasty's greatest guardian, its staunchest defender, the rock at the centre of a broken family and, above all, through her blood and divine protection from on high, she carried the authority of the most powerful royal house of the Iberian Peninsula of the time: the Leonese monarchy.

The Royal Protectresses
of León and the Legends
of the Grail

So far we have studied the biblical liturgy, documents and chronicles of the Lord's Cup, the testimonies of pilgrims who came to worship it in Jerusalem, and the story of its transfer to Iberia as a token of friendship from the Emir of Dénia to King Ferdinand I of León. We now move on to the Holy Chalice's first appearances in medieval European literature; as the Holy Grail of Arthurian legend. In these accounts we find many intriguing details that could be connected to the history of León.

León's territorial gains in the eleventh century, particularly the conquest of Toledo by Alfonso VI (1085), attracted many European noblemen seeking fame, honour and fortune at the open border against Islam. Many such knights came from Languedoc, in the Midi-Pyrénées, and troubadours from this area of France came to play key roles in forging Grail legends.[276] A main source of the epic poem *Parzival* (*c.*1207),[277] by Wolfram von Eschenbach (1170 to *c.*1220), is said to have been the poet Kyot or Kiot, known as 'the Provençal', who discovered an ancient Arabic manuscript written in Toledo by Flegetanis, revealing the secrets of the Holy Grail.[278]

There has been some debate over whether or not Kyot was Guiot de Provins (*c.*1105 to *c.*1208), a French popular poet and troubadour who travelled widely across Europe and to Jerusalem. Guiot is believed to have taken part in the Third Crusade, having written of it in terms that demonstrate direct knowledge.[279]

Interestingly, during this same era, there is evidence that Leonese and Galician noblemen were present in Palestine; men such as Count Rodrigo Álvarez, who adopted the habit of the Templar order for a time and was a direct descendant of King Alfonso VI of León. His presence in Jerusalem is well known; he founded the Order of Mountjoy, whose headquarters were next to the Holy City. So it is not inconceivable that the troubadour Guiot de Provins would personally have known some of these knights.[280] We have to acknowledge that many scholars now believe Kyot to have been a character invented by von Eschenbach as a fictional device. However, there are other features in the Grail legends that resonate with the history of León.

Von Eschenbach, for his part, sets certain events from *Parzival* in Spain. In one of them, the protagonist's father, whose chivalry and physique he praises, is battling Muslims in the East and in Africa. His hunger for adventure leads him across the Strait of Gibraltar to meet with his cousin, 'the king of Spain', after a quick journey from Seville to Toledo.

The emphasis placed on Toledo within the 'the kingdom of Spain' is also relevant. Although there were in fact various kingdoms in the peninsula during von Eschenbach's lifetime, the expressions *rex Hispaniae* and *imperator totius Hispaniae* are traditionally used to refer to the kings of León, particularly during the eleventh and twelfth centuries when Ferdinand I, Alfonso VI and Alfonso VII each held the title. Following the conquest of Toledo in 1085, the latter two started to include the city's name within their formulaic titles, which became *imperante in Toleto et in Hispaniae*.[281] The once Visigothic city obviously provided the Leonese monarchs with a key piece of territorial recognition, but the most significant development came in 1135 when Alfonso VII was crowned at León Cathedral, received the vassalage of the noblemen Ramón Berenguer of Barcelona, the Count of Toulouse, García the King of Navarre and 'many counts and dukes of Gascony and France became his obedient servants'.[282]

The more deeply we analyse the early legends and poems that recount events related to the Grail, the more connections we find between the historical backdrop which informed their authors and Spain. Of course, it can be difficult to untangle the elements of fiction and allegory in these legends: they often carry spiritual messages and they vary widely as to the nature of the Grail itself, but it is nonetheless interesting to look at the ways in which they relate to the historical records. Specifically, there are allusions to northeastern Iberia and its relationship to the political development of France, the birthplace of Guiot de Provins and Chrétien de Troyes, inspirations to von Eschenbach, Robert de Boron and other medieval authors who wrote about the Holy Grail.

It is here that the Leonese monarchy becomes entwined with the medieval literary context against which the traditional Grail legends developed. In the work *Titurel*, a prequel to *Parzival*, von Eschenbach places the Grail (which in this version of the legend is a stone rather than a cup) in the hands of a royal dynasty; the same one to which the so-called 'kings of Spain' belong. A similar idea appears in the work of Chrétien de Troyes (although there we find the Grail being described differently again, as a dish or platter).

By examining the points at which the French and German versions of the tale overlap, we can trace the dynasty's story as follows: the old king Titurel founds a temple to safeguard the Grail. Already advanced in years, he entrusts the Grail and all it symbolizes to his son, Frimutel. His early death means it ends up in the hands of another descendant, Anfortas, whose love affairs break the sacred bond of trust placed in the guardians of the

Grail. This king is left crippled by a serious leg wound. Because of his sins the kingdom finds itself barren, without a male heir, causing no end of problems when the chivalrous heroes arrive in search of the Grail.

The fiction is almost a carbon copy of the political events in the time of Ferdinand I: the king built San Isidoro, the place which housed the Lord's Cup, whose first-born son, Sancho of Castile, died young, turning the second-in-line, Alfonso VI, into the monarch and protector of the Isidorian temple and its contents. Alfonso VI also suffered a serious wound to the thigh during the Battle of Sagrajas (1086), a year after conquering Toledo, and the product of his romantic exploits were his two bastard daughters Teresa of Portugal, wife of the Frenchman Henry of Burgundy, and her sister Elvira, wife of Count Raymond of Toulouse, who accompanied him on the crusades. Towards the end of his life, the sovereign lost his only son at Uclés (1108), and his kingdom was left devoid of any male heir. The line of succession passed, therefore, to a widowed woman, his eldest legitimate daughter Urraca, and the king looked to find her a husband among all of the best-known knights of León, Castile, Galicia, Aragón and Navarre. Finally, King Alfonso I the Battler was chosen.

The parallels between the early Grail poems and historical events are intriguing, and there is another notable detail: the role of maidens directly assigned to guard the Lord's Cup. According to Chrétien de Troyes, Perceval (as he is called in this version) was awarded the honour of meeting the Fisher King (elsewhere identified as Anfortas). At the king's castle, Perceval finds himself in the presence of a strange cortège: a young man carrying a spear is followed by two pages holding candelabra. Behind them is a beautiful maiden of noble descent, displaying the golden Grail adorned with gems so dazzling that they illuminate the whole room. Finally, bringing up the rear of the procession, a second maiden carries a tray.[283]

The eastern Muslim authors who wrote about the Lord's Cup and the early Grail texts both describe a shining vessel. As for the regal maiden carrying the treasure of gold and jewels, historical precedent suggests that she might be a fictionalized version of a holder of the *infantazgo (or infantado) leonés,* the right to the Leonese royal line. She may even be Princess Urraca Fernández, who bequeathed her personal collection of jewels to create an appropriately grand framework for the most sacred of Christian relics when it arrived in her father Ferdinand I's kingdom.

This female institution, so particular to León and so unfamiliar to outsiders, has its origins in the tenth century, and it is worth a brief digression to go back over this period for an overview of its history.

The León monarch Ramiro II the Great, having defeated the Caliph Abd al-Rahman III, founded a specifically feminine tradition to secure the future stability and legitimacy of his dynasty: the *infantado.* This medieval institution gave significant power to a dynasty of unmarried princesses, who ruled over the religious and cultural heritage of the crown and received a 'dowry' of towns and property. The first *domina del infantado* (protectress of the *infantado*) was his daughter Elvira Ramírez, and its original seat of power was the San Salvador de Palat de Rey Monastery (León).[284]

As their power became more widely acknowledged, the *dominas* often acted as political arbitrators of their time. To take control of this lucrative inheritance, which included lands and monasteries with their attendant income, these illustrious women generally had to commit to remaining unmarried. In contrast to those who took religious vows, this actually allowed these women to govern their own destinies, without having to depend on men.[285]

This was not always the case, however. The unwritten moral rule was broken on three occasions: by Sancha, wife of Ferdinand

I; her granddaughter Queen Urraca; and finally by Princess Sancha, wife of Sancho VI of Navarre, who received the entire principality from her brother Ferdinand II: 'All that belongs to the *infantazgo*, just as our aunt Princess Doña Urraca had it'.[286]

The territorial power of these women, as well as their moral authority and their role in representing the kingdom's legitimacy at times of heightened tension, led the academic and abbot of San Isidoro, Antonio Viñayo, to define the *infantazgo* as almost 'a kingdom within a kingdom'.[287]

Elvira Ramírez (*c.*934–86), the first *domina*, was sister to the kings Ordoño III and Sancho I. Following Sancho I's death, she was forced to act as the regent because her nephew Ramiro III was still a child. For nearly a decade, until 975, she governed León with a firm hand, sent ambassadors to the caliph of Córdoba and reined in the aristocracy. She was often given the title 'queen'. After the fall of San Esteban de Gormaz (975), the tables turned[288] and her name was relegated to second billing, but this did not stop her from championing the monarchy, guaranteeing the dynastic authority of its ancestors and supporting her blood relative on the throne.

Two key events which took place nearly seventy years apart are central to the history of the *infantazgo*: the transfer of the relics of the boy martyr San Pelayo (Saint Palayo) and the arrival of the remains of Saint Isidore from Seville, under Ferdinand I. After the first event, at the time of Elvira Ramírez, a new temple was built to house the relics, beside another dedicated to Saint John the Baptist. Given the level of devotion for the saint, who was widely known across the whole of Europe, Elvira decided to move the *infantazgo*'s power base from San Salvador de Palat to this new monastery.[289]

In the latter half of the tenth century, the de facto ruler of Al-Andalus was Almanzor, the *hajib*[290] of Córdoba. From 981 CE until about 1000 CE he launched a series of devastating military campaigns against the Christian kingdoms, especially León and Castile. These years brought chaos to the kingdom and its capital. Led by their new Mother Superior, the widowed queen Teresa Ansúrez, the nuns of San Pelayo fled for Oviedo with the martyr's remains, to protect them from desecration.[291] The *infantado* remained there until the reign of Alfonso V (999–1028), when peace and order were re-established. This was largely a result of the death of Almanzor, as well as his sons and heirs, which triggered a civil war in Al-Andalus that culminated in the separation of the caliphate into taifa kingdoms.

Alfonso V rebuilt some of the monasteries that had been damaged by Almanzor, Saint John the Baptist among them, and included two cemeteries: one for his parents and himself, between the building and the outer Roman wall, and another to bury his predecessors and bishops, at the church's sanctuary end. For a while the new *domina* was his own sister, Teresa Vermúdez, who died in 1039.[292]

The third great *domina* of the *infantazgo* was Sancha (*c.*1013–67), Alfonso V's daughter and future queen of León. While she was in charge of the institution, she was engaged to García Sánchez, the Count of Castile, who was assassinated in León in 1029. Sancho III Garcés, the sovereign of Navarre, had opposed the wedding, which would have increased Leonese power in Castile. As we have seen, he now took advantage of this unexpected death to nominate his second son, the Prince Ferdinand, for Sancha's hand and as successor to the county of Castile.

These events took place during Bermudo III's reign as king of Leon. He was the son of Alfonso V and, therefore, Sancha's brother. As we have seen, when Ferdinand killed him in 1037 he had no offspring, meaning that Ferdinand and his wife, Princess Sancha of León, became heirs to the throne.[293] Within a year, Ferdinand was anointed king of León, claiming the irrefutable rights of his wife Sancha.[294]

The fourth great *domina* was Princess Urraca Fernández, first-born daughter of Ferdinand and Sancha. San Isidoro had by now replaced San Pelayo as the headquarters of the Leonese *infantazgo*. Born when her father was Count of Castile, around 1033, near-contemporary accounts attest to her moral integrity and praise Ferdinand's commitment to his children's education:

> King Ferdinand educated his sons and daughters,
> instructing them firstly in the liberal disciplines, of which
> he himself had been a learned student, and later arranged
> for his sons, at the right age, to learn the equestrian arts,
> military exercises and hunting in the Spanish style, and his
> daughters, far from being idle, were instructed in honest
> womanly virtues.

Urraca's mediating role came into the spotlight shortly after the death of her father in 1065. Ferdinand I's distribution of his territories (Castile for Sancho, León for Alfonso, Galicia for García and the seigneury of Zamora and de Toro respectively for Urraca and Elvira, who were made queens as well as sharing the *infantazgo)* meant that his daughters were, to some extent, on a par with his sons.

We have seen how Sancho, a first-born son aggrieved at his inheritance, openly declared war on his siblings as soon as Ferdinand I's widow Sancha had died (1067). García of Galicia was captured and imprisoned, and Alfonso's life was only spared thanks to Urraca interceding on his behalf. Lastly, Sancho overcame Elvira de Toro, leaving only Urraca and Zamora in his way. The princess and her city endured nearly seven months under siege, until a plan hatched by the noble Zamoran knight Vellido Dolfos saw the belligerent monarch slain in the entranceway now known as the Gate of Loyalty.

Sancho died without heir, so the throne passed to the exiled

Alfonso of León, who united Castile and refused to return Galicia to its rightful ruler, García, who would languish in prison for the rest of his life. With his territories reunified, Alfonso embarked on a campaign to conquer territory and secure his position, while his sister Urraca became his most loyal and faithful advisor, enjoying his complete trust and confidence until her death in 1101.[295] Their sister Elvira, with whom she had shared the *infantazgo*, died two years later.[296]

Over those years, in her role as guarantor of the dynasty, Urraca focused her efforts on expanding the Basilica of San Isidoro, home to the Leonese kings and the vaults of their ancestors. Since she had not married or had children, a good proportion of her riches remained in the Isidorian treasury. Her personal collection of jewels was among them, including those decorating the chalice that bore her name and which contained the Lord's Cup that had arrived from the Orient in her father's time.

The penultimate great *domina* of the *infantazgo* was Sancha Raimúndez,[297] Urraca Fernández's great niece and the daughter of Queen Urraca and her husband Count Raymond of Burgundy.[298] She succeeded her illustrious predecessors as the head of the institution and advised her brother, the Emperor Alfonso VII. As patron of the Isidorian temple and loyal guardian of all it contained, it is to Sancha Raimúndez that we owe part of the cloisters, the chapter house and the bell tower, the renowned Torre del Gallo.[299] It was under her *infantazgo* that the San Pelayo female convent was replaced by a male community of Canons Regular of Saint Augustine and became an abbey, a status it still holds today.

Thanks to the generosity of her brother Ferdinand II of León, her niece Sancha, Queen of Navarre was to be the last great *domina*. With the convent's conversion into an abbey, San Isidoro ceased to be a female space, and its role was definitively curtailed by the union of the crowns of Castile and León in 1230.

The maiden-guardians of the kings' souls were lost forever, and the detailed memory of a Leonese bloodline, its kingdom in the era of Ferdinand I, and the Grail, died with them. This historical reality, imbued with a trace of myth and legend, naturally appealed to medieval troubadours and poets: the history of Christ's Chalice, and the Legend of the Holy Grail.

The Grail . . . Hidden in Plain Sight All Along

Why was the Holy Chalice's presence in León kept secret? When the relic was bequeathed to him, Ferdinand I had reached a critical stage in his reign. Why the silence? The scarcity of documentary evidence is odd and makes this a difficult question. There is, however, proof that the royal family was aware of the gift it had received, since Urraca donated her own jewellery to decorate and venerate the chalice that bore her name, within which the Holy Cup was housed and protected.

The object's importance demanded serious prudence from Ferdinand I. Despite his political and military advantages, announcing the Holy Chalice's presence in León would have created religious and political tensions, as it had been appropriated from the Church in Jerusalem. One possibility is that revealing it might have harmed the development of the Camino de Santiago pilgrimage, which was steadily growing in popularity. (This is a traditional route, known as the Way of St James in English, in which pilgrims make their way to the cathedral of Santiago de Compostela, where the remains of the saint are reputedly buried.) This was a time of conflict, with threats from rival kingdoms and the Moors on all sides. The papacy, who might not have appreciated negative stories about 'stolen relics', had the power to excommunicate a king, meaning that his vassals would no longer feel obliged to obey him, and his treasures could end up being plundered by neighbouring powers. (Indeed, this fate nearly befell the Chalice only fifty years later, when Alfonso I the Battler, King of Aragón, attacked San Isidoro and plundered the altars of their silver and gold. The Chalice was saved only because it had been hidden.) There was, then, a very real fear of it disappearing, and in the circumstances it was unsafe to draw the wrong kind of attention.

The Muslim texts describe the disdain for the Chalice felt by 'Jews and men of science'. Aversion to the Cup in Iberia is also evident, in the Emir of Dénia's letter of thanks. Could these shadowy enemies of the Cup have been behind Ferdinand's caution? One can imagine what these vague threats would mean in the eleventh century for a king as powerful as Ferdinand. Given the medieval mindset, it is significant that while silence was maintained around the Holy Chalice, clues were left for the initiated.

One significant clue is to be found in the frescoes of the Royal Vaults at the Basilica of San Isidoro. This extraordinary scheme, one of the most valuable works in the Hispanic Romanesque style, is composed of various scenes. The scene depicting the Last Supper is extremely interesting. It comprises fifteen figures in an architectural context that represents the Cenacle, or Upper Room, where the event is believed to have been held. The specific identities of these figures is beyond all doubt, not least because each of their names is marked (except Jesus and Peter, whose names have been lost).

On either side of Jesus, with halos marked with the cross, are the disciples Peter and John. Peter is holding a dagger and to his left are Andrew, holding a clay cup, Bartholomew, with his hands outstretched and Philip, with a cup of wine and a piece of bread. Next to John is James, with a bowl and spoon, followed by Thomas, engaged in conversation with James, then Matthew to his right, eating with a knife in hand and finally the other James, engaged in an impassioned discussion with Matthew.[300]

In the lower section of the scene, below a table filled with food, are Judas, in the middle without a halo, and at the edges, Simon holding a pot and Matthias filling a vessel from a wine jar. At this point a series of discrepancies begin to emerge in the painting, given that there is no explanation for the appearance of Matthias. It is possible that the artist simply wanted to represent Matthias, the thirteenth apostle, who although not present at the Last Supper, was elected by the other eleven to replace Judas Iscariot after Jesus's death and Ascension. But this is not the only curious feature of the painting.

In the upper section there are two figures: Thaddaeus on one side, who has no halo and is holding a bowl with fish, and Marcialis Pincerna on the other. In all, there are eleven people with a halo, excluding Jesus himself. The three depicted without haloes are Judas, Thaddaeus and Marcialis.

The appearance of Marcialis Pincerna, Saint Martial of Limoges, as Martial the cupbearer is out of context, but may be explained by an eleventh-century theological dispute. There was a disproportionate and inexplicable interest in portraying the patron and first bishop of Limoges as having been one of Christ's apostles or disciples. Various monks from the Abbey of Saint Martial of Limoges, where he had taught, propounded this outlandish theory, and its most vigorous advocate at the beginning of the eleventh century was the French monk Ademar de Chabannes (989–1034). Ademar put forward a series of arguments, mostly questionable if not plain false, for Martial's apostolicity.

This theory drew on the writings of Gregory of Tours,[301] which actually describe Martial as a missionary sent to Gaul by the Pope in the mid-third century (meaning he clearly couldn't have been alive in Christ's time); later he became the first bishop of Limoges. In texts that can be dated to the late Carolingian period, towards the end of the ninth century, his life was increasingly aggrandized and he was referred to as a disciple of Saint Peter, who had personally granted him the mission of evangelizing in Gaul. Later hagiographers, in the early eleventh century, hypothesized that Martial might have been Peter's youngest cousin. Thus, a new cult was fostered and spread from the Abbey of Limoges, elevating him to the status of a saint.[302]

Martial's apostolic status came to a temporary end in 1029 when Benedict of Chiusa, a wandering monk from Lombardy, exposed the imposture in a public debate, declaring that it had all been a mere excuse for the greed of the monks of Limoges.

The battle lost, Ademar retired to Limoges and devoted himself to compiling a collection of texts that he believed would lead him to triumph by demonstrating Martial's apostolicity to future generations; he spared no expense in falsifying papal letters, council acts and sermons. By the end of the eleventh century he had rehabilitated Martial's reputation and had persuaded the monks to reassert their patron's apostolic status. Astonishingly, it was not until the 1920s that Louis Saltet and other researchers finally uncovered this plot.

In one of the many meetings, councils and documents he is named as having been the cupbearer at the Last Supper, and therefore a disciple. The only way to become an apostle was to have been present in the cenacle, the Upper Room, even in a secondary role, such as the wine pourer, just as Martial is depicted in the Leonese painting. This is how he is described in his biography, presumably written by Ademar himself and falsely attributed to the Bishop Aurelianus. Aurelianus was Saint Martial's supposed successor, and would allegedly have been able to testify to his presence at the Last Supper and subsequently the Crucifixion.[303]

This controversy appears to coincide with the construction of the Royal Vaults, a lengthy process with an uncertain timeline. Whether the painter came from France via pilgrim routes or from a local studio, he must have heard these theories, seen their

King Arthur battles the Saxons in an image from the *Rochefoucauld Grail*.

Medieval illumination depicting Perceval, one of the Arthurian knights involved in the quest for the Grail.

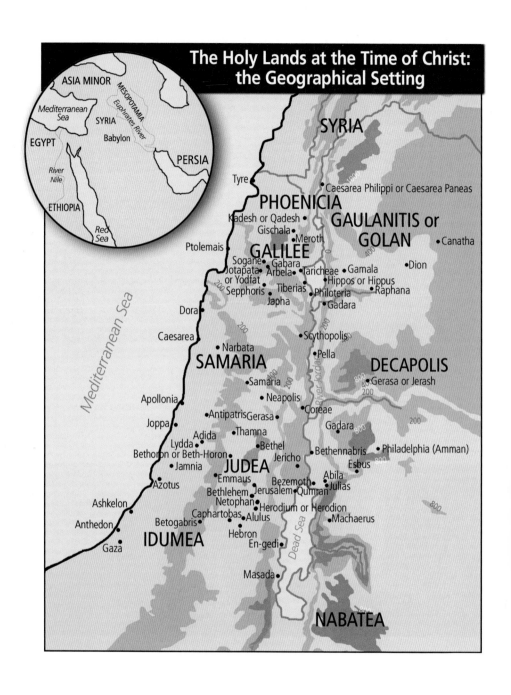

The Holy Lands at the Time of Christ: the Geographical Setting

ASIA MINOR

Mediterranean Sea

MESOPOTAMIA

SYRIA

Euphrates River

Babylon

EGYPT

PERSIA

River Nile

ETHIOPIA

Red Sea

SYRIA

Tyre

• Caesarea Philippi or Caesarea Paneas

PHOENICIA

GAULANITIS or GOLAN

Kadesh or Qadesh •

• Canatha

Gischala •

Meroth

Ptolemais •

GALILEE

• Dion

Sogane •

Gabara

Jotapata •

Arbela • Taricheae • Gamala

or Yodfat

• Hippos or Hippus

Sepphoris •

Tiberias •

Philoteria

• Raphana

Japha •

• Gadara

Dora •

Caesarea •

• Scythopolis

• Narbata

SAMARIA

• Pella

DECAPOLIS

• Samaria

• Neapolis

• Gerasa or Jerash

Apollonia •

• Coreae

Joppa •

• Antipatris Gerasa •

Gadara •

Adida •

• Thamna

200

Lydda •

• Bethel

Bethoron or Beth-Horon •

Jericho •

• Bethennabris

• Philadelphia (Amman)

• Jamnia

JUDEA

• Esbus

• Emmaus

Bezemoth •

Abila

Azotus •

Bethlehem •

Jerusalem • Qumran •

• Julias

Netophan •

• Herodium or Herodion

Ashkelon •

Caphartobas •

Alulus

Anthedon •

Betogabris •

Machaerus •

Hebron •

Gaza •

IDUMEA

En-gedi •

Masada •

NABATEA

Mediterranean Sea

River Jordan

Dead Sea

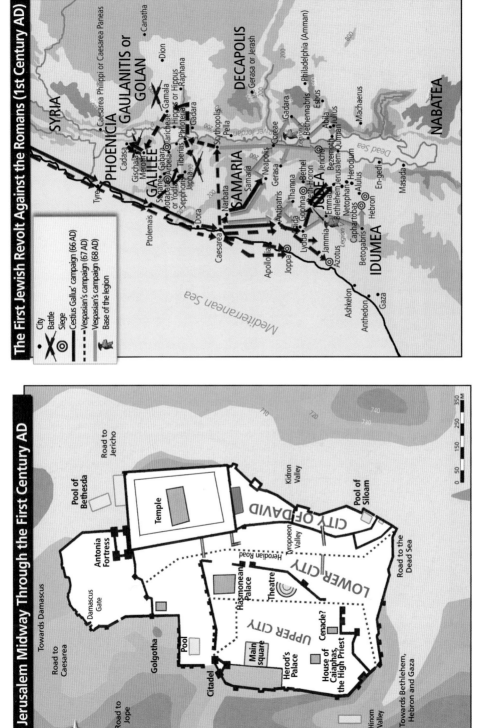

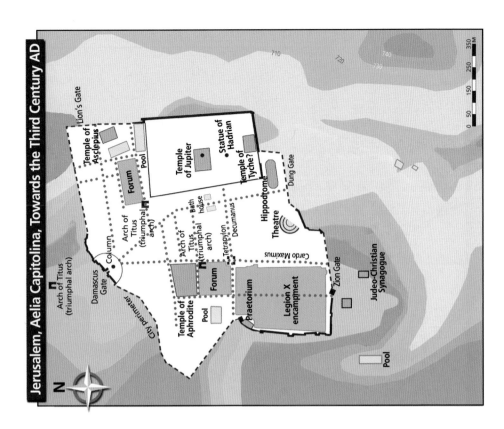

Jerusalem, Aelia Capitolina, Towards the Third Century AD

Arch of Titus (triumphal arch)

Damascus Gate

Column

City perimeter

Temple of Aphrodite

Pool

Forum

Arch of Titus (triumphal arch)

Praetorium

Legion X encampment

Zion Gate

Judeo-Christian Synagogue

Pool

Temple of Asclepius

Lion's Gate

Forum

Pool

Arch of Titus (triumphal arch)

Bath house

Decumanus

Tetrapylon

Cardo Maximus

Temple of Jupiter

Statue of Hadrian

Temple of Tyche?

Hippodrome

Theatre

Dung Gate

710

720

740

730

710

0   50   150   250   350   M

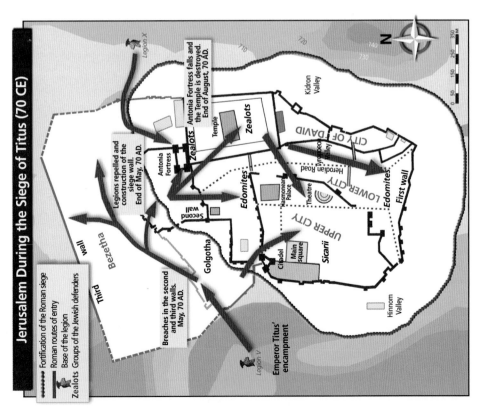

Jerusalem During the Siege of Titus (70 CE)

Legion X

Antonia Fortress falls and the Temple is destroyed, 70 AD.

Legions repelled and construction of the siege wall. End of May, 70 AD.

Third wall

Bezetha

Zealots

Zealots

Antonia Fortress

Temple

Zealots

Kidron Valley

CITY OF DAVID

Second wall

Edomites

Golgotha

Theatre

Hasmonean Palace

Tyropoeon Valley

Herodian Road

LOWER CITY

Edomites

First wall

Breaches in the second and third walls. May, 70 AD.

UPPER CITY

Sicarii

Citadel

Main square

Hinnom Valley

Emperor Titus' encampment

Legion V

Fortification of the Roman siege

Roman routes of entry

Base of the legion

Zealots   Groups of the Jewish defenders

710

720

740

730

0   50   150   250   350   M

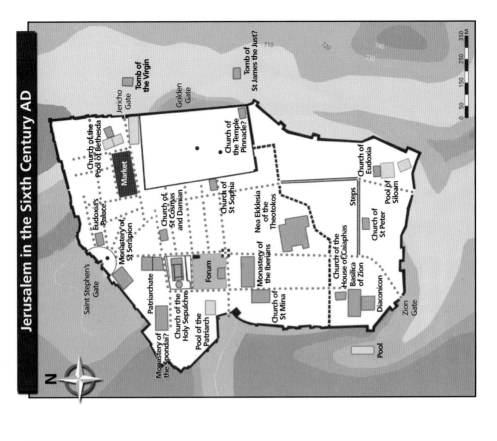

Jerusalem in the Sixth Century AD

Saint Stephen's Gate

Monastery of the Spondai?

Monastery of St Serapion

Eudoxia's Palace

Patriarchate

Church of the Holy Sepulchre

Pool of the Patriarch

Forum

Church of St Cosmas and Damian

Church of St Sophia

Monastery of the Iberians

Church of St Mina

Nea Ekklesia of the Theotokos

Church of the House of Caiaphas

Basilica of Zion

Diaconicon

Zion Gate

Pool

Steps

Church of St Peter

Church of Eudoxia

Pool of Siloam

Church of the Temple Pinnacle?

Market

Church of the Pool of Bethesda

Jericho Gate

Golden Gate

Tomb of the Virgin

Tomb of St James the Just?

710 720 730 700

0 50 150 250 350 M

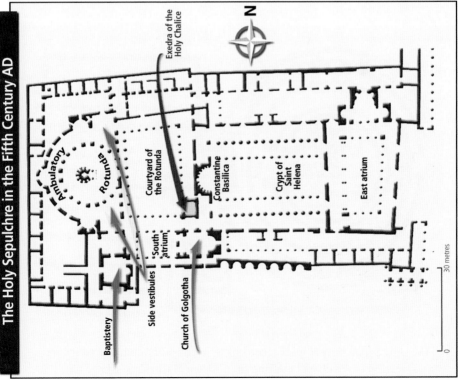

The Holy Sepulchre in the Fifth Century AD

Baptistery

Side vestibules

Church of Golgotha

Ambulatory

Rotunda

Courtyard of the Rotunda

South atrium

Exedra of the Holy Chalice

Constantine Basilica

Crypt of Saint Helena

East atrium

0 30 metres

Reconstruction of the entrance to the Basilica of the Holy Sepulchre (see page 60).

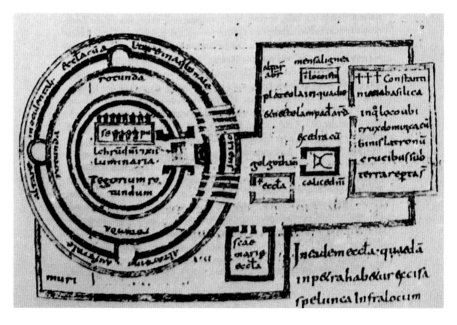

The Holy Sepulchre complex according to Arculf and Adomnan, showing the location of the chapel housing the Chalice of Christ (see page 66).

Reconstruction of the Courtyard of the Rotunda facing east. In the centre is the Exedra of the Lord's Cup (see page 67).

Possible Route of the Holy Chalice (1056 AD)

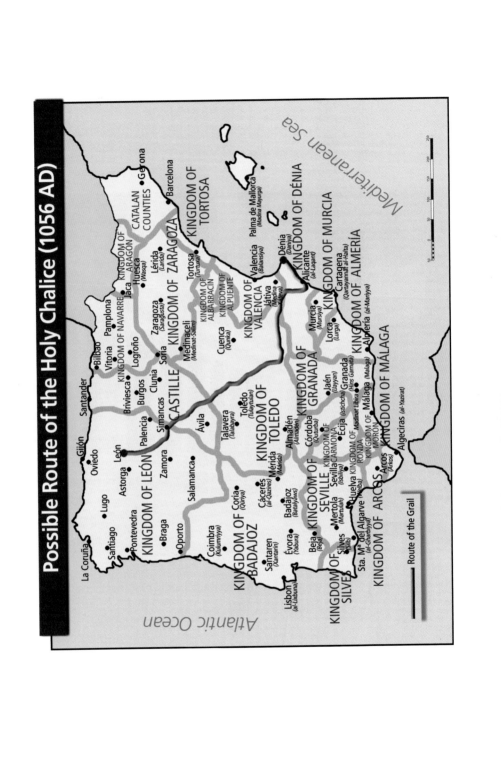

Top: Royal Vaults of San Isidoro, León (see page 126).

Above: The Last Supper, Royal Vaults of San Isidoro, León (see page 126).

Right: Marcialis Pincerna , Royal Vaults of San Isidoro, León (see page 127).

Above: Christ
Pantocrator of the
Royal Vaults of San
Isidoro, León (see page
130).

Left: Crucifixion of
the Lord with chalice
detail, Royal Vaults of
San Isidoro, León (see
page 131).

Point of impact and the break line in the agate-onyx.

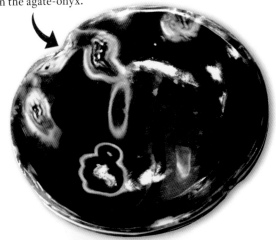

View of the upper cup of the Chalice of Doña Urraca (see pages 133–5)

Otto III's infant crown, year 983, Essen Cathedral Treasury, Germany. To the right, a detail from the outer part of the crown that surrounds the cup of the Chalice of Doña Urraca (see page 136).

Pottery from Qumran, c. 1–70 AD (see page 136).

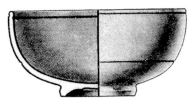

Roman pottery: Ritterling Hofheim Form 8, c. 30/40-70 AD (see page 136).

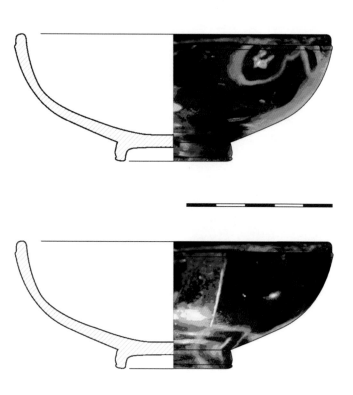

Chalice of Doña Urraca (see page 137).

Roman agate cup, *c.* 1–200 AD in the Paul Getty Museum (see page 138).

Agate cup from the Crescent Gallery in Tokyo (see page 138).

Nielloed silver casket of Sadaqa ibn Yusuf, vizier of the Fatimid Caliph Al-Mustanṣir, mid-11th century, kept at the Basilica of San Isidoro Museum, León (see pages 91, 144).

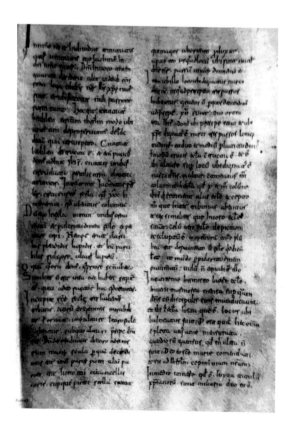

Original account of the pilgrimage of the cleric Jacinto (Hyacinth, according to his anglicised name) to Jerusalem in the 11th century, preserved in the Cathedral of León's archive (see page 87).

Front and overhead views of the casket of Sadaqa ibn Yusuf.

The Chalice of the Princess Doña Urraca, daughter of Ferdinand I the Great, San Isidoro Museum (see pages 133–6).

Detail of the 11th century medieval mounting placed over the broken part of the cup (see page 135).

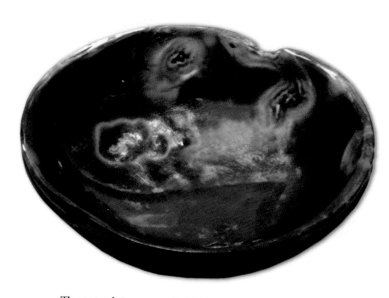

The actual Cup revealed (shown from above), without the added medieval elements (see page 91).

representations in another artwork, or have been influenced by the designer of the iconic project. In the tenth century, the cult of Saint Martial spread as far as Asturias and León.

We know that the Holy Chalice was transferred from Jerusalem to León in the presence of a Frankish bishop from the region. We also know that, in the same year, Elinand, Bishop of Laon, made the pilgrimage to the Holy City. Could this painting portray Saint Martial holding the actual Holy Chalice? The painting offers a clue. Jesus Christ, who occupies the central space, does not have the Holy Chalice in front of him, as is usually depicted. Instead we see a huge bowl, larger than those containing bread and other foods. Judas is attempting to take a fish from Jesus, symbolizing the act of betrayal that he was soon to commit.

Martial, however, is holding a jug, and a small bowl exactly like the Holy Chalice. It is not a cup like the one Philip holds, but a bowl that he proffers to Jesus, gazing at him with arm outstretched. Eyes and hands were depicted disproportionately large in Romanesque art, because they are, in spiritual terms, the most expressive parts of the human anatomy. Romanesque painters knew that their paintings could not convey movement. To understand the language of such scenes, the action must normally be construed by tracing the direction of the gaze. In this case, Martial 'the cupbearer' is clearly looking at the scene's central figure: Jesus Christ. The action is therefore taking place in this direction. Furthermore, to avoid any doubt, the painter who recreated the Last Supper scene at the request of the Leonese monarchs chose to place the chalice in Martial's hands in its pure form, just as it arrived from the East, i.e. the simple stone Roman cup of agate-onyx, without the medieval additions that the kings and their servants placed around it in order to protect the Holy Cup after its arrival in León.

The Romanesque artist makes the importance of the cup proffered to Jesus by Martial even clearer: it is the only one depicted in a dark colour, the same colour as the Roman cup within the Chalice of Doña Urraca, while the other cups held by the apostles are white. The Leonese monarchs who commissioned the paintings in the Royal Vaults shortly after the Lord's Cup's arrival in León wanted to leave clear evidence to future generations that they possessed the true chalice of the Last Supper and, let us not forget, images and paintings were, in those times of widespread illiteracy, the best way to leave a clear message for posterity. The message was very simple: the kings of León knew that the chalice worshipped in Jerusalem for centuries as the one used at the Last Supper was the very same one that they had been given by the Muslim Emir of Dénia. Therefore, they decided to honour it by adorning it with gold and jewels, and leave a record of it painted at the Royal Vaults of San Isidoro, the very heart of the Leonese monarchy. The creator of this iconography chose to show us a Frankish bishop as the bearer of the Holy Grail, an object that was already to be found at San Isidoro.

Within the complex Romanesque iconography, Saint Martial could well symbolize the Frankish bishop, who travelled with the Holy Chalice. Martial has a twofold connection to the story: there was a cult to Saint Martial in León, and Marcialis Pincerna was an Asturo-Leonese construct that suited the monks of Limoges.

This possibility calls for new readings of the entire iconography of the Royal Vaults of San Isidoro. Interestingly, these paintings replaced earlier works, and must have been added when work on the building was complete.[304] The *Last Supper* is placed next to the *Pantocrator* (the title given to typical full-faced icons of Christ holding a bible in his left hand and making a gesture of blessing with his right hand), which occupies the central dome as dictated by tradition. In León and San Isidoro, Doña Urraca's Chalice was clearly believed to be the Holy Chalice, as can be deduced from the message that was displayed in the most important position in the whole basilica complex.

Also pertinent is the Crucifixion scene, where Christ appears with kings at his feet. In this image, Joseph of Arimathea appears to hold the cup, and its shape is identical to Doña Urraca's chalice.

Undoubtedly, the best way to hide a treasure of such magnitude is the one chosen by the kings of the Grail: keep it in plain sight.

The Grail of San Isidoro:
The Basis of a Sacred Relic

The cup that had become known as the Chalice of Doña Urraca, after the Leonese princess who bequeathed it to the Basilica of San Isidoro, gained fame in the Middle Ages. In the thirteenth century, the historian Lucas, who was Bishop of Tuy and previously Canon of San Isidoro, alluded to its great value and prestige. In his account of the wedding of King Alfonso I, the Battler of Aragón, to Queen Doña Urraca of León he describes the 'chalice of sardonyx decorated in gold and precious stones'.[305]

The humanist and historian Ambrosio de Morales (1513–91) also depicts the cup in great detail in his celebrated *Viages*:

> A Chalice of Agate in three parts, one for the cup,
> another for the base, and a third for the handle, joined
> and mounted in very delicate, old gold work, and set with
> many fine small stones, although they are not precious.
> The cup is gold plated on the inside, so that blood does not
> touch the stone when it is blessed. It is said that the paten
> [a plate or shallow dish, on which the host is laid during
> the Eucharist] was very precious, and was carried by the
> king of Aragón. It is now silver-gilt.[306]

Jumping ahead to the eighteenth century, another description differs only in a detail of the cup's original owner. Fray Tomás de Granada and Father José Manzano mention the Cup in their work *The Life of San Isidoro, Archbishop of Seville*:

The Chalice is made of the stone they call Agate, all adorned
in purest gold: around the vase there are ten and six precious
stones, of various colours; the handle at the centre has
thirteen, some large and some small . . . Tradition says that
the Chalice belonged to the glorious Saint.[307]

For over nine centuries, the chalice survived medieval
conflicts, French invasions and Carlist Wars, and today marks
a reference point for art and Leonese society. On display at the
Museum of San Isidoro of León, it is made of two pieces of agate-
onyx, joined by a gold framework. The upper part, in the form
of a cup, is coated in a hemisphere of gold, attached to a crown-
shaped ring embellished by precious and semi-precious stones,
pearls and a cameo depicting a face.

Its dimensions are typical of medieval Hispanic pieces that
were used in the liturgy: 18.5 cm in height, the diameter of mouth
and base are 11.5 cm and 12 cm respectively. The upper cup is
11.1 cm at its maximum width and 4.4 cm in height.

The lower part of this treasure is a shallower cup, inverted to
serve as the base, surrounded by a band of gold. Four crosspieces,
similar to those found on the upper part of the chalice, connect
it to the central node. This rests on a round plate bearing an
inscription of the donor in gold filigree: +In D(om)mine Vrraca
Fredina(n)di.

The gold node is decorated with four diamond-shaped sections
in relief, containing Greek crosses with green enamel fleur-de-
lis. Fine gold filigree threads, pearls and various precious and
semi-precious cabochons cover its surface.

In 2010 Rafael Moreno, an expert goldsmith from Granada
who restored the Chalice of the Catholic Monarchs at Granada
among other pieces, made a replica of the Doña Urraca Chalice in
honour of the 1,100[th] anniversary of the León kingdom. While he
was working, he discovered some previously unnoticed details.[308]

These included the broken part of the upper cup; a rivet to hold the cameo to the gold lining protecting the agate-onyx cup, the rough placement of which suggests it was a later addition; that some of the piece's original stones are missing; and that small gold hoop-like mountings run around the gold band to hold a string of small pearls which has since disappeared.

The most noticeable fact is that the broken part of the cup was removed with skill, preventing any greater split or damage.[309] The break was made by a square blow from a pointed object, causing a small fragment to chip off.

This finding agrees with Saladin's account of the Cup's transfer from Egypt to Dénia. As we have seen, the ruler ordered for:

> (. . .) a piece of the holy stone to be sent, which had been cut from it with a kommeyya by the leader of Banī-l-Aswad's men in the year 447, when the wicked al-Mustanṣir named him head of the expedition to Dénia in the far West (. . .) The shard taken from the Cup was sent to Salah ad-din.[310]

Saladin's account perfectly corresponds to the broken piece of the Doña Urraca Chalice. Although the fragment is missing, its shape indicates that it was removed before the Romanesque construction of the chalice; it pre-dates the gold covering and the three sections being mounted together.

When the replica was being made, the upper part of the piece was partly detached from its lining to record its original dimensions. This revealed further details: the rough way that the inner gold cup had been affixed to the upper decorative gold band; the modern replacement of a pair of staples that held the crosspieces in place – neither of which was in a noble metal, and one of which was partly broken; and the fastening of the cameo, which is visible and pierces the internal golden part of the piece.

The cup and base of the chalice place it in the Greco-Roman era, making it around two millennia old and contemporary with Christ, and also the same age as that other great religious vase kept in Valencia Cathedral (which has also been proposed as a candidate for being the Grail). Antonio Beltrán,[311] professor of Archaeology at the University of Zaragoza, who has studied the Valencian chalice, has already noted this similarity.

The gold framework references the Ottonian style, a prime example of which is Otto III's infant crown (983 CE), kept in Essen Cathedral Museum. Similar examples can be found in Germany, Italy and France.[312] There is also the tradition of the Visigothic votive crown, a practice first used by Emperor Justinian, which consisted of the royal diadem given as an offering to a temple, to cement a personal connection.[313]

The most interesting detail is the cup of the chalice itself. As Professor Beltrán has observed, it conforms to the Hellenistic-Roman style and resembles similar examples from the period in agate, sardonyx, onyx and glass, giving us an approximate date between the second century BCE and the first century CE.

This chronology is supported by numerous examples in ceramic and glass found in excavations of the Holy Land and throughout the Roman world, but these are only secondary to dating carried out on more closely related materials. Given the obvious difference between ceramics and semi-precious stone, we have followed the latter methodology. Semi-precious stone artefacts have more in common with pieces shaped in glass, as well as with existing examples in the same material.[314]

Among the Romans, common drinking vessels were usually ceramic.[315] The owner's wealth dictated the quantities of noble materials, such as glass or metal, used in a cup's manufacture.

That a whole piece was carved from semi-precious stone not only tells us that its owner was thriving financially, but also that he or she was connected to the elite. For the upper classes living in first century BCE to first century CE, objects sculpted in a semi-precious stone such as agate or sardonyx were desirable, fashionable and luxurious. Rising demand led to the use of glass as a less costly material.[316] Seneca wrote of the popularity of onyx, agate or fluorite vases – known as murrhine ware – among the nobility:

> I see men using murrhine vases, because it would be
> insufficient luxury to raise a toast in anything but
> gemstones, carved to hold the wine they later vomit.[317]

In the Middle Ages and beyond it was customary to reuse Roman pieces, incorporating them into new chalices, salt-cellars and reliquaries. One of many comparable examples is the Roman cup made of sardonyx that was turned into an oil lamp, now kept in the National Gallery of Canada.[318]

The Chalice of Abbot Suger of Saint-Denis, in the collection of the National Gallery of Art in Washington,[319] is also made from sardonyx. It is first documented as belonging to the Abbey of Saint-Denis between 1137 and 1140.[320] Although Abbot Suger does not specify its origins, it is most likely to have been acquired from merchants or a wealthy Jewish moneylender.[321] The basic core of the consecrated vase is a cup in this same variety of agate, sculpted between the second and first centuries BCE, probably in Alexandria (Egypt).[322]

There is another excellent example in Stockholm: the reliquary of Saint Elizabeth of Hungary, who was canonized in 1235. The upper part is a Roman agate cup decorated by a wide gold rim set with various gems that give it a chalice-like form, although it had a different devotional purpose.[323]

From the same approximate period, and embellished with gems like the Chalice of Doña Urraca, is a collection of extraordinary quality held in the J. Paul Getty Museum, some of which is, at the time of writing, exhibited at the Getty Villa in Malibu (United States). This was part of the trove discovered in the outskirts of Koptos (Qift), on the borders of the Nile in southern Egypt.[324] The significance of the Koptos settlement is that it was on a trade route connecting the Arabian Sea with the Mediterranean. In antiquity, agate was transported this way from its main source, India,[325] to reach Koptos and Egypt, where it was worked and shipped across the Roman Empire.[326]

Particularly comparable to the example in San Isidoro, in terms of the stone used, is a Roman Agate Cup dated between the first and second century CE, at the J. Paul Getty Museum (catalogue number 72.AI.38).

More recently, Christie's auctioned an agate cup from Ancient Greece (third to first century BCE) from the Crescent Gallery in Tokyo, which is similar in shape to Doña Urraca's chalice.

The chalice preserved in Valencia Cathedral is a similar example.[327] It is made of three separate pieces – two cups made of agate joined by a gold framework from the late medieval period (around the late fourteenth and early fifteenth centuries). The legend of San Lorenzo (Saint Lawrence) links the upper cup with the chalice used by Christ at the Last Supper. Unembellished and smooth, it measures 9.5 cm in diameter, 7 cm from the bottom to the rim, with a base one centimetre deep.[328] It dates from the Greco-Roman period, earlier than the first century CE according to Dr Beltrán, who had the honour of examining this fabulous work of art.

As to whether this piece is the grail, Professor Beltrán says: 'The question of the chalice's authenticity rests entirely on the cup itself'.[329] In his view, it is irrelevant whether the rest of it was made later, or even, as in the case of the upturned cup that forms the base, whether it is the product of Hispanic Muslim artisans.

The chalice still commands significant devotional interest, but the earliest historical reference appears to date from 1135, when Ramiro III the Monk, King of Aragón, offered a valuable donation to the monastery of San Juan de la Peña in exchange for certain of their items,[330] among them 'that chalice of precious stone'.[331] It is entirely possible that this could be the chalice now found in Valencia Cathedral.

Despite the close relationship between sovereign and church,[332] and the significant role played by San Juan de la Peña within the Aragonese dynastic system, Ramiro did not identify this sacred vase as that used by Christ at the Last Supper.[333] The piety of this Aragonese king is well documented. It would therefore be surprising if he had refrained from comment.

In 1322, the Aragonese monarchs saw no link between this beautiful chalice and the Cup of Christ. In fact, as we shall see in more detail below, they appealed to the ruler of Egypt to send the Holy Chalice to them, having heard that it was – or had at some point been – in Egyptian lands.

Almost eighty years later, in 1399, King Martín requested that San Juan de la Peña deliver him the Chalice of Jesus Christ, referring to that which would come to be called the Valencia Chalice, for his chapel in the palace of Aljafería, offering another richly made cup of gold and enamel in its place. This is nothing short of astounding given that only a few years earlier, the Aragonese dynasty had been unaware of both its properties and its link with San Juan de la Peña.

This document, from the cusp of the fifteenth century, is the first reference to the cup's alleged journey to Huesca in Aragón (in northeastern Spain). As with so many medieval traditions, we must be cautious about its authenticity.[334] The text describes the sovereign coming to secure the sacred object:

> For his royal chapel he diligently sought to obtain the chalice made of stone in which Our Lord Jesus Christ blessed his own precious blood at His Last Supper and

which Saint Lorenzo, who received it from Saint Sixtus, then His Holiness the Pope, of whom he was a pupil and deacon at Santa María in Dominica, sent with a letter he had written to the monastery and convent of San Juan de la Peña, set in the mountains of Jaca in the kingdom of Aragón.[335]

This Cup reached its final destination in Valencia Cathedral where it is still worshipped, thanks to another king of Aragón, Alfonso V the Magnanimous. It was deposited there as security for a loan that he could not afford to pay back, and would remain there until the present day, in the city on the banks of the Turia.[336]

In 2005, Dr Catalina Martín Lloris published an interesting doctoral thesis about the Chalice at the University of Valencia. It examines the historical documents, taking a fresh look at the traditions that follow the chalice's arrival in Valencia and on its supposed link with the papacy in Rome. She argues that researchers have sometimes been so obsessed with identifying the Valencian cup as the one used at the Last Supper that they have failed to step back and separate myth from reality.[337]

Without wishing to delve into this debate, from a purely archeological standpoint Dr Antonio Beltrán's description still applies.[338] This was reiterated by his successor at the University of Zaragoza, Dr Martín Bueno, at the First International Conference on the Holy Chalice held in 2008.[339] The Professor of Archaeology identifies it as an agate cup from the Greco-Roman period, like the one at San Isidoro in León.

One Chalice of Christ in Jerusalem and another in Hispania?

Beltrán's detailed study of the types of sacred vessels used by early Christians is called into question by this realization: in order to favour the Valencian Cup, Beltrán overlooks certain key contradictory sources that he himself has examined. Dr Martín Lloris states:

> Many of those who have investigated the relic of the Holy Chalice of the Last Supper have upheld (the Valencian Chalice's) authenticity over all the other chalices found in Europe. The desire to prove that it is the true cup has led certain researchers to lose real perspective and repeatedly confuse legend with reality. Indeed, the only thing that this historiography has been able to achieve, through a lack of rigorous research, is to damage its credibility.[340]

Beltrán tiptoes around older references to 'supposed chalices of the Holy Supper' and firmly states that 'none of them merit even the least credit'. He casually dismisses, without supporting arguments, the presence in Jerusalem of a chalice that contemporary eyewitnesses recognized as 'The Lord's'. He cites the testimony described in the *Jerusalem Breviary*, 'also known as the Itinerarium of the bogus Antonino de Piacenza, who says (*c.*570 CE) that the chalice of the Last Supper was onyx and was kept in the Constantine Basilica of Jerusalem'. He adds that 'another' chalice in Jerusalem 'repeatedly cited as the Lord's Chalice is the one named by Venerable Bede, who many other authors copied', such as Arculf (730) or the pilgrim priest Adomnan.[341]

Offering a précis of every cup he finds unconvincing, he goes on to cover other medieval examples.[342] In the process he waters down the documentary evidence for the Chalice's presence in Jerusalem, from the testimony of pilgrims who visited the Holy Lands from the fourth century onwards. Meanwhile, Beltrán clings to the legend which places the cup in the Pyrenees throughout this period of history, having been taken from Jerusalem to Rome by St Peter in the first instance. As we have seen in Christian sources, the historical documents are far more convincing than Beltrán would like to admit. He bases his thesis on the legends of the Grail, rather than contemporaneous accounts of people who worshipped the piece in Jerusalem up to the eleventh century.

When it comes to the 1135 document in which Ramiro III offered a donation to San Juan de la Peña for a chalice of stone, Beltrán himself expresses misgivings about the chalice at San Juan de la Peña, and doesn't believe it to be the same chalice that ultimately settled in Valencia. While, as an archaeologist, he has no doubts about identifying the Valencian Chalice as an oriental Roman cup, the broad chronology of which allows us to locate it in the time of Christ, as a historian he cannot avoid the fact that in 1135 the kings of Aragón did not believe this chalice to be the one from the Last Supper. In fact, subsequent source material from the beginning of the fourteenth century demonstrates that the kings of Aragón could *not* have been in possession of the Lord's Cup since 1135, given that they appealed to the sultan of Egypt for it at the beginning of the fourteenth century. If they requested it, this must be because they did not have it. The Chalice of San Juan de la Peña belonging to the kings of Aragón, and kept in their own royal chapel before going on to be donated to Valencia Cathedral, cannot therefore be the Cup used at the Last Supper, for nobody would petition a foreign kingdom for what they already have in their own. These weighty, documentary evidence-based arguments were assessed by Beltrán, and, troubled by the dates in question, he tried to find any way he could to try to salvage the identification of the Valencian Chalice as the Cup of Christ. As a historian he did what he could, but the documents that he was aware of dictated a single truth: the kings of Aragón did not view the San Juan de la Peña chalice as the Chalice of Christ, given that, in the fourteenth century, they asked the sultan of Egypt for the Last Supper Cup, in the knowledge that the holy relic was, or had been, kept in his lands.

This contradiction at the heart of Beltrán's study raises its head elsewhere. This is not because of his repudiation of the references in the accounts of the Venerable Bede and other medieval testimonies that locate the Chalice in Jerusalem, but quite the opposite: by his reference to an account which excludes the possibility of the Cup having been present in Spain, at a time that is alarmingly close to the announcement made by Martín I in 1399.

This is the previously mentioned source, from the Records of the Royal Chancellery kept in the Crown of Aragón Archive, dated 1322, during the reign of Jaime II. It concerns the diplomatic missive which, as Beltrán concedes, is problematic, since it describes how, in 1322, the Aragonese monarch sent an ambassadorial envoy to the Sultan of Egypt, requesting relics of the True Cross and Christ's Chalice, from the Islamic Treasury.[343] It would be odd if the Seigneur of Aragón, who enjoyed clear dominion over the Mediterranean and a strong political presence in Iberia and across Europe, a devotee of the True Cross, felt the need to ask the Sultan of Egypt for a relic that was supposedly stored at San Juan de la Peña.

It is important to consider this account in more detail because it also shows us that Jaime II knew that the Chalice was, or had at some point been, in Egyptian territory. The relationship between Iberia, the sultans of Egypt and their predecessors, the caliphs, goes back some way. We have seen how, during the eleventh-century reign of the High Imam al-Mustanṣir, Ferdinand I of

León's contemporary, a fleet from the Emir of Dénia landed on the shores of Egypt, loaded with goods to help endure a devastating famine. The Fatimid caliph of Cairo was grateful to this Muslim prince of southeastern Spain and showered him with gifts, some of which found their way into the treasuries of cathedrals and monasteries, such as León's San Isidoro or Astorga Cathedral.[344] In the case of the latter, it was the Fatimid glass bottle in the Chalice of Saint Toribio, or Our Lady's Goblet. And, as we have mentioned, the nielloed silver casket of Sadaqa ibn Yusuf, vizier to al-Mustanṣir of Egypt, along with other lesser objects, is still preserved within the Isidorian treasury.

How could the treasures that al-Mustanṣir gave to the Emir of Dénia have found their way to León, unless they were sent in payment of the tribute, or to win over King Ferdinand I and his son and heir Alfonso VI? The presence of the Sadaqa casket provides clear evidence, as does the Lord's Cup, chipped by a double-edged *kommeyya* as described by the Islamic sources, and carved from agate-onyx, like the one the pilgrims worshipped in Jerusalem. And when dated, the Isidorian chalice perfectly matches the type used by Christ.

Blinded by the legends of the Grail, the researchers who have focused on the Valencia Chalice also miss out on clues that might help establish its true identity. Of the pilgrims that travelled to the Holy Land, one source is worth highlighting. The anonymous pilgrim of Piacenza, author of the aforementioned *Itinerarium Antonini Placentini*, writes about another extremely important object that was also present at the Last Supper. In his text, when describing the Church of Zion, he reveals a significant detail:

> The Cup of the Apostles is there, which they used to celebrate Mass after the resurrection of the Lord.[345]

So it appears that there was another venerable chalice in Jerusalem at the end of the sixth century. A few years later, during the Persian invasion, the church was destroyed and the 'Chalice of the Apostles' was never heard of again. Jerusalem had a considerable Iberian community, significant enough to support a *'monasterium Iberum Hierosolymis'*,[346] as Procopius tells us. Knowing this, and given that a number of Iberian pilgrims with names like Turribus, Antonius, Sergius and Legati[347] made the journey to the Holy Land along with the famous Egeria of Hispania, could it be that the Chalice of the Apostles escaped Jerusalem in the opposite direction to the Persian attack, towards Visigothic Hispania? Could this be the very same cup that is stored in the Cathedral of Valencia?

The so-called Holy Chalice of Valencia Cathedral fits this hypothesis perfectly. Knowing that the Persian invasion caused devastation in Jerusalem, that there was a substantial Iberian community there and that relations between the Visigothic kingdom and the Byzantine Empire had improved significantly since 615, there is nothing to stop us from supposing that the Chalice of the Apostles is indeed the Holy Chalice of Valencia. Furthermore, this hypothesis would be corroborated by Beltrán's research, as well as by many of the later studies, which have only been able to establish that there is no real evidence of the chalice's presence before the ninth century at San Juan de la Peña, and that it was not documented until some centuries later. Legend, lest we forget, links this cup to the apostle Peter and his successors.

However, our purpose in this book is not to further examine the Valencian Chalice, but to focus on the Holy Chalice of Jesus Christ.

The Other Grails

The search for the Holy Grail became a myth at the height of the Middle Ages. The path pioneered by Robert de Boron, Wolfram von Eschenbach and Chrétien de Troyes was an individual quest in search of purification and even redemption. This quest transformed the Chalice into a symbol of Christian chivalry, an exemplar of the sublime virtues of Arthurian legend or the adventures of Parzival and Galahad at their respective medieval courts. Perhaps because this fiction has lived on in the popular imagination, Holy Grail sightings have been documented across Europe in places as diverse as Italy, England, Denmark and Ireland. That is to say nothing, of course, of the crackpot theory known as *Sang Réal* ('Royal Blood'), which posits Mary Magdalene's womb as the true receptacle of the Grail. This is a distant descendant of the Grail story told by Robert de Boron. He emphasized the reality of Christ's blood because he was writing in the early years of the thirteenth century, at a time when the Catholic Church was keen to reject the Cathar belief that Christ was a spirit, without a physical body.

De Boron's legend claims that the Holy Grail left Palestine for Roman Britain in the hands of Joseph of Arimathea,[348] so we will begin our tour of the other grails in Great Britain.

The Grails of Britain and Ireland

No fewer than three cups stake their claim on the title in the British Isles, if we include the example in Ireland: the Nanteos Cup, the Chalice of Ardagh and the Grail of Hawkstone Park.

The Nanteos Cup

This medieval wooden bowl is kept at Nanteos Mansion in Aberystwyth, Wales, by the Powell family who claim that it came from the former Glastonbury Abbey. In de Boron's version, Joseph of Arimathea brought the Grail, the vessel from the Last Supper that was also used to catch the last drops of Christ's blood, to Avalon, which has been identified with Glastonbury.

The first references to it appear during the reign of King Henry VIII. At odds with Rome over his desire to annul his marriage to Catherine of Aragón and marry Anne Boleyn, Henry broke with the Roman Catholic Church and set off on the path that would lead to Britain's permanent religious separation from the continent.

For the monarchy, Catholic abbeys and monasteries became pockets of resistance that required strict monitoring. In 1539 a group of confidants of the king arrived without warning at Glastonbury, on the orders of Thomas Cromwell. Following conversations with the abbot, the monks supposedly decided to hide some of their most prized possessions, including a cup carved out of olive wood with the same dimensions as the one at Nanteos. We know that Glastonbury was subsequently sacked and its monks escaped in the direction of Strata Florida Abbey in Cardiganshire. Pursued by Henry VIII's men, they made contact with the Powell family, who gave them shelter.

They stayed at Nanteos for many years until the last of the monks, close to death, confessed a secret to Lord Powell: the olive wood cup was really Christ's Chalice, brought to Britain by Joseph of Arimathea. From this moment on, the Powell bloodline became the guardians of the chalice, until the Holy Roman Church claimed its dues.

In 1739 Thomas Powell rebuilt the mansion and the cup was stored in a glass box in a room on the upper floor.

George Powell invited Richard Wagner, who was composing *Parsifal* at the time, to visit in 1855. At Nanteos, he admired the cup and heard tales of its healing properties. Generations of believers flocked there to benefit from its health-giving properties. Members of the Powell family who fell ill, or those that were sent to their home, would be given water blessed by the cup.

On 5 July 1934, Tom MacDonald, a journalist from the *Western Mail and South Wales News*, wrote an article collecting testimonies from those who had been cured by the cup, some of which were recent.

In 1952 the Powells let go of Nanteos, and the supposed Grail passed on with their estate to the Mirylees family. In an article published in the *Martinist Review* in 1959, Marjory Mirylees described the cup and how water placed within it acquired a yellowish hue and even took on the taste of wine, a phenomenon which, she said, had nothing to do with the wood from which the bowl was carved.

The chalice was recently analysed. Sadly, the history of this illustrious relic dates back no further than the fourteenth century. Nanteos Mansion has been turned into a B&B. The cup has ended its days in a Lloyd's safety deposit box in Herefordshire.[349]

The Hawkstone Grail

Just as the Nanteos Cup laid claim to a centuries-old Grail tradition in spite of its actual age, the story of the Hawkstone Grail is barely a hundred years old and its peculiar association with Christ is obscure and unexpected. Made from alabaster with the proportions of an eggcup, it has been evaluated to be a genuine antique, possibly even Roman in origin, but its use as a chalice has been ruled out due to its diminutive size.

Kept for two centuries at Hawkstone Manor in Shropshire,

the first trace of it, according to several inconsistent accounts, takes us back to the nineteenth century when the Manor's owner ordered a park to be built. Then, at the beginning of the twentieth century a local dealer called Walter Langham acquired some statues from Hawkstone Park. As the items were being moved, the cup fell from a secret compartment hidden in one of the statues, and was kept by the family.

Graham Phillips, who has conducted most research into the cup, defends an alternative version of events based on the work of the historian Thomas Wright and his wife, whose family can be traced back to the Middle Ages.

This version of the story begins in the nineteenth century when Wright hid the cup in the base of an eagle statue which was made of stone and had been commissioned for an artificial cave in the gardens of Hawkstone Park. He wrote an epic poem describing his wife's ancestors' relationship to the Grail, which he embellished with enigmatic figures and words. The claim is that Walter Langham, who was his wife's grandson, subsequently deciphered the secret code and recovered the relic in 1920, with news of the discovery being subsequently published in a local walking guide, *Shropshire Rambles* (1934). The current owner is Langham's great granddaughter, a graphic designer named Victoria Palmer.

Thomas Wright was already well known in Shropshire for his claim to the Holy Grail, which he said had been handed down by his wife's family, the Peverels of Shropshire, since the Middle Ages. In the mid-nineteenth century he announced that he had hidden the relic, having left sufficient clues for it to be found: the epic poem was one of these.

In 2004 Graham Phillips was writing a book about King Arthur when he discovered the piece and believed it could be the Holy Grail, having followed a trail of clues that led him to the theory. Previously, this former BBC reporter had specialized in the history of the Knights of the Round Table, identified some Roman ruins as Camelot and located the tomb of the Virgin Mary on the Isle of Anglesey.

Phillips claims to have consulted experts from the British Museum who identified the small cup as a Roman vial for scent or ointment, probably from the first century CE. It is carved from green alabaster, 'also known as onyx' according to Phillips, which was a popular material for Palestinian artisans two thousand years ago. Given that Jesus lived in Palestine and the dates correspond, he identifies the Hawkstone Cup as an object potentially linked to Jesus. Specifically, he maintains that although its proportions mean that it can't be the chalice used at the Last Supper, it could be an object belonging to Mary Magdalene, the so-called Marian Chalice in which she is said to have caught Christ's blood.[350]

The Irish Ardagh Chalice

In the peculiar and eccentric search for 'the unknown' and the Holy Grail up and down the British Isles, no shortage of commentators have claimed to find a good candidate across the water on the Emerald Isle: the Ardagh Chalice (*Cailís Airgid Ardach*).

Although historians have dismissed its authenticity, we will briefly relate its story. The cup was found in 1868 in Reerasta Rath, County Limerick, by two young men, Jim Quinn and Paddy Flanagan, who were working in a potato field. It had apparently been hidden in the tenth century[351] to prevent its destruction. It is a beautiful piece in silver, bronze-gilt, glass and gilding, dating from the period of early Christianity in Ireland.[352] Kept in the National Museum of Ireland,[353] it is an eighth-century chalice with a ministerial function, used during the celebration of the Eucharist to offer wine to the congregation. Double-handled, it measures 17.8 cm high by 19.5 cm wide.

The Italian Grails

The *Sacro Catino*

In the Treasury Museum at San Lorenzo Cathedral in Genoa, there is an ancestral relic known as the *Sacro Catino* (the sacred bowl), which has been identified for some time as the Holy Grail. It is a hexagonal bowl once believed to be made of emerald, but now known to be green glass.

In the *Golden Legend,* which contains traditional stories of saints' lives compiled in the thirteenth century by the Archbishop of Genoa, Jacobus de Voragine, it is claimed that it was brought to Genoa by the chevalier Guglielmo Embriaco after the conquest of Caesarea in 1101, as it was believed to have been a piece of the tableware used by Jesus.[354] In his work from the end of the twelfth century, the chronicler Guillermo de Tiro wrote that the bounty won by the Genoese included a bowl of brilliant green that shone like an emerald.[355]

It went on to become part of the Cathedral Treasury in 1327, when Cardinal Luca Fieschi acquired it in payment for a loan made to the city. From that moment, it was ordained that under no circumstances should it leave the temple. There it stayed, worshipped by the faithful right up until the conquest of Genoa by Napoleon's troops, who took it to Paris. Ten years later it was returned to the Italian city, albeit in several pieces.

A story that can be traced back as far as the seventeenth century claims that it was either the cup or the plate that Jesus used during the Last Supper.[356] It is said that a rich Jew from Metz accepted the *Sacro Catino* as a deposit for a loan of the value of 100,000 crowns. Years later, when the Genoese who had pawned this valuable treasure tried to reclaim it, they discovered that the Hebrew had fabricated a number of copies and made a profit on all of them.

After several restorations, the most recent studies of the *Sacro Catino* have found it to be a glass piece of Byzantine or Islamic origin, which cannot have been produced any earlier than the ninth century.

The *Sacra Catina*

This cup, as in the case above, reached Genoa after the First Crusade. Its dimensions and form reveal it to be a small stone bowl, dateable to the time of Roman rule in Palestine. Crusaders' accounts from the time do not, however, make any suggestion of it being identified as the Chalice of Christ.[357]

The North American Grail: the Antioch Chalice

This quick overview must also mention the Antioch Chalice, kept in the rich collection of the Metropolitan Museum of Art of New York, and exhibited in their Syrian gallery. Acquired in 1950, it is believed by some English-language commentators to be Christ's Chalice. The museum actually dates it to between 350 and 500 CE. In spite of this it has formed the centrepiece of a number of exhibitions in Europe and America.

The story of the Antioch Chalice's discovery reaches us from Eustache de Lorey, the High Commissioner of Antiques to Syria. De Lorey initially questioned its authenticity, but ended up convinced. His testimony describes how it was found by workers who were digging a well in a garden near Hama, in modern-day Syria. Opening up an alcove in the back wall to shelter themselves from falling stones, they revealed a cavity containing what would come to be known as the Treasure of Antioch. Sold to a local antiques dealer, it was sold on to an

Armenian from New York, Fahid Kouchakj, in 1912.

The treasure consisted of a cross, a cup, a chalice and three embossed book covers. The Antioch Chalice was an almost hemispherical silver cup within another of the same shape, also made of silver, but gilt. The interior cup contains no inscription or symbols, while Jesus and the Apostles appear embossed on the outer cup.

Recent enquiries, published in *Arte y Antigüedades* magazine,[358] indicate that the Greek Cypriot goldsmith and forger Constantin Christodoulos made it in 1910, the very year it was discovered in Syria. The article describes a private interview between Christodoulos and a representative of the British Museum in Damascus in 1938, during which he confessed to the forgery of this most prized piece. It also adds that the Armenian buyer was Christodoulos's cousin.

With its authenticity thus ruled out, the theory placing it at the Last Supper lay in tatters.

The Agate Bowl of the Austrian Emperors

The *Achatschale*, or agate bowl, of Austria, believed to be the largest of its kind in the world, measures 58–58.5 cm in diameter and 76 cm wide, including its two handles. Linked to the imperial House of Habsburg,[359] it has been dated to the fourth century CE, and is said to have originated from either Trier or Constantinople. The latter seems more likely since, following the sacking of the city in 1204,[360] various Byzantine artefacts passed into the House of Burgundy and, through marriage, ended up in the hands of the Habsburg dynasty.

A misread inscription supposedly led to its being mistaken for the Grail. The inscription was taken to read 'B. XRISTO. RI.XXPP', suggesting that it was somehow connected to Jesus

Christ. However, during its restoration in 1951, the art historian Rudolf Egger recognized this word as ARISTO, perhaps the name of the artisan who made the bowl, although some regard the lettering as little more than an optical illusion.[361]

So, our journey ends in Vienna. We shall omit other alleged grails such as the reliquary of Saint Elizabeth of Hungary or the Iron Cup that two Italian authors, Gabriella Agrati and Maria Letizia Magini, have identified as the grail, without any attempt to substantiate their claim. Considering the precarious basis on which each claim is based, even the most confident assertions fall down, whether chronologically, as in the case of the Nanteos Cup or the Achatschale, or because of their form, such as the Hawkstone Grail. Others are plain forgeries, such as the Antioch Chalice. The only evidence for others to be regarded as the Grail are the unfounded intuitions of researchers and commentators.

We chose not to include the Valencia Chalice in this brief précis of the other grails because it deserves its place within the archaeological evidence supporting the identification of the Chalice of Doña Urraca as the Lord's Cup. Its antiquity and importance set it apart from the story of the other grails, which ends here.

Conclusion

This marks the end of a centuries-old search: the discovery of the Chalice of Christ, the Cup used by the Lord at the Last Supper with his disciples before his crucifixion. This is how it was described by Jerusalem's early Christian communities, in accounts which reveal that it was to be found in a dedicated chapel within the church that epitomizes the Holy Lands: the Holy Sepulchre. We know, thanks to Jewish customs of the time, that it could not have been made of a porous material, pottery or wood. The earliest Christian sources that touch on the treasured relics guarded in the Holy City are specific about the Chalice's material: the very same as ours, which distinguished archaeologists have dated to the time of Christ.

The first clues reached us fortuitously, via the parchments from Egypt. Both manuscripts confirm the chalice's presence in León, Spain, the result of the Emir of Dénia's desire to court the most powerful monarch of the time: Ferdinand I 'The Great' or 'al-Kabir', as he is known in the Islamic texts.

The original object was a simple Eastern Roman agate cup, small, broken and worn, which one day around the middle of the eleventh century, the powerful and legendary Queen Urraca of Zamora, daughter of Ferdinand I, deemed worthy of protection and embellishment with her own jewels, turning it into a reliquary chalice which, thanks to her, we are still able to admire in San Isidoro in León today. It is an object graced with gold and adorned with gems, as described in some of the first medieval descriptions of the Grail.

This sacred cup was chipped by a clean blow from a *kommeyya*, a blow delivered by an Egyptian of noble extraction, a member of the Banu Aswad family who had been entrusted with leading the expedition in the name of the Fatimid caliph. He was accompanied by a Frankish bishop from the lands of *Yalaliqa* – the name the Arabs used to describe the Kingdom of León – the chalice's guardian during the perilous journey from East to West, across the Mediterranean from Egypt to Dénia, on the Levant coast of modern Spain. This was its last stop-off before its final resting place in León, where it has remained for nearly one thousand years.

The remains of Ferdinand I, the first Western monarch to own the cup, were laid to rest beneath a scheme of excellent frescoes which have been described as the 'Romanesque Sistine Chapel', presided over by the Last Supper scene in which, as we have seen, a person offers Christ a dark-coloured cup, unlike the ones used by the Apostles, and yet remarkably similar in colour and shape to the broken Roman cup that travelled from Cairo to León.

The Grail kings exercised caution about showcasing such a precious gift, but they had no hesitation in displaying it to friends and visitors in the enclave where they were to be buried, in the place that, along with Compostela (the pilgrims' destination on the Way of St James), was the monarchy's spiritual heart: San Isidoro.

Thousands of pages have been written about the sacred relic which was kept and worshipped in Jerusalem from at least 400 CE onwards. We know that Christians had been persecuted by Rome and suffered martyrdom, but that the fourth century was a turning point, thanks to the emperors Constantine and Theodosius I. By the year 400, when we find the first confirmed account of the chalice, Christianity had become the official religion of the Roman Empire. It now no longer needed to be concealed, and was ready to be put on show. It was then that the Lord's Cup first appeared, worshipped for six centuries in its own chapel, '*exedra cum calicem Domini*' in the Church of the Holy Sepulchre, before being taken away, around the middle of the eleventh century, and delivered to the Muslim Emir of Dénia. Perhaps he is the true star of this story, since it was he who would change the course of history by offering such a sacrosanct object as a gift to the Christian king, Ferdinand I.

The Holy Grail is an object of power, faith and veneration, the existence of which has been the subject of much controversy. Without any scientific basis, works of fiction and an overactive imagination have made outlandish associations, for instance conflating the Passover Cup with Mary Magdalene's womb. This is an absurd idea that we can finally dismiss for good: the object physically exists, just as was believed by early Christians, and accepted by contemporary Muslims.

The troubadours and jongleurs who forged the Grail myth, based on both the material and spiritual quest for the Lord's Cup in the Middle Ages, left us clues that might have helped us to track the cup down, identify its location and understand its environment. But the grail legends were a complex mix of fact, rumour and fiction, and the clues that they contained were not easy to follow, even though it was all there: Spain, the King and Queen of the Grail (Ferdinand I and Sancha), Anfortas (Alfonso VI) and the maiden of the Grail (Doña Urraca, its guardian). The painters who left clues in the Royal Vaults did so with the artistry of a teacher setting a pupil on his own path to knowledge. The Holy Chalice was pictured in the Royal Vaults of San Isidoro, in full view of visiting knights, yet we had lost the key that was needed to interpret the composition. Fortunately, the new evidence from the Islamic texts means that we no longer have to rely solely on these hints and clues.

Hidden for one thousand years in Jerusalem, the Holy Chalice spent nearly another millennium lost in the sands of time, myth and legend, within reach of faith and now, thanks to fate, available to readers and academics too. The agate cup was sheathed in gold, for no priest would have dared to conduct mass by placing their lips where Christ's might once have touched. This was a blessed relic with the power to heal, as the chronicles and Sultan Saladin himself remind us.

If you visit León, look upon it with admiration, devotion or curiosity, and know that shining before your very eyes is the Cup of Power that played a historic role one Passover at the beginning of the first century: the Holy Chalice of Jesus Christ, the relic revered by early Christians above all others.

Appendices

Converting Dates Between the Islamic and Christian Calendars

Formulae can be used to convert Muslim and Gregorian years, but establishing the exact correspondence between specific dates is practically impossible. The discrepancy is due to the fact that the Muslim calendar is regulated by the observable lunar cycle. For quick calculations the following formulae should suffice.

To go from a Muslim year to the Gregorian:

$$G = H + 622 - \frac{H}{33}$$

To go from a Gregorian year to the Muslim:

$$H = 1{,}03125\,(G - 622)$$

Where:

G = Gregorian year
H = Muslim year (Hijra)

Study of the Islamic Texts

First Manuscript Text

Context

The Emir of Dénia receives Christ's Chalice, which had previously been kept in Jerusalem, in return for giving aid to Egypt (1055). His intention is to ingratiate himself with Ferdinand, King of Léon.

Location of the Source and its Characteristics

In 2006 Dr Gustavo Turienzo Veiga, responsible for both translations, located the manuscript in the National Library of Egypt. In 2010, it was found in the Al-Azhar Library in Cairo, on the third floor, manuscript section, general catalogue number 8781. We would like to thank Gustavo Turienzo for his meticulous translation, the result of months of work, along with the other Arabists who were subsequently kind enough to review it.

Probably late medieval (approximately fourteenth century).

Thirty-two lines of text: sixteen on each side of the document.

Dimensions: 28.5 × 18.1 cm

Written area (of each the front and the back of the document): 22.5 × 14.5 cm

Translation:

Al-Qifti tells us that the cup that the Christians call the Cup of the Messiah – peace be upon him – used during the celebration with his disciples – may God have mercy on them – was found in one [stain] of the small churches that are on the outskirts of Jerusalem – may Allah return it to the nation of Islam. This church is famous because of the presence of relics of the Bishop Jacob [stain], the Messiah's true disciple – peace be upon him. And there the cup was found, under the protection of some brave Rumis, who had sworn an oath to protect it, hidden behind a pair of small curtains, in a niche between the walls, far from view. The Christians insist that this cup has extraordinary medicinal powers [stain], a rumour that is revealed [stain] by the tongues of both Christians and Muslims, heightening the cup's fame and popularity. But men of science and doctrine disregard it, and certain Muslims even strongly reject the claim that any such church exists [stain] healing.

In the year of the great famine (447), Ali bnu Muyahid ad-Danii sent a boat with a great supply of provisions to the country of Egypt. And as he had already heard something of the power of the Cup, he asked the High Imam al-Mustanṣir for it, in exchange for whatever was necessary to offer him for handing it over [stain] since his intention was to send it to the King of León, Ferdinand al-Kabir, [stain] king of this land, in 429, to strengthen their alliance. This king already suffered gravely with the disease of the stones, which would cause him to die a painful death.

There are others, however, who say that Ali was really a Christian and his mother was still living in Christian lands, but that he had not been able to accompany her.

The infidel guardians feared that the Cup might fall into Muslim hands during its movement from one place to another. Knowing the antipathy that the Jews and the men of science and doctrine felt towards the cup and [stain] the act of pilgrimage [stain], they entrusted it to a Frankish bishop from Al-Yalaliqa, who al-Masûdi mentions in his book, was in Jerusalem at the time on pilgrimage. Accompanied by some of the custodians of the Cup, and his own men, the bishop [stain] gathered up what was necessary for the journey, and quickly set forth [stain]. And it is known that during the journey [stain] . . .

Second Manuscript Text

Context

Saladin demands to be sent the 'fine shard' of the Cup that an ancestor of the Banī-l-Aswad family had chipped off with a *kommeyya* during its journey towards the west, where it would be given to the Emir of Dénia by the Caliph al-Mustanṣir.

Location of the Source and its Characteristics

As in the case above, it was found in the Al-Azhar Library in Cairo in 2010, on the third floor, manuscript section, general catalogue number 8781.

Fifteen lines of text on one side of the document.

Probably late medieval (approximately fourteenth century).

Dimensions: 21.8 × 24.9 cm (at the widest points)

Translation

Given the state of our daughter's health, who as you know suffers from diseased blood flow and the sickness of the stone, and having previously taken advice from the physicians and mufti of Jerusalem, we ordered a piece of the holy stone to be sent, which had been cut from it with a kommeyya by the leader of Banī-l-Aswad's men in 447, when the wicked al-Mustanṣir named him head of the expedition to Dénia in the far West [stain]. And it is known how doing so darkened his face and hands [stain].

The shard taken from the Cup was sent to Salah ad-din, may God have pity on him, and after his daughter was healed by the piece of stone placed upon her body, he ordered for it to be kept in a cabinet in the House of Wealth (the Islamic public treasury).

Notes

1   The Battle of Atapuerca (1054) took place between King García Sánchez III of Navarre and King Ferdinand I of Castile. The area is a mountain range in Northern Spain near Burgos, known for its limestone caves rich in fossils and early human remains.

2   For further details, refer to SAFRAI, S. and STERN, M. (eds), *The Jewish People in the First Century,* 2 vols, Assen, 1974–1976.

3   By way of an overview, see: HORSLEY, R.A., *Archaeology, History and Society in Galilee: The Social Context of Jesus and the Rabbis*, Valley Forge, 1996.

4   APPLEBAUM, S., *Judea in Hellenistic and Roman Times: Historical and Archaeological Essays*, Leiden, 1989.
The following works by Reich and Herbert are also of interest:
REICH, R., *Archaeological Evidence of the Jewish Population at Hasmonean Gezer, I.E.J.* No. 31 (1981), pp. 48–52.
HERBERT, S., *Tel Anafa I. Final Report on Ten Years of Excavation at a Hellenistic and Roman Settlement in Northern Israel*, Ann Arbor, 1994.

5   The elements listed from here on appear in the excavations undertaken in the city of Nazareth, very closely linked to the life of Jesus (BAGATTI, B., *Excavations in Nazareth,* Vol. I: *From the Beginning till the XII Century,* Jerusalem, 1969).

6   HESSE, B. and WAPNISH, P., Can Pig Remains Be Used for Ethnic Diagnosis in the Ancient Near East?, in

SILBERMAN, N.A. and SMALL, D. (eds), *The Archaeology of Israel: Constructing the Past, Interpreting the Present,* Sheffield, 1997, pp. 238–270.

7   MAGEN, Y., Jerusalem As a Center of the Stone Vessel Industry during the Second Temple Period, in GEVA, H. (ed.), *Ancient Jerusalem Revealed,* Jerusalem, 1994, pp. 244–256.

8   Ritual bath known as the *Miqwaot* (SANDERS, E.P., *Judaism: Practice and Belief 63 B.C.E.–66 C.E.,* Philadelphia, 1992, pp. 222–229; BAUMGARTEN, J. M., *The Purification Rituals in DJD 7,* in DIMANT, D. and RAPPAPPORT, U., *The Dead Sea Scrolls: Forty Years of Research,* Leiden-Jerusalem, 2002, pp. 199–209; WRIGHT, B., Jewish Ritual Baths – Interpreting the Digs and the Texts: Some Issues in the Social History of Second Temple Judaism, in SILBERMAN, N.A. and SMALL, D., *The Archaeology of Israel: Constructing the Past, Interpreting the Present,* Sheffield, 1997, pp. 190–214).

9   REED, J.L. *Archaeology and the Galilean Jesus. A Re-examination of the Evidence,* Harrisburg, 2000, pp. 44–48.

10   Take, for example, Nazareth and Capernaum. The first is linked to the early years of Christ's life, while the second, greater in size and relevance, was where he spent many of his later years and is believed by many to have been his home as an adult (REED, J.L., *Archaeology and the Galilean Jesus,* pp. 160–161).

11   It should be remembered that Roman military units were present in the area, as indicated by the references to the Roman centurion in Capernaum in the gospels. These were troops from the Tenth Legion of the Sea Strait (*Legio X Fretensis*) and others, under the region's Roman command. On this subject, see Safrai's work on the presence of the Roman army in Galilee (SAFRAI, Z., The Roman Army

in the Galilee, in LEVINE, L.I. (ed.), *The Galilee in Late Antiquity*, New York, 1992, pp. 103–114).

12 Matthew 9:11.

13 Mark 1:21, 2:1, 9:33.

14 Luke 2:12; 4:23; 4:46; 6:17; 24.

15 John 6:59.

16 CHARLESWORTH, J., *Jesus within Judaism: New Light from Exciting Archaeological Excavation*, New York, 1988.

17 A good survey of the origin, evolution and coexistence of these four groups can be found in: NEWMAN, H. and LUDLAM, R.M., *Proximity to Power and Jewish Sectarian Groups of the Ancient Period: A Review of Lifestyle, Value and Halakhah in the Pharisees, Sadducees, Essenes and Qumran*, Leiden, 2006.

18 Acts 23:6.

19 Acts 4:2.

20 There are numerous references to the Essenes and Zealots in the work of Flavius Josephus. With regard to the Zealots, specifically, Yigael Yadin's analysis is interesting (YADIN, Y., BALLESTEROS GAIBROIS, M. and TORRE, V. DE LA, *Masada: la fortaleza de Herodes y el último bastión de los zelotes*, Madrid, 1992).

21 In addition to the Newman and Ludlam text mentioned above, the contributions of the following two works in Spanish are of interest:
STEGEMANN, H., *Los esenios, Qumram, Juan el Bautista y Jesús,* Madrid, 1996.
MONTES PERAL, L.Á., *Tras las huellas de Jesús: seguimiento y discipulado en Jesús, los Evangelios y el 'Evangelio de dichos Q',* Madrid, 2006.

22 We recommend the following reading about the Zealots: BORG, M., The Currency of the Term 'Zealot', *Journal of Theological Studies,* 22 (1973), pp. 504–512.

GOODMAN, M., *The Ruling Class of Judea: The Origins of the Jewish Revolt against Rome, A. D. 66–70,* Cambridge, 1987.

HENGEL, M., *The Zealots: Investigations into the Jewish Freedom Movement in the Period from Herod I until 70 A. D.,* London, 2010.

HORSLEY, R. and HANSON, J., *Bandits, Prophets and Messiahs: Popular Movements in the Time of Jesus,* Minneapolis, 1985.

BRANDON, S.G.F., *Jesus and the Zealots: A Study of the Political Factor in Primitive Christianity,* Manchester, 1967.

23 Exodus 12: 'The Lord spoke to Moses and Aaron in the land of Egypt, saying, 2 "This month shall be to you the beginning of months. It shall be the first month of the year to you. 3 Speak to all the congregation of Israel, saying, 'On the tenth day of this month, they shall take to them every man a lamb, according to their fathers' houses, a lamb for a household; 4 and if the household is too little for a lamb, then he and his neighbour next to his house shall take one according to the number of the souls; according to what everyone can eat you shall make your count for the lamb. 5 Your lamb shall be without blemish, a male a year old. You shall take it from the sheep, or from the goats: 6 and you shall keep it until the fourteenth day of the same month; and the whole assembly of the congregation of Israel shall kill it at evening. 7 They shall take some of the blood, and put it on the two doorposts and on the lintel, on the houses in which they shall eat it. 8 They shall eat the flesh in that night, roasted with fire, and unleavened bread. They shall eat it with bitter herbs. 9 Don't eat it raw, nor boiled at all with water, but roasted with fire; with its head, its legs and its inner parts.10 You shall let nothing of it remain until the morning; but that which remains of it

until the morning you shall burn with fire. 11 This is how you shall eat it: with your waist girded, your shoes on your feet, and your staff in your hand; and you shall eat it in haste: it is the Lord's Passover. 12 For I will go through the land of Egypt in that night, and will strike all the firstborn in the land of Egypt, both man and animal. Against all the gods of Egypt I will execute judgments: I am the Lord. 13 The blood shall be to you for a token on the houses where you are: and when I see the blood, I will pass over you, and there shall no plague be on you to destroy you, when I strike the land of Egypt. 14 This day shall be to you for a memorial, and you shall keep it a feast to the Lord: throughout your generations you shall keep it a feast by an ordinance forever. 15 "'Seven days you shall eat unleavened bread; even the first day you shall put away yeast out of your houses, for whoever eats leavened bread from the first day until the seventh day, that soul shall be cut off from Israel. 16 In the first day there shall be to you a holy convocation, and in the seventh day a holy convocation; no manner of work shall be done in them, except that which every man must eat, that only may be done by you. 17 You shall observe the feast of unleavened bread; for in this same day have I brought your armies out of the land of Egypt: therefore you shall observe this day throughout your generations by an ordinance forever. 18 In the first month, on the fourteenth day of the month at evening, you shall eat unleavened bread, until the twenty-first day of the month at evening. 19 Seven days shall there be no yeast found in your houses, for whoever eats that which is leavened, that soul shall be cut off from the congregation of Israel, whether he be a foreigner, or one who is born in the land. 20 You shall eat nothing leavened. In all your habitations you shall eat unleavened bread.'"
21 Then Moses called for all the elders of Israel, and said to

them, "Draw out, and take lambs according to your families, and kill the Passover. 22 You shall take a bunch of hyssop, and dip it in the blood that is in the basin, and strike the lintel and the two doorposts with the blood that is in the basin; and none of you shall go out of the door of his house until the morning. 23 For the Lord will pass through to strike the Egyptians; and when he sees the blood on the lintel, and on the two doorposts, the Lord will pass over the door, and will not allow the destroyer to come in to your houses to strike you. 24 You shall observe this thing for an ordinance to you and to your sons forever. 25 It shall happen when you have come to the land which the Lord will give you, according as he has promised, that you shall keep this service. 26 It will happen, when your children ask you, 'What do you mean by this service?' 27 that you shall say, 'It is the sacrifice of the Lord's Passover, who passed over the houses of the children of Israel in Egypt, when he struck the Egyptians, and spared our houses.'"

The people bowed their heads and worshipped. 28 The children of Israel went and did so; as the Lord had commanded Moses and Aaron, so they did.

24   Deuteronomy 16:1: 'Observe the month of Abib, and keep the Passover to the Lord your God; for in the month of Abib the Lord your God brought you forth out of Egypt by night'.

25   John 2: 13–23: '13 The Passover of the Jews was at hand, and Jesus went up to Jerusalem. 14 He found in the temple those who sold oxen, sheep, and doves, and the changers of money sitting. 15 He made a whip of cords, and threw all out of the temple, both the sheep and the oxen; and he poured out the changers' money, and overthrew their tables. 16 To those who sold the doves, he said, "Take these things out of here! Don't make my Father's house a marketplace!" 17 His disciples remembered that it was written, "Zeal for your

house will eat me up." 18 The Jews therefore answered him, "What sign do you show us, seeing that you do these things?" 19 Jesus answered them, "Destroy this temple, and in three days I will raise it up." 20 The Jews therefore said, "Forty-six years was this temple in building, and will you raise it up in three days?" 21 But he spoke of the temple of his body. 22 When therefore he was raised from the dead, his disciples remembered that he said this, and they believed the Scripture, and the word which Jesus had said. 23 Now when he was in Jerusalem at the Passover, during the feast, many believed in his name, observing his signs which he did.'

26 John 6:1–6: 'After these things, Jesus went away to the other side of the sea of Galilee, which is also called the Sea of Tiberias. 2 A great multitude followed him, because they saw his signs which he did on those who were sick. 3 Jesus went up into the mountain, and he sat there with his disciples. 4 Now the Passover, the feast of the Jews, was at hand. 5 Jesus therefore lifting up his eyes, and seeing that a great multitude was coming to him, said to Philip, "Where are we to buy bread, that these may eat?" 6 This he said to test him, for he himself knew what he would do.'

27 The period that begins with Jesus' visit to his friend Lazarus (John 11–12). John tells us that as Passover was approaching, many Jews would head to Jerusalem to purify themselves. The High Priests and Pharisees looked for Jesus, aware of the danger he presented. Suspecting he was likely to appear in the Holy City given the dates, they ordered that if anybody knew where he was they should tell them, so he could be arrested. Six days before Passover, Christ walked to Bethany, where he met with Lazarus, whose family members honoured him with a dinner. John's account goes on to explain that the following day, the crowds that had

gathered in Jerusalem for the festival learned that Jesus was on his way to the city and took branches of palm trees to welcome him as the King of Israel. In John 13 the whole ritual of the Last Supper is described. He begins by telling us that these events take place 'before the feast of the Passover' (John 13:1).

28 John 18: 28.

29 This custom can be neither proven nor verified, although it is likely that it did occasionally happen.

30 John 18:39.

31 Mark 14.

32 Mark 14:3. John's account describes a meal given in the Messiah's honour by his friend Lazarus and his family.

33 Mark 14:12–26.

34 Matthew 26.

35 Luke 22.

36 PIÑEIRO, A. and GÓMEZ SEGURA, E., *La verdadera historia de la Pasión. Según la investigación y el estudio histórico*, Madrid, 2007, pp. 222–224.

37 This is the origin of the sacramental host used during the Eucharist.

38 It is not clear whether before the fall of the Second Temple (70 CE), *Seder* was conducted with four cups or just one. 'Cup' does not mean the physical object itself, but its contents. This custom was practised after Titus and his legions conquered Jerusalem, but there is some doubt over whether it was already in place prior to Titus' invasion. Nevertheless, it is certain that at least one cup of wine was used as part of the ritual practised at the time of Christ.

39 The *Torah* (Exodus 6: 6–7) specifies that there were four promises symbolizing the freedom granted to Israel by God: 'I am the Lord, and I will bring you out from under the burdens of the Egyptians, and I will rid you out of their

bondage, and I will redeem you with an outstretched arm, and with great judgments: 7 and I will take you to me for a people, and I will be to you a God; and you shall know that I am the Lord your God, who brings you out from under the burdens of the Egyptians.'

This is the origin of the custom whereby every Jew must drink four cups of wine, to represent the four expressions of freedom. At this special dinner, everybody serves wine to the person next to him or her, which must be red, in memory of blood. The custom of offering a cup to the Prophet Elijah was introduced after the period that concerns us.

40 These words are very similar to the ones spoken by priests during the Eucharist. This would suggest that the ritual of the four cups was already in use around the time of Christ, although this cannot be verified.

41 ST JUSTIN MARTYR, *Letter to the Emperor Antoninus Pius*, c.155 CE.

42 'No-one feeds his guests on himself; that is what the Lord Christ did, being himself the host, himself the food and drink' (ST AUGUSTINE, Sermon on the Day of the Martyrs, 1–2).

43 I Corinthians 10:16–17.

44 Although we have gone into some detail about these aspects, our arguments essentially involve starting with the Gospels and the book of Acts themselves, and trying to address these basic elements through their subsequent transcendence (Matthew 14:19; 15:36; 26:26; Mark 8:6–19; Luke 24:13–35; Acts 2:42–46; 20:7–11; 1 Corinthians 11:24).

45 1 Corinthians 5: 7–8.

46 Luke 24:30–35.

47 Acts 2:42; 2:46; 20:6.

48 The *Didache* or *the Teaching of the Twelve Apostles* was written between 65 and 80 CE, although some specialists

have dated them a little later, either around 90 CE or in the second century. It could be seen as the earliest form of the catechism, highly esteemed by the Fathers of the Church and of clear didactic value for the faithful. Chapters 9 and 10 hint at an outline for the primitive celebration of the Eucharist:

'9:1 Concerning the Eucharist, give thanks this way. 9:2 First, concerning the cup: We thank you, our Father, for the holy vine of David your servant, which you made known to us through Jesus your servant. To you be the glory forever. 9:3 Next, concerning the broken bread: We thank you, our Father, for the life and knowledge which you made known to us through Jesus your servant. To you be the glory forever. 9:4 Even as this broken bread was scattered over the hills, and was gathered together and became one, so let your church be gathered together from the ends of the earth into your kingdom. To you is the glory and the power through Jesus Christ forever. 9:5 Allow no one to eat or drink of your Eucharist, unless they have been baptized in the name of the Lord. For concerning this, the Lord has said, 'Do not give what is holy to dogs.' *Chapter 10* 10:1 After the Eucharist when you are filled, give thanks this way:10:2 We thank you, holy Father, for your holy name which you enshrined in our hearts, and for the knowledge and faith and immortality that you made known to us through Jesus your servant. To you be the glory forever.10:3 You, Master Almighty, have created all things for your name's sake. You gave food and drink to all people for enjoyment, that they might give thanks to you; but to us you freely give spiritual food and drink and life eternal through Jesus, your servant.10:4 Before all things we thank you because you are mighty. To you be the glory forever.10:5 Remember, Lord, your church. Deliver it from all evil and make it perfect in your love, and gather it from the four winds sanctified for your kingdom which you have prepared for it. For Yours is the power and the glory forever.10:6 Let grace come, and let this world pass away!Hosanna to the Son of David! If anyone is holy, let him come; if anyone is not holy, let him repent. Maranatha! Amen 10:7 But permit the prophets to make thanksgiving as much as they desire.' (See also MILAVEC, A., *The Didache. Text, Translation, Analysis, and Commentary*, Collegeville, 2003).

49 Pliny states that the Christians would meet on a given day, before sunrise, sing a hymn to Christ and then separate after making certain promises, before coming together again later to eat: '(...) they were in the habit of meeting on a certain fixed day before it was light, when they sang in alternate verses a hymn to Christ, as to a god, and bound themselves by a solemn oath, not to any wicked deeds, but never to commit any fraud, theft or adultery, never to falsify their word, nor deny a trust when they should be called upon to deliver it up; after which it was their custom to separate, and then reassemble to partake of food, but food of an ordinary and innocent kind'. (GAIUS PLINIUS CAELILIUS SECUNDUS, *Epistolarum ad Traianum Imperatorem cum eiusdem Responsis liber X*, 96).

50 Acts 13:2–3; 14:23; Matthew 2,20; Didache 8,1.

51 Acts 21:21.

52 Acts 10:14.

53 Acts 2:46; 3:1–5,43; 10:9.
    REED, J.L., *Archaeology and the Galilean Jesus: A Re-examination of the Evidence*, Trinity Press International, Harrisburg, 2000, p. 24.

54 Acts 2:1; 16:13; 18:4; 20:16.

55 Acts 2:38–41; 8:12–13, 16, 36–38.

56 Acts 2:42–46.

57 Acts 20:7; 1 Corinthians 16:2; Revelation 1:10; Didache 14:1; Epistle of Barnabas 15:8–9.

58 Acts 4:32, 5:11.

59 GUIJARRO OPORTO, S., *El Jesús histórico* (online – accessed 25 February 2011).
Available at: http://www.jesus.teologia.upsa.es/default.asp

60 1 Corinthians 11:23.

61 Acts 1:13–14.
We should add to these the group comprised of women, which is cited regularly in the early years and always independently of the other groups.

62 The figure of St James the Just or St James of Jerusalem has been discussed extensively over the centuries. This is firstly because of the confusion that exists between him and the apostle James the Less, and secondly because many early texts describe him as Jesus Christ's brother. Some authors, such as the Fathers of the Church like Tertullian, maintain that he was Joseph and Mary's son, and therefore Jesus' blood brother. Others believe that he was Joseph's son from a previous marriage, while yet others maintain that 'the brother of the Lord' simply means cousin or other relative, something that was common in both the Aramaic and Hebraic languages. The issue is that the Gospels of Mark and John and the Letter to the Galatians were all written in Greek and the word 'adelfos', which is used to refer to St James as the brother of the Lord, does not mean any sort of relative, but only actually brother. Equally, the use of the term 'brother' by Flavius Josephus in a non-Jewish text raises important questions (FLUSSER, D., *Jesús en sus palabras y su tiempo*, Madrid, 1975, p. 136 onwards; MCDOWELL, J., *Más que un carpintero*, Miami, 1997, p. 60; STROBEL, L., *El caso del Jesús verdadero*, Miami, 2008; KLAUSNER, J., *Jesús de Nazaret*, Buenos Aires, 1971).

63 Galatians 1:19.

64 1 Corinthians 15:7; Acts 1:13–14.

65 Acts 6:1–14; 7:1–53.

66 Acts 8:1.

67 Galatians 2:10; Romans 15:26.

68 Acts 10–11.

69 Acts 11:22–23.

70 Acts 11:25; 13–14.

71 Acts 14:27.

72 Acts 15:3.

73 Acts 15; Galatians 2.

74 Acts 12:1–17.

75 Acts 21:20.

76 Although this is the name by which the meeting is commonly known, it is not counted as such by the Catholic Church. The first official council would be the Council of Nicaea in 325 CE.

77 Acts 11:26.

78 Acts 15:4.

79 It is worth remembering the nature of this group's religious belief, as described in previous pages.

80 Acts 15:6.

81 Acts 15:7–11.

82 Acts 15:12.

83 Acts 15:13–20.

84 See Deuteronomy 32:17; Leviticus 18:6–18 and 17:10–12.

85 Acts 1:15–26.

86 Although it might seem as though the Council of Jerusalem completely solved the Church's internal problems, this was not the case. Some groups, generally of Pharisee descent, (Acts 15:5) were not content with being the only group that kept Jewish Law and wanted to make it obligatory for others, even gentiles, taking their behaviour and attitude

to an almost sectarian and heretical extreme. These so-called 'judaizing' groups were St Paul's bitter rivals. The apostle meets with them in Antioch (Acts 15:1), Jerusalem (Acts 15:5), Galatia (Galatians) and Corinth (2 Corinthians 3:13–18; 4:2–4; 10:1–17; 11:4–5, 22–23; 12:11–15).

87   For more on this: GIRI, J. *Les nouvelles hypothèses sur les origines du christianisme: Enquête sur les recherches récentes*, Paris: Kartala, 2010, p. 200 onwards.

88   In the Gnostic Gospel of Thomas, the disciples tell Jesus: 'We know that you are going to leave us. Who will be our leader?' Jesus said to them, 'No matter where you are you are to go to James the Just, for whose sake heaven and earth came into being' (Gospel of Thomas, 12).

89   Matthew 16:18–20.

90   The group of women, whose presence is clearly distinguished in the text, probably took on a key role in this regard. To find out more about how they influenced the early church see: OSIEK, C., MACDONALD, M. and TULLOCH, J.H., *El lugar de la mujer en la iglesia primitiva. Iglesias domésticas en los albores del cristianismo*, Salamanca, 2007.

91   FLAVIUS JOSEPHUS, *Antiquities of the Jews*, 20.9.1.

92   EUSEBIUS OF CAESAREA, *Historia Eclesiástica*, II, 23.

93   James the Just was succeeded in the office of bishop of Jerusalem by Simeon, Justus (107–113), Zaccheus or Zacharias, Tobias, Benjamin, Matthias (*d*.120), Philip, Senecas, Justus II, Levis, Ephram, Joseph and Judas Cyriacus.

94   There are many authors who believe that there was a link between early Christianity and the Zealots. (BRANDON, S.G.F., *The Fall of Jerusalem and the Christian Church*, London, 1957).

95   FLAVIUS JOSEPHUS, *The Jewish War*, 6, XII.

96   There was resistance in Machaerus (in Perea, modern

Jordan), Herodium (close to Bethlehem) and Masada (on the Dead Sea).

97 Luke 21:20–21.

98 LANGE, N. de, *El Judaísmo*, Madrid, 2006, p.134.

99 Nazarenes and heretics.

100 Talmud Bavli, Megillah 17b, Berachot 28b.

101 CASSIUS DIO, *Historia de Roma*, LXVIII.32.

102 HOLDER, M., *History of the Jewish People*, New York, 2000, pp. 50–56.

103 According to Numbers 24:17.

104 CASSIUS DIO, *Historia de Roma*, LXIX.XIII, 1–2.

105 While it was long held that the annihilation of the Roman Twenty-Second Deiotariana Legion should be included in these losses, this is no longer considered certain (SCHÄFER, P., *The Bar Kokhba War Reconsidered: New Perspectives on the Second Jewish Revolt against Rome*, Mohr Siebeck, 2003, p. 118).

106 We refer to the following works of interest:
ESPARCIANO, E., *Vida de Adriano, Biógrafos y panegiristas latinos*, Madrid, 1969.
BLÁZQUEZ, J.M., *Adriano*, Barcelona, 2008.
BIRLEY, A., *Hadrian. The Restless Emperor*, London, 1997.

107 Ibid., 14:3.

108 EUSEBIUS DE CAESAREA, *Ecclesiastical History*, XXXIX, 6.3.

109 It is important to bear in mind that ritual prostitution was practised by *hierodules* in temples dedicated to Aphrodite.

110 GIBSON, S. and TAYLOR, J.E., *Beneath the Church of the Holy Sepulchre: The Archaeology and Early History of the Traditional Golgotha*, London, 1994.

111 THEODORET DE CYR, *Histoire ecclésiastique*, 2 vols, Paris, 2006 and 2009.

112 We should not discount the possibility that a section of the

community lived on the outskirts of Jerusalem and even had contact with Romans. Historically, a group of civilians would live on the edges of Roman military camps, employed in their service.

113 EUSEBIUS OF CAESAREA, *Life of Constantine*, III, XXVI.

114 There is an inscription in the periphery of the Holy Sepulchre, which depicts a boat with a broken main mast and the following words: *'Domine ivimus'* (Lord, we came). The message is not difficult to understand: they were Western pilgrims (Greek was the language of the Orient), at the point of perishing in a storm on the way to Jerusalem, but who finally reached the destination of their pilgrimage, Calvary. The date of this inscription is not clear, but we can tell that it was at a time when there was no access to the Holy Sepulchre, since it was found on an external wall that supported the Temple of Aphrodite. It tells us, therefore, that the location of the place where Christ died was already known about even as far back as the era of the Temple of Aphrodite (135–325 CE).

115 In his *Ecclesiastical History*, I, 2.

116 Peter underwent a genuine *conversion* brought about by the episodes of Simon, the tanner, and the centurion Cornelius. Thanks to them he came at last to understand that Jesus' message made no distinction between pure and impure Jews, like Simon, or circumcised and uncircumcised men. It was a universal message, and the apostle resolved to risk even his life by confronting the strict views of the Community of Jerusalem led by James the Just, to whom he was obliged to explain his change of heart (RIUS-CAMPS, J., *De Jerusalén a Antioquía. Génesis de la Iglesia Cristiana. Comentario lingüístico y exegético a Hch* 1–12, Córdoba, 1989, pp. 246–271).

117 The Church's recognition by the Jewish authorities following

the initial period of persecution by the Sadducees was owed, to a large extent, to the intervention of the Pharisee Gamaliel. For a while, thanks to him, Christians were respected.

118 On the development of the Aelia settlement, see:

ESHEL, H., The Date of the Founding of Aelia Capitolina, in: *The Dead Sea Scrolls, Fifty Years after their Discovery*, Jerusalem, 2000, pp. 637–643.

KINDLER, A., Was Aelia Capitolina Founded before or after the Outbreak of the Bar Kokhba War? A Numismatic Evidence, *Israel Numismatic Journal*, 14 (2000–2002), pp. 176–179.

CASSIUS DIO, *Roman History*, LXIX 12, 1–2.

EUSEBIUS OF CAESAREA, *Ecclesiastical History*, IV, 6.

ELIAV, Y.Z., The Urban Layout of Aelia Capitolina: A New View from the Perspective of the Temple Mount, in: P. SCHÄFER, *The Bar Kokhba War Reconsidered*, Tübingen, 2003.

MESHORER, Y., *The Coinage of Aelia Capitolina*, Jerusalem, 1989.

GEVA, H., Jerusalem. The Roman Period, in: *The New Encyclopedia of Archaeological Excavations in the Holy Land*, II, Jerusalem, 1993, pp. 758–767.

BAR, D., Aelia Capitolina and the Location of the Camp of the Tenth Legion, *Palestine Exploration Quarterly*, 130 (1998), pp. 8–19.

VINCENT, H. and ABEL, F.M., Jérusalem, recherches de topographie, d'archéologie et d'histoire. II. *Jérusalem nouvelle*, Paris, 1914.

BELAYCHE, N., Dimmenticare... Gerusalemme. Les paganismes à Aelia Capitolina du IIe au IVe siècle de notre ère, *Revue des Etudes Juives*, 1 58/3–4 (1999), pp. 287–348.

ARNOULD, C., Les arcs romains de Jérusalem : architecture, décor et urbanisme, *Novum Testamentum et Orbis Antiquus*,

35 (1997), pp. 9–147.

L'espace urbain d'Aelia Capitolina (Jérusalem): Rupture ou continuité?, *Histoire urbaine* 2005/2 – No. 13 (2005), pp. 85–100.

KATZ, S.T. (ed.), *The Cambridge History of Judaism. The Late Roman–Rabbinic Period*, vol. 4, Cambridge, 2006.

119 Melito of Sardis (who died around 180 CE) held the bishopric of the city of Sardis, close to Smyrna in Asia Minor, and was one of the Fathers of the Church.

120 IBÁÑEZ IBÁÑEZ, J. and MENDOZA RUIZ, F., *Melitón de Sardes. Homilía sobre la Pascua*, Pamplona, 1975, pp. 204–207.

121 EUSEBIUS OF CAESAREA, *Ecclesiastical History*, VI, 11.2

122 FINNEGAN, J., *The Archeology of the New Testament*, Princeton, 1978.

123 MITRE, E., *Ortodoxia y herejía: Entre la Antigüedad y el Medievo*, Madrid, 2003, pp. 60–61.

124 LLORCA VIVES, C.B., *Historia de la Iglesia Católica. I: Edad Antigua: la Iglesia en el mundo grecorromano*, Madrid, 1990, p. 388.

125 The word 'Invention' is derived from the Latin *inventare* meaning to find, come upon or discover, rather than to invent.

126 EUSEBIUS OF CAESAREA, *Life of Constantine*, III, 26–28.

127 While some experts believe the *Didache* was composed in the second half of the first century CE, most believe it took shape in the second century. Its remarkable value lies in its relationship with Jewish and early Christian sources, such as the Gospels. It contains the first known instructions on the liturgy of baptism and the Eucharist. The codex was found in Istanbul, in the library of the Monastery of the Holy Sepulchre, in 1873. Later, fragments from other sources which contained parts of the *Didache* such as those

contained in the Papyrus Oxyrhynchus 1782 (1922) were added to it, bolstering the antiquity and relevance of this key work in the history of early Christianity. We refer the interested reader to the following key texts, which go into some depth on this subject:

AYÁN CALVO, J.J., *Didaché*, Madrid, 1992.

DRAPER, J., *Ritual Process and Ritual Symbol in Didache 7–10*, *Vigiliae Christianae*, 54, nº 2 (2000), pp. 121–158.

128 *Didache* IX, 2.

129 *Didache* IX, 3.

130 Without wishing to stray into provocative arguments, the existence of such pieces of *Lignum Crucis* (wood of the True Cross) across the length and breadth of the Christian world has given rise to numerous critiques of their authenticity. Although it is true that wood can acquire the status of relics through contact, this does not explain the existence of a veritable forest of crosses, rather than one or a single piece. The Romans, nothing if not pragmatic, tended to reuse any material possible for executions, meaning that the cross would probably have remained in service after Christ's death. In the same way, the lance that pierced his side, far from belonging to the legionnaire, would have been the property of the military unit he served, and would naturally have returned to the *armamentarium* to be used again later. Given the Jewish mentality of the time, it seems unlikely that Christ's relatives and first disciples would have petitioned the Roman authorities to hand these objects over to them, objects used for his torture and murder.

For this information about the use of Roman weaponry we are grateful to Dr Á. Monrillo Cerdán, Professor of Archaeology at the Universidad Complutense of Madrid and undoubtedly the most highly recognized national expert in the fascinating field of Roman Legions.

131 '*A sinistra autem parte est monticulus golgotha, ubi dominus crucifixus est. Inde quasi ad lapidem missum est cripta, ubi corpus eius positum fuit et tertia die resurrexit; ibidem modo iussu constantini imperatoris basilica facta est, id est dominicum, mirae pulchritudinis*' (TEUBNER, B.G. (ed.), *Itinerarium Burdigalense,* Stuttgart, 1990, 593–594).

132 This does not mean that she was Galician in today's sense. When we are looking to locate a historical figure, it is essential to disregard modern geographical appellations. Don Pelayo was not Asturian, but *astur,* and Egeria was not from one of the four modern Galician provinces, but *Gallaecia,* the fourth-century limits of which included a large part of the contemporary autonomous regions of Castile and León, as well as Asturias.

   Unfortunately, geographical simplification, whether biased or not, often leads to these kinds of misunderstandings.

133 The author, a high-ranking aristocrat, would have been able to afford the great personal expense, as well as that of her entourage. She also carried a letter of safe passage and could rely on the support of the authorities, such as a military guard, in some cases.

134 EGERIA, *Itinerarium,* 37.4. We used the Arce translation (ARCE, A. (ed. and trans.)), *Itinerario de la Virgen Egeria (381–384),* Madrid, 1996).

135 EUSEBIUS OF CAESAREA, *op. cit.,* III, 30.

136 The writings of Saint Jerome about Saint Paula (35 CE), the original *Breviarius* of Jerusalem (400 CE), the letter of Echerius to Faustus (430 CE), Rufus' life of Peter the Iberian (500 CE) and Theodosius on the Topography of the Holy Land (518 CE) do not give us any relevant information on the subject.

137 The *Breviary* can be seen as a topographical description of part of Jerusalem. There are two versions, which survive

in three manuscripts. One of them comes from Milan, and was copied in the twelfth century (*Codices Ambrosianus* M. 79). The other, which agrees with it, appears in a manuscript kept in Oxford, dated from between the eighth and ninth centuries (*Oxoniensis Laud.* Misc. 263). Lastly, the final version was produced in 811 and is stored in the treasury of Sant-Gall (*Sangallensis* 732).

In his study of the sources that include accounts of pilgrimages to the Holy Land before the First Crusade (1099), Wilkinson approaches the subject of how each text was transmitted and its level of accuracy and rigour when evaluating the data contained within them. In his view, the original source should be reconstructed on the basis of the Milan and Oxford texts, and can be traced back, through the clues it contains, to the end of the fourth or beginning of the fifth centuries (J. WILKINSON, *Jerusalem Pilgrims*, pp. 3–4, 8–9).

138 *Breviarius A* in: WILKINSON, J., *Jerusalem Pilgrims Before the Crusades,* Oxford, 2002, p. 119.

139 J. WILKINSON, *op. cit.* p. 119.
There is also a reference to this church in PRINGLE, D., *The Churches of the Crusader Kingdom of Jerusalem, vol. 3. The City of Jerusalem,* Cambridge, 2007, p. 384.
It is also mentioned in *Conmemoratio* 20 (as the Martyrium of Saint Theodore) and the *Anonymous Pilgrim of Piacenza,* 46.

140 CASTIGNOLI, P., *Piacenza e i pellegrinaggi lungo la Via Francigena,* Piacenza, 1999, pp. 181–200.

141 Two versions of this key source exist, of which only one has been translated. The other is secondary, and simply seeks to clarify certain unclear aspects of the first text. Some authors, such as C. W. Wilson, in his notes on the translation completed by A. Stewart, suggest that the first version contained some additions, although later studies have

demonstrated that there is only one word which can said with certainty to have been added later (J. WILKINSON, *op. cit.*, pp. 12–13).

The main philological and codicological studies of this source locate it at the end of the nineteenth century and the middle of the twentieth, although debates around it persist (GEYER, P., *Kritische und sprachliche Erlaiterungen zu Ant. Plac. Itin.*, Augsburg, 1892; VERMEER, G.F.M., *Observations sur le Vocabulaire du Pèlerinage chez Egérie et chez Antonin de Plaisesance*, Nijmegen, 1965).

142 *Anonymous Pilgrim of Piacenza*, 20. The wood of the Cross (v. 173).

We have used the P. Geyer edition of this text (GEYER, P., *Antonini Placentini Itinerarium*, in *Itineraria et alia geographica,* Turnhout, 1965, pp. 127–174).

143 The first chalices were generally made of glass, in the Roman domestic tradition (RIGHETTI, M., *Manual de Historia Litúrgica*, vol. I, Madrid, 1955. p. 185).

144 There are various authors who play down the destruction of Jerusalem under Persian rule, or describe it as having been limited to certain areas:

VALLEJO GIRVÉS, M., Miedo bizantino: las conquistas de Jerusalén y la llegada del Islam, in *Milenio: Miedo y religión*. IV Simposio Internacional de la SECR, Sociedad Española de Ciencias de las Religiones, La Laguna, 3rd – 6th February 2000 (viewed online: www.ull.es/congresos/conmirel/VALLEJO.htm).

WALTER, E., *Byzantium and the Early Islamic Conquests*, Cambridge, 1995, p. 451, n. 59.

SCHICK, R., *The Christian Communities of Palestine from Byzantine to Islamic Rule. A Historical and Archaeological Study*, Princeton, 1995, pp. 33–39 and 327–338).

145 WILKINSON, *op. cit.*, pp. 13, 14, 15 onwards.

146 SOFRONIO DE JERUSALÉN, *Anacreontica*. G 125 47. 614.
We have used the edition by Marcello Gigante (GIGANTE,
M. (ed.), *Sophronius Anacreontica*, Rome, 1957).

147 This leads us to believe that Sharvaraz's desire to avenge the
staunch resistance of the city's Christian population was
behind this sacrilegious looting.

148 In later chapters we will show that the Chalice was hidden
in the outskirts of the city during the era of Arab rule.

149 DASXURANCI, M., *The History of the Caucasian Albanians*,
II, 51, London, 1961.

150 The *Armenian Guide* includes the testimony of one of the
pilgrims from Armenia who were received in Jerusalem by
the Abbot Modesto shortly before the city was taken by the
Persians. Some experts maintain that the text should be read
in relation to the first version of the *Guide of the Greek Monk
Epiphanius*, which is from the same century, studied by H.
Donner, whose reflections we have drawn on (DONNER,
H., Die Palästinabeschreibung des Epiphanius Monachus
Hagiopolita, *Zeitschrift des Deutschen Palästina-Vereins*, 87
(1971), pp. 45–92).

151 J. WILKINSON, *op. cit.*, pp. 16 and 17.

152 J. WILKINSON, *op. cit.*, p. 165.

153 It is important to bear in mind that there were some pilgrims
who became so elated in their worship that strict measures
needed to be taken; for example, they tried to bite the Holy
Cross when kissing it in an attempt to take away a piece of
it for themselves.

154 Other sources confirm that the lance was moved to
Constantinople on 26 October 614 CE, six weeks after the
sponge and four months after Jerusalem was conquered by
the Persians (MORERI, L., *El gran diccionario histórico o
miscelánea curiosa de la historia sagrada y profana*. Vol. V,
París, 1753, p. 479).

155 Khalid bin al-Waleed was one of Mohammed's companions (AKRAM, A.I., *The Sword of Allah: Khalid bin al-Waleed – His Life and Campaigns*, Oxford, 2004).

156 Regarding the Muslim army and conquest:
LOCK, H.O., *The Conquerors of Palestine through Forty Centuries*, New York, 2010.
GIL, M., *A History of Palestine, 634–1099*, Cambridge, 1997.
JANDORA, J.W., Developments in Islamic Warfare: The Early Conquests, *Studia Islamica*, 64 (1986), pp. 101–113.
WALTER, E., *Byzantium and the Early Islamic Conquests*, Cambridge, 1995.
NICOLLE, D., *Yarmuk 636 A.D.: The Muslim Conquest of Syria*, Oxford, 1994.
NICOLLE, D., *The Great Islamic Conquests AD 632–750*, Oxford, 2009.
PALMER, A., *The Seventh Century in the West-Syrian Chronicles*, Liverpool, 1993.

157 This must have been the first siege where Jerusalem came up against Muslim troops.

158 It seems there was an attempt to impersonate the caliph, but that Sophronius did not fall for it.

159 Qur'an, Surah XVII.

160 This expression appears in the Bible in reference to the crucifixion (Acts 5:30, 10:39).

161 Ancient Roman measure of liquid, equivalent to 546 ml, or just under one pint.

162 MEEHAN, D. (ed. and trans.), *Adomnan's De locis sanctis*, Dublin, 1983. v. 235.

163 The different traditions of this text have led to some surprising misunderstandings. The 'French gallon' or the English 'quart' must always be translated as a sextarius. Some authors have gone so far as to say that the capacity of the object was eight litres.

164 As has been mentioned, Adomnan's text was widely distributed across Europe, along with his maps. The four preserved today are from the ninth century (WILKINSON, J., *op. cit.*, p.371). Wilkinson states clearly that this was the object in question: '*The Lord's Cup Is Evidently the Holy Grail of Later Legend*' (J. WILKINSON, *ibid.*, p. 174).

165 DONNER, H., Die Palästinabeschreibung des Epiphanius Monachus Hagiopolita, *Zeitschrift des Deutschen Palästina-Vereins*, 87 (1971), pp. 42–91, p. 83 no. 6.
Also found in WILKINSON, J., *op. cit.*, p. 208.

166 EPIPHANIUS HAGIAPOLITA, *La Ciudad Santa y los Santos Lugares*, 3 (Cf. WILKINSON J., *op. cit.*, pp. 207–215).

167 WILKINSON, J., *op. cit.*, p. 21.

168 '*In platea, quæ martyrium et Golgotha continuat, exedra est, in qua calix Domini in scriniolo reconditus, per operculi foramen tangi solet et osculari. Qui argenteus calix, duas hinc et inde habens ansulas, sextarii Gallici mensuram*' (WILKINSON, J., *op. cit.*, p. 218). Just as Doña Urraca would adorn the cup with gold and her jewellery, increasing its size with the golden cup that protects it, at the time of the Latin source it could well have been covered in silver, with two handles.

169 In subsequent chapters we will see how this was possibly the system referred to in the description as a 'hole in the door'.

170 THE VENERABLE BEDE, *Historia eclesiástica del pueblo de los anglos*, Madrid, 2013.

171 Others deny this statement (HOYLAND, R., *Seeing Islam As Others Saw It.*, Princeton, 1996, p. 481).

172 WILKINSON, J., *op. cit.*, p. 253.

173 For a clearer outline of the dynasty, see the family tree on p. 83.

174 CAHEN, C., *El Islam. Desde los orígenes hasta el comienzo*

del Impero Otomano, Madrid, 2002, pp. 254–255.

175 Taqi al-Din al-Maqrizi (1364 – 1442 CE). Born in Cairo, he studied theology and was a *qadi*. He is the author of various key collections, foremost among which are his studies of the Fatimids. He was a meticulous and prudent copyist who had access to the original archives when writing his works. Our thanks to Gustavo Turienzo for his translation of the two Arabic parchments and for helping us to understand the work of al-Maqrizi. (RONART, S. and RONART, N., Maqrizi, in *Concise Encyclopaedia of Arabic Civilisation. The Arab East*, New York, 1985, p. 348).

176 17 September 1007 to 5 September 1008. To convert dates between the Christian and Islamic calendars, see the Appendix.

177 The almozala (*al-musala*) is a wide, open and flat space, which serves as an Islamic place of open-air worship; its purpose is to provide an outdoor venue for celebrating large collective Muslim religious festivities and, of course, special prayer processions.

178 Muslim chroniclers referred to the Church of the Resurrection in Jerusalem (Kanisaal Qiyama bi-l Quds) as Kanisa al Qumama (Church of Rubble) because it amused them to swap the word 'qiyama' (meaning resurrection) for the work 'qumama' (rubbish, remains, rubble).

179 A qa'id or caid is an Islamic local governor or leader, particularly in North Africa or Moorish Spain. Also see note 206.

180 Translator's note: Or this could equally mean 'fat' or 'oil'. Our translation of the phrase '(...) they always came together in great numbers to celebrate the anniversary of the Resurrection, displaying their crosses with pride and carrying over-spilling candles in their hands' is hypothetical, and is an approximate reconstruction based on the parts

of the sentence, the deliberately complex construction of which requires some interpretation. To achieve this, we have arbitrarily connected the word 'al-za'ibaq' with the verb 'za'b' (to fill up, to overfill). It is however perfectly plausible that these two words are not related at all, and that 'al-za'ibaq' actually means 'cup' or 'chalice' (another possible meaning of the word), which would mean the phrase would translate as: 'they always came together in great numbers to celebrate the anniversary of the Resurrection, displaying their crosses with pride and carrying candles with wicks oiled in the chalice'. On this point, and considering its importance, we ought to remember the clear revulsion with which Muslim chroniclers and geographers often refer to Christians. Such revulsion could well have influenced the deliberate complexity of the phrase in question, whose author may have purposely referred only obliquely to the Holy Chalice. On the other hand, the Orthodox Church currently celebrates the offices of Holy Week with a particularly emotive rite whereby every believer taking part in the day's rites must carry a small candle: this candle is lit from a flame which has been transported for this express purpose all the way from the Church of the Holy Sepulchre (or Resurrection) in Jerusalem.

181 Jerusalem's population was fundamentally Christian. In 985 CE a notable Arab geographer gave this description: '(...) in Jerusalem there are few learned men, but there are instead many Christians, and their constant presence in public places, absolutely repulsive, is as obvious as it is odious' AL-MUQADDASI, M., *Ahsan at-Taqasim fi Ma`rifat il-Aqalim*, Leiden, 1906, p. 167).

182 AL-MAQRIZI, *Itti`at al-Hunafa bi-l-ajbar al-Amirat al-Fatimiyyin al Jirafa*, vol. II, Cairo, 1973, p. 74.

183 25 August 1009 to 15 August 1010.

184 AL-MAQRIZI, *Itti`at al-Hunafa bi-l-ajbar al-Amirat al-Fatimiyyin al Jirafa*, vol. II, Cairo, 1973, p. 81.

185 MURPHY O'CONNOR, J., *The Holy Land, An Oxford Archaeological Guide from Earliest Times to 1700*, Oxford, 1998, pp. 49–53.

186 23 July 1012 to 13 July 1013.

187 Or perhaps forearm (*dirra*).

188 AL-MAQRIZI, *Itti`at al-Hunafa*. pp. 94–95.

189 These adjectives are exclusively used in reference to Allah.

190 Ya'far Ibn Muhámmad al-Sadiq (700–765 CE) is, for Shi'ites, one of the greatest Imams.

191 *Qa'b jasab* can also be translated as 'wooden chalice'.

192 *Sa'f wa qadara* can also be 'pan', 'platform', or 'bed', in its more modern sense.

193 Or indeed bed.

194 This inscription is, without doubt, fraudulent, intended to legitimize al-Hakim's destruction of the Church of the Holy Sepulchre, and is probably related to the events of 388 of the Hijra/995 CE, when the Imam al-Aziz, al-Hakim's predecessor, dismissed his Christian vizier Isa iben Nesturus, under an accusation of treason and disloyalty (IBN AL QALANISI, *Dhail* or *Mudhayyal Ta'rikh Dimashq*, Damascus, 1983 p. 57). Shortly afterwards he was reinstated to his position following the intercession of Sitt al-Mulk on his behalf, al-Aziz's powerful grandmother (CORTESE, D. and CALDERINI, S., *Women and the Fatimids in the World of Islam*, Edinburgh, 2006. p. 119).

195 AL-MAQRIZI, *Itti`at al-Hunafa*, pp. 118–119.

196 11 February 1027 to 1 January 1028.

197 '*Rumi*' was the name given by Moors to Christians.

198 '*Fataha*' is a verb that can also mean 'go straight for' or 'conquer'.

199 AL-MAQRIZI, *Itti`at al-Hunafa*, p. 176.

200 He died on 15 June 1036 (15th of Shaaban, 427 of the Hijra).

201 14 October 1037 to 3 October 1038.

202 In the royal stables, which had contained as many as 10,000 horses, only three were now left. Following a revolt by the caliphate's Turkish troops, he was found in his ruined chambers with three slaves and two loaves of bread.

203 AZUAR RUIZ, R., La Taifa de Denia en el comercio mediterráneo del siglo XI, *Anales de la Universidad de Alicante. Historia medieval*, No. 9 (1992–1993), pp. 39–52

204 VIGUERA MOLINS, M.J., *Los Reinos de Taifas y las invasiones magrebíes (Al-Andalus del XI al XIII)*, Madrid, 1992, p. 85.

205 2 April 1055 to 20 March 1056.

206 Qadis are judges in Muslim communities, who rule according to shariah law. Also see note 179.

207 The term '*malik*' used in this phrase implies the exercising of temporary power not issued by the caliph, by delegation, and lies outside of any Islamically recognized politico-religious institutional hierarchy, such that it can be considered a way of exercising power of a non-religious nature both within and outside of Islamic territory (BOSCH VILÁ, J., *Historia de Sevilla. La Sevilla islámica 712–1248*, Sevilla, 1984, p. 66, note 46).

208 Theodora Porphyrogenita (980–1056 CE) and her sister Zoe (978–1050 CE) were daughters of Constantine VIII. Zoe was married three times: to Romanos III Agyros, emperor from 1028 to 1034, Michael IV the Paphlagonian, who governed from 1034 to 1041, and to Constantine IX Monomachos, emperor from 1042 to 1055. After his death Theodora became empress until she died the following year. She adopted the future Michael VI as her successor, who only ruled for two years, 1056 and 1057, bringing the Macedonian Byzantine dynasty to an end.

209 AL-MAQRIZI, *Itti`at al-Hunafa,* II, p. 230.

210 When looking at this era, it is important to remember that 1054 was the year of the Great Schism of East and West, in which the Orthodox and Latin branches of the Church separated. An experienced reader will realize that the proximity of the dates cannot simply be by chance since, for the first time, Islam's enemies were divided in two.

211 A relationship with Egypt that was sustained over time then, according to documents from the Genizah in Cairo, which state that Dénia was one of the three al-Andalusian ports that were licensed to trade with the land of the Nile (AZUAR RUIZ, R., *La Taifa de Denia en el comercio mediterráneo del siglo XI,* p. 43).

212 Muslim experts in doctrine.

213 AL-SANTARINI, A. and ABBAS, I., *Al-Dajira fi mahasin ahl ahl-Yazira,* Tunis, 1989, III, 1, p. 393 onwards.

214 AZUAR RUIZ, R., *La Taifa de Denia,* p. 43.

215 RUBIERA MATA, M.J., *La Taifa de Denia,* Alicante, 1985, p. 101.

216 The full and formal details of this extraordinary unpublished text are included in the appendices chapter. We owe the translation and news of its appearance in Egypt to Dr. Gustavo Turienzo Veiga, who in the course of the investigation that gave rise to this study, travelled to Al-Azhar, funded by the research project, to examine possible documents or chronicle accounts which made any reference to links between the Kingdom of León and the Fatimid Caliphate. His translation of the two parchments included here, reviewed by other Arabic scholars, is proof of his meticulous work.

217 *Vita Lietberti Episcopi cameracensis auctore Radulfo Monacho S. Sepulchri Cameracensis,* Hannover, 1934, pp. 838–868.

218 MARTINET, S., Elinand, évêque de Laon méconnu (1052–
1098), *Fédération des Sociétés d'Histoire et d'Archéologie de
L'Aisne*. Mémoires, vol. XXXVI, Saint-Quentin, 1991, pp.
58–78.

219 The original of which we were able to access and consult
thanks to the generosity of the archivist at the Cathedral of
León, Manuel Pérez Recio. In the appendices we include
the front of the first folio of this document.

220 AL-SANTARINI and ABBAS, *Al-Dajira fi mahasin,* pp.
394–396.

221 The relationship between Ali Iqbal al-Dawla and Ferdinand
I was a close one. Some Muslim chroniclers report that he
came to his aid in the siege of Valencia in 1065.

222 At the end of Abu-l-Hasan Ali ibn Yusuf ibn al-Qifti's text,
it also says 'and it is known that during the journey'. This
probably refers to the same episode.

223 For a complete overview of this process, we recommend
two key chronicle sources:
IBN BASSAM AL-SANTARINI, *Al-Dajira fi Mazzini ahl
al-yazira*, 8 vols, Tunis-Libya, 1989, vol. 1, part 3, pp. 370–
371.
AL-MAQQARI, *Abu-l-Abbas, Nafh al-Tib min gusn al-
Andalus wa-l-ratib, wa dikr wisirahu Lisan al-Din ibn al-
Jatib,* 10 books in 5 volumes, Cairo, 1959, vol. 5, part I, p. 16.

224 AL-MAQQARI, *Nafh al-Tib min gusn al-Andalus wa-l-ratib*,
vol.5, part I, p. 16.

225 Translator's note: The word used for this type of Moorish
curved blade in the Spanish edition of this book is 'gumía',
which is a hispanicized spelling of 'kommeyya'. Kommeyya
is given as the Moroccan Arabic spelling of the word by the
Real Academia Española. As this is a transliteration, one can
find alternative, equally valid spellings, including 'koumaya'
and 'khoumiya'.

226 The formal analysis of the unpublished text is covered in the appendices chapter.

227 BARAULT-BERCASTEL, A.H. de., *Historia de la Iglesia*, vol. XIV, Valencia, 1831. p. 184.

228 2 April 1055 to 20 March 1056.

229 See the chapter 'The Grail of San Isidoro: The Basis of a Sacred Relic', concerning the archaeological study of the Cup. Regarding the Bani-l-Aswad family, it ought to be noted that since the conquest of Jerusalem by the Caliph Omar, they had held the privilege of guarding the keys to the main door of the Church of the Holy Sepulchre (GERAMB, P. Mª J. de, *La Tierra Santa, el Monte Líbano, El Egipto y Monte Sinaí, vol.* I, Barcelona, 1851, p. 260.).

230 KEPPIE, L., Legiones Britanniae. Legiones II Augusta, VI Victrix, IX Hispana, XX Valeria Victrix, in WOLFF, C. and LE BOHEC, Y., *Les légions de Rome sous le Haut-Empire*, Lyon, 2000, pp. 25–37.
   RODRÍGUEZ GONZÁLEZ, J., *Historia de las legiones romanas (2 vols)*, Madrid, 2003.
   MORILLO CERDÁN, Á. and GARCIA MARCOS, V., Nuevos testimonios acerca de las legiones VI Victrix y X Gemina en la region septentrional de la Península Ibérica, in WOLFF, C. and LE BOHEC, Y., *Les légions de Rome sous le Haut-Empire*, Lyon, 2000, pp. 589–607.

231 PALAO VICENTE, J.J., *Legio VII Gemina (Pia) Felix. Estudio de una legión romana*, Salamanca, 2006.

232 As confirmed by the Professor of Medieval History Ángel Martín Duque in his recent biography of Sancho III Garcés, in which he states that 62.5% of the Navarran's ancestors were in fact Leonese. Added to these are the ones contributed by his wife, Muniadomna of Castile, daughter of the Count of Castile and Beni Gómez, a woman descended from the Saldaña-Carrión county bloodline (MARTÍN DUQUE, Á.,

Sancho III el Mayor de Pamplona. El rey y su reino (1004–1035), Pamplona, 2007, p. 94).

233 TORRES SEVILLA, M., Una intervención leonesa en el Califato de Córdoba. A propósito de la identificación del conde Ibn Mama Duna al-Qumis, *Estudios Humanísticos,* 18 (1996), pp. 239–249.

234 FERNÁNDEZ LADREDA, C. and REDÓN HUICI, F., *La arqueta de Leyre y otras esculturas medievales de Navarra*, Pamplona, 1983.

235 TORRES SEVILLA, M., Los aliados cristianos de Almanzor: las redes familiares como base del sistema clientelar amirí, *Cuando las horas primeras. En el milenario de la batalla de Calatañazor,* Colección Monografías Universitarias, 13 (2004), pp. 89–114.

236 Documented biographies of both monarchs can be found in the work of Fernández del Pozo (FERNÁNDEZ DEL POZO, J.M., *Alfonso V (999–1028) y Vermudo III (1028–1037)*, Burgos, 1999). We refer the reader to this work for the background to and general aspects of the geopolitical setting.

237 Regarding the so-called 'Navarran split' in León, see our work in collaboration with the late professor Fernando Galván about the Countess Sancha de Cea (GALVÁN FREILE, F. and TORRES SEVILLA, M., La condesa doña Sancha. Una nueva aproximación a su figura, *Medievalismo,* 5 (1995), pp. 9–29).

238 D'ABADAL, R. and GALTIER MARTÍ, F., *El condado independiente de Ribagorza*, Zaragoza, 1981.

239 MARTÍN DUQUE, Á., Definición de espacios y fronteras en los reinos de Asturias-León y Pamplona hasta el siglo XI, *Los espacios de poder en la España Medieval. XII Semana de Estudios Medievales de Nájera,* Logroño, 2002, pp. 315–339.

240 SALAZAR ACHA, J., Una hija desconocida de Sancho el

Mayor reina de León, *Primer Congreso General de Historia de Navarra,* vol. 2, *Comunicaciones,* Príncipe de Viana, Pamplona, 1988, pp. 183–192.

241 SÉNAC, P., *La frontière et les hommes, VIIIe–XIIe siècle: le peuplement musulman au nord de l'Èbre et les débuts de la reconquête aragonaise,* Paris, 2000, pp. 288–289.

242 With regard to this unusual division and its immediate consequences, we found Martín Duque's book about Pamplona useful (MARTÍN DUQUE, Á., *Sancho III el Mayor,* pp. 342–350).

243 NÚÑEZ CONTRERAS, L., Colección diplomática de Vermudo III, rey de León, *Historia, instituciones, documentos, 4* (1977), pp. 381–514, doc. 18.

244 The monarch of Navarre had not yet died, however. We can date his death precisely to 18 October 1035 (MARTÍN DUQUE, Á., *Sancho III el Mayor,* p. 340).

245 NÚÑEZ CONTRERAS, L., Colección diplomática, doc. 19.

246 NÚÑEZ CONTRERAS, L., Colección diplomática, doc. 20.

247 Bermudo III's tombstone is preserved in the Royal Vaults of San Isidoro in León. It has the following inscription: *HIC EST CONDITUS VEREMUDUS JUNIOR, REX LEGIONIS, FILIUS ADEFONSIS REGIS. ISTE HABEBIT GUERRAM CUM COGNATO SUO REGE MAGNO FERNANDO, ET INTERFECTUS EST AB ILLO IN TAMARA PRAELIANDO. ERA MLXXV.*

248 This is the description of events given in the *Historia silense* (PÉREZ DE URBEL, J. and GONZÁLEZ RUIZ ZORRILLA, A. (trans. and ed.), *Historia silense,* Madrid, 1959).

249 TORRES SEVILLA, M., La monarquía leonesa, in *La Historia de León,* vol. II, *Edad Media,* León, 1999, pp. 105–137, p. 106.

250 MARTÍN, G., La Historia Legionensis (llamada Silensis) como memoria identitaria de un reino y como autobiografía,

e-Spania, Revue interdisciplinaire d'études hispaniques médiévales et modernes, 14 (2012), pp. 1–22.

251 *Historia silense* (Cf. TORRES SEVILLA, M., *La monarquía leonesa,* pp. 107–108).

252 MARTÍN DUQUE, Á., *Sancho III el Mayor,* p. 358.

253 While it is true that he had used this title earlier, in the manner of the Leonese kings, and was even recognized as such by his brothers, it is nevertheless clear that he used it with greater frequency from this point onwards.

Using the title of 'imperator', in comparison with the ones used by his own brothers, reveals, in the words of Sánchez Candeira: 'not only his effective imperial status, but also his recognition as such by the sovereigns of Aragón and Navarre' (SÁNCHEZ CANDEIRA, A., *Castilla y León en el siglo XI: estudio del Reinado de Fernando I,* Madrid, 1999, p. 121).

254 In 1045, Gonzalo, Count of Ribagorza and Sobrarbe, had been assassinated and his territories absorbed into those of Ramiro of Aragón.

255 MENÉNDEZ PIDAL, R., *La España del Cid,* vol. 1, Madrid, 1969, pp. 159–163.

256 MARTOS QUESADA, J., *Los reinos de Taifas en el siglo XI,* in CARRASCO, A.I., MARTOS, J. and SOUTO, J.A., *Al-Andalus,* Madrid, 2009, pp. 147–272.

257 VIÑAYO, A., *Fernando I, el Magno (1035–1065),* Burgos, 1999.

258 Diplomatic and military relations between the kingdoms of León and Toledo are covered in detail in the following recommended papers:

BOLOIX GALLARDO, B., La Taifa de Toledo en el siglo XI: Aproximación a sus límites y extension territorial, *Tulaytula: Revista de la Asociación de Amigos del Toledo Islámico,* 8 (2001), pp. 23–57.

WASSERSTEIN, D. J., *The emergence of Taifa Kingdom of*

Toledo, Al-qantara, 21 *Fasc.* 1 (2000), pp. 17–56.

259 VÁZQUEZ ATOCHERO, A., *Badajoz árabe, el reino aftasí*, Badajoz, 2004.

260 RUIBERA MATA, M.J., *La taifa de Denia*, Alicante, 1986; AZUAR RUIZ, R., *Denia Islámica. Arqueología y poblamiento*, Alicante, 1989.

261 CORRAL, J.L., *Historia de Zaragoza. Zaragoza musulmana (714–1118)*, Zaragoza, 1998.

262 TURK, A., *El Reino de Zaragoza en el siglo XI de Cristo (V de la Hégira)*, Madrid, 1978.

263 VIÑAYO, A., *Fernando I*, pp. 158–161.

264 VIÑAYO, A., La llegada de San Isidoro a León, *Archivos Leoneses*, 17 (1963), pp. 65–112, and 18 (1964), pp. 303– 343.

265 Based on the chronicles, Antonio Viñayo describes the frustration Sancho, future King of Castile, felt at this division (VIÑAYO, A., *Fernando I*, pp. 209–211).

266 The *Historia silense* tells us that a miracle took place in Compostela during this campaign: the apostle James appeared to Peter, a monk of eastern origin and pilgrim who had arrived from Jerusalem. This is a new piece of information to take into account regarding the presence of religious men from the Holy Land in the Leonese kingdom. There was an open communication route between the two, certainly by sea and probably not dissimilar to the one undertaken by the Chalice to reach Dénia, its first stop on the way to León. This remained an active route between East and West. This is without doubt the most relevant information to take from this account (BARKAI, R., *El enemigo en el espejo. Cristianos y musulmanes en la España medieval*, Madrid, 2007, p. 113).

267 BISHKO, C. J., The Liturgical Context of Fernando I's Last Days according to the so-called *Historia silense*, in *Hispania Sacra. Miscelánea en memoria de Dom Mario Férotin, 1915–*

1964, XVII–XVIII (1965), pp. 47–59.

See also: CALDWELL, S.H., Queen Sancha's 'Persuasion': A Regenerated León Symbolized in San Isidoro's Pantheon and its Treasures, in ROSS, S.D., *The Gift of Self: Shattering Emptiness, Betrayal,* Binghamton, 2000, p. 1–48.

268 Which we owe to Ramiro II (d. 951), and around which the feminine institution that became known as the *infantado* was created, whose first incumbent was the founder's daughter, Elvira Ramírez, as recalled by the bishop of Astorga and royal historian Sampiro (PÉREZ DE URBEL, J., pp. 329–332).

269 If we consider the relationship between members of the Royal House buried there, as described by Ambrosio de Morales, it appears there were no ancestors of Alfonso V, other than his parents. That said, we are able to appraise the remains that were moved from within the capital itself, because although they are not identified on tombstones like Alfonso's predecessors, the same source, quoting Rodrigo Ximénez de Rada and Lucas de Tuy, maintains that Alfonso IV and his children, Ramiro II and his sons Ordoño III and Sancho I were all moved there (MORALES, A. de, *Viage de Ambrosio de Morales por orden del rey Phelippe II a los Reynos de León y Galicia y principado de Asturias para reconocer las reliquias de santos, sepulcros reales y libros manuscritos de las cathedrales y monasterios,* Madrid, 1765, pp. 57–60).

The information related to Bermudo II (d. 999) and his wife Elvira is particularly relevant, which confirms the account given by Morales and is explicitly referred to in Lucas de Tuy's chronicle (FALQUE, E., *Lucas Tudensis, Chronicon Mundi, Corpus Christianorum continuatio mediaevalis LXXIV,* Turnhout, 2003, p. 275).

270 Whose jaw, which supposedly came from Rome following a request made by Alfonso V, is still kept in the current San

Isidoro Basilica today (FERNÁNDEZ DEL POZO, J.M., *Alfonso V (999–1028) y Vermudo III (1028–1037)*, Burgos, 1999, pp. 225–226).

271 The remains of the boy martyr Pelayo were requested by Sancho I of León and his sister Elvira, both children of Ramiro II. They arrived in the capital in 967 CE where '(...) *cum religiosis episcopis in civitate Legionensi tumulavit'*. (PÉREZ DE URBEL, J. and GONZÁLEZ RUIZ-ZORRILLA, A., *Historia silense*, p. 340).

For more about this monastery and its religious community we refer the reader to: COLOMBÁS, G.M., *San Pelayo de León y Santa María de Carvajal. Biografía de una comunidad femenina*, León, 1982.

Regarding the Princess Elvira Ramírez and her key role in Leonese politics over various decades, see: CARRIEDO TEJEDO, M., Una reina sin corona en 959–976. La infanta Elvira, hija de Ramiro II, *Tierras de León*, XLIX–113 (2001), pp. 118–137.

272 '*Interea, domini regis coloquium Sancia regina petens ei in sepulturam regum ecclesiamfieri Legione persuadet ubi et eorundem corpora iuste magnificeque humari debeant ... porro Sancia regina, quoniam in Legionenssy regum ciminterio pater suus digne memorie Adefonsus princeps et eius frater Veremundus serenissimus rex in Christo quiescebant, ut quoque et ipsa et eiusdem vir cum eis post mortem quiescerent, pro uiribus laborabat'*. (*Historia silense*, p. 197).

273 Although it was traditionally believed that the envoy of ambassadors set off from León, thanks to Ferdinand I's official records we now know that the decision was in fact taken by the sovereign following a victorious campaign in Mérida. To this clarification we are also able to confirm the tradition that associates the movement of St Isidore's body

with his appearance to the Bishop Alvito of León, in which the Bishop's death was foretold. He died in fact, as stated in a royal bequest, in the city of Guadalquivir (BLANCO LOZANO, P., *Colección Diplomática de Fernando I (1037–1065)*, León, 1987, doc. 67).

274 Translation by Viñayo of document 125 of the Archive of San Isidoro of León (VIÑAYO, A., *Fernando I*, pp. 201–202): '(...) a façade of pure gold, worthily worked, with emeralds and sapphires; three facades in silver, one for each altar; three golden crowns, one of them with six alpha Moroccan pendants on the outer and inner ring; another in *anemmates* gold with crystals; the third gold crown is the diadem of mine own head. A small glass casket, covered in gold. A gold cross adorned in glass and stonework. Another in ivory with the likeness of Our Lord on the cross. Two incensories in gold with a gold *naveta* [a small shuttle or ship-shaped ceremonial vase or box, used in church to administer incense]. Another heavy weight silver incensory. Chalice and paten of gold with crystals. Gold stoles with silver trim and goldwork. Another in silver with a glassy trim. An ivory casket with goldwork. Two more ivory chests with silverwork, one of which holds three smaller boxes in the same material. Two carved diptychs in ivory. Three façades bordered in gold. A large *lotzorí* [a type of Arabic textile] veil for the temple, and other smaller ones in ermine. Two capes edged in gold, one being an *alguexi* [an Arabic cloth or brocade woven in gold, from Southern Spain] with goldwork, the other byzantine in *indimisso* purple [from the Latin *indimissus*, meaning the purple is dyed fast and will not fade]. A chasuble with a gold trim and two dalmatics, similarly finished. Another *alguexi* gold cloth. A dinner service, that is to say: salt cellar, platters, tongs, ladle and ten spoons. Two gold candlesticks. Gold emblem. Carafe. All these utensils are in gilded silver,

and the aforementioned carafe bears two handles'.

275 Urraca, present at her parents' royal bequest to San Isidoro, which included a chalice and paten 'of gold with crystals', was already the de facto *domina* of the *infantado*, since Ferdinand I had revealed his desire to divide up his kingdoms and leave an endowment to his daughters, according to the *Historia silense*, around the time of the arrival of St Isidore's body in the capital and the consecration of the temple (*Historia silense*, pp. 204–295).

On the occasion of the consecration, the main barons and clerics assembled in the city, as well as the king's wider family members, such as his mother Muniadomna and his sister Jimena. The historical sources closest in date to the events taking place, such as the *Historia silense*, the *Cronicon Compostelano* or the account by Pelayo de Oviedo (VIÑAYO, A., *Fernando I*, pp. 209–211), include descriptions of these facts.

Given the significance of the moment, and the fact that there was no other chalice donated that could be described as having similar features to the one delivered by the *muyahid* of Dénia after its return to the Peninsula, our view is that the so-called 'Chalice of Doña Urraca' comprised two eastern Roman cups, was enriched with gold, stones and crystals and was offered to San Isidoro on behalf of the *domina* of the *infantado* on the day that her parents were making their bequest to the Basilica. This act undoubtedly constituted the crowning moment of Ferdinand's construction of his kingdom-empire, expressed both in the building of the monastery and temple as well as in the division of his territories.

276 Essential reading on this subject is the work of RESINA, J. R., *La búsqueda del Grial*, Barcelona, 1988.

277 We owe the excellent translation of this work into Spanish

to Antonio Regales (ESCHENBACH, W. VON, *Parzival*, Madrid, 1999).

278 'Kiot begged me to remain silent... Kiot, the renowned master of the poetic arts, found the first version of this account in a forgotten Arabic manuscript. He first had to learn to read the strange writing'. Verses 452–453 of this fragment of the poem *Parzival* remind us of the importance of this mysterious figure.

279 ORR, J., *Les oeuvres de Guiot de Provins, poète lyrique et satirique*, Manchester: University Press, 1915.

280 We refer the reader to our work on the presence of Leonese and Castilian crusaders and pilgrims: TORRES SEVILLA, M., Cruzados y peregrinos leoneses y castellanos en Tierra Santa (ss. XI–XII), *Medievalismo*, 9 (1999), pp. 63–82.

281 See the part related to the political history of the kingdom of León. See also the works of Mínguez on Alfonso VI (MÍNGUEZ FERNÁNDEZ, J.M., *Alfonso VI: poder, expansión y reorganización interior*, Hondarribia, 2000) and Reilly concerning the Royal Chancery of Alfonso VII where royal manuscripts were kept (REILLY, B.F., The chancery of Alfonso VII of León-Castilla: the period 1116–1135 reconsidered, *Speculum*, 51–2 (1976), pp. 243–261). Lastly, we would also suggest the work of A. Gambra: GAMBRA GUTIÉRREZ, A., *Alfonso VI, cancillería, curia e imperio*, 2 vols, León, 1997 and 1998.

282 PÉREZ GONZÁLEZ, M. (trans.), *Crónica del Emperador Alfonso VII*, León, 1997, p. 84.

283 REAL, E., Perceval de Chrétien de Troyes. El nacimiento de un mito, in RAPOSO FERNÁNDEZ, B. (ed.) and ANDERSEN, K., FERRER MORA, H., GUTIÉRREZ KOESTER, I. and KASPER, F. (eds), *Parzival. Reescritura y transformación*, Valencia, 2000, pp. 11–34, particularly pp. 24–26.

284 The terms *infantzago* or *infantado* term do not have an English equivalent, although they can mean 'principality', or the little-used word borrowed from the French: 'appanage'. The terms refer to the land and power passed on to an infante/a, royal prince or princess, but also to a more intangible system of inheriting rights, rank and the carrying of the bloodline. It is worth noting that 'protectress' is not the only translation of 'domina' – it can mean 'mistress' or 'ruler', and therefore refers to the fact that the *domina* was also in charge of the monastery which was the headquarters of the *infantado* (this was first Palat del Rey and subsequently moved to San Pelayo, close to San Isidoro). According to the *Historia silense* and Lucas de Tuy's *Chronicon Mundi*, being an unmarried virgin was a prerequisite for the role of *domina* (although this was not always adhered to), which creates a clear parallel with the role of the noble maidens of Grail legend.

285 Despite its key role in supporting the reigning dynasty during the tenth to twelfth centuries, there is as yet no book which addresses the importance of the *Infantazgo*. A paper on the subject published in Spanish by Therese Martin has an abstract in English: http://e-spania.revues. org/12163?lang=en (MARTIN, T., Hacia una clarificación del infantazgo en tiempos de la reina Urraca y su hija la infanta Sancha (ca. 1107–1159) *e-Spania* Online, 5 June 2008).

286 We owe this piece of information, which is useful for better understanding this Leonese female institution, to Patrick Henriet's research. We have chosen to translate the original source, which is as follows: '(...) *dono vobis unice Sorori mee quantum infantadigum in Toto regno meo est, videlicet in Toleto et in toto Alenserra, in Extremadura, Legione, in Beriz, in Gallicia, et in Asturiies, villa, Castella, hereditates,*

monasteria et Omnia que ad infantadigum pertinente, habeatis ergo illud quomodo melius habuit avia Nostra infantissa domna Sancia...' (HENRIET, P., Deo votas. L'Infantado et la fonction des infants dans la Castile et le León des xe–XIIe siècles, in HENRIET, P. and LEGRAS, A.M. (ed.), *Au cloître et dans le monde: Femmes, hommes et sociétés (IXe–XVe siècles), Mélanges en l'honneur de Paulette L'Hermite-Leclercq* (Cultures et Civilisations médiévales No. 23), Paris, 2000, pp. 189–203, pp. 202–203).

287 VIÑAYO GONZÁLEZ, A., *L'Ancien royaume de León roman*, Paris, 1972, p. 35.

288 RODRÍGUEZ FERNÁNDEZ, J., *Ramiro II, rey de León*, Burgos, 1998, pp. 279–281.

289 VIÑAYO GONZÁLEZ, A., *Reinas e Infantas de León, abadesas y monjas del monasterio de San Pelayo y de San Isidoro, Semana de historia del monacato cántabro-Asturleonés*, Oviedo, 1982, pp. 123–135.

290 This is an honorific title by which Almanzor was known in his later years, similar in rank to a vizier, chancellor or court chamberlain.

291 Teresa Ansúrez was Sancho I's wife and mother to Ramiro III of León (died 985).

292 A plethora of legends and few concrete facts surround this princess, although some were recorded by the chroniclers Pelayo de Oviedo or Rodrigo Ximénez de Rada. She was supposedly given in marriage to a Muslim prince, either by her father Bermudo II, or her brother Alfonso V. Some believe her husband was none other than Almanzor himself, or one of his favoured sons. Others, however, point to a supposed king of Toledo ... when the taifa of Toledo did not exist. Whatever the truth, although the possibility that a princess had been given to an Amiri (a relative or descendant of Almanzor ibn Abi Aamir, the last ruler at the height of Al-

Andalus, whose successors, the Amiri, presided over the fall of the caliphate of Cordoba at the beginning of the eleventh century, and the founding of the taifas) or an Umayyad was in fact highly probable, one thing is certain: Teresa was well documented in León and later Oviedo, the city where she died and her epitaph is still preserved today, leaving little room for doubt about her existence: '*Tarasia Christo dicata, proles Beremundi regis et Geloriae Regina*' (monasterio de San Pelayo de Oviedo).

293 SÁNCHEZ CANDEIRA, A., *Castilla y León en el siglo XI. Estudio del reinado de Fernando I*, Madrid, 1999.

294 FERNÁNDEZ DEL POZO, J.M., *Alfonso V (999–1028) y Vermudo III (1028–1037)*, Burgos, 1999, pp. 231–235.

295 Her tomb in San Isidoro bears the following epigraph:
H. R. DOMNA URRACA REGINA DE ZAMORA, FILIA REGIS MAGNI FERDINANDI. HAEC AMPLIFICAVIT ECCLESIAM ISTAM, ET MULTIS MUNERIBUS DITAVIT. ET QUIA BEATUM ISIDORUM SUPER OMNIA DILIGEBAT. EJUS SERVITIO SUBJUGAVIT. OBIIT ERA MCXXXVIIII...NOBILIS URRACA JAceT HOC TUMULO TUMULATA HESPERIAEQUE DECUS HEU TENET HIC LOCULUS HAEC FUIT OPTANDI PROLES REGIS FREDENANDI. AST REGINA FUIT SANCTIA QUAE GENUIT cENTIES UNDECIES SOL VOLVERAT ET SEMEL ANNUM CARNE QUOD OBTECTUS SPONTE
(ARCO GARAY, R. DEL, *Sepulcros de la Casa Real de Castilla*, Madrid, 1954, pp. 187–188).

296 Although she received a burial in the same Royal Vaults as Urraca and her parents, she did not die in León, but Távara, a town within her estate. In her will, set down on 11 November 1099, she left her share of the *infantazgo* of San Pelayo, San Isidoro and Covarrubias to her niece,

the Princess Sancha Raimúndez, the last great *domina* of the *infantazgo* and associated estates and seigneuries (MARTIN, G., Le testament d Elvire. (Tábara, 1099), *e-Spania, revue interdisciplinaire d'études hispaniques médiévales et modernes*, 5 (2008)).

297 See the family tree, p. 103.

298 A study by Ana Isabel Cerrada Jiménez looks at the highly significant role played by these women: Doña Sancha, the Princess Urraca and the queen of the same name, including Teresa of Portugal. It offers an interesting perspective on the women who had access to power in an era dominated by men (CERRADA JIMÉNEZ, A.I., Tres generaciones de mujeres en el poder: Urraca de Zamora, Urraca de Castilla, Teresa de Portugal y doña Sancha, in SEGURA GRAIÑO, C. and CERRADA JIMÉNEZ, A. I. (ed.), *Las mujeres y el poder: representaciones prácticas de vida*, Madrid, 2000, pp. 99–106).

299 This opinion, expressed by Therese Martin, is one that we share (MARTIN, T., Hacia una clarificación del infantazgo en tiempos de la reina Urraca y su hija la infanta Sancha (*c*.1107–1159, *e-Spania. Revue interdisciplinaire d' études hispaniques médiévales et modernes*, 5 (2008) p. 9).

300 SUREDA PONS, JOAN, Arte Románico, in *Historia del Arte de Castilla y León*, II, Valladolid: Ámbito Ediciones, 1994, pp. 232–233.
See also: VIÑAYO, A. *Pintura románica. Panteón de San Isidoro*, León, 1979.
VIÑAYO, A., *Pintura románica del Panteón de Reyes. San Isidoro de León*, León, 1993.
CRUZ MARTÍN, A., *Pinturas románicas del Panteón Real de San Isidoro de León*, León, 1959.

301 TOURS, GREGORY OF. *De Gloria Confessorum*, cap. XXVII e Historia Francorum, i, 28.

302 Our thanks to Sergio Pérez for the information on this subject.

303 To find out more, see:

LANDES, R.A., (1995)., *Relics, Apocalypse, and the Deceits of History: Ademar of Chabannes, 989–1034*, Harvard University Press.

LITTLE, LESTER K., and ROSENWEIN, B.H. (eds), *Debating the Middle Ages: Issues and Readings*, (Oxford: Blackwell, 1998). (Trans: *La Edad Media a debate* (Madrid: Akal, 2003)).

SALTER, L., Une discussion sur Saint Martial, *Bulletin de Littérature Ecclésiastique*, 26 (1925), pp. 161–186.

SALTER, L., Une prétendue letter de Jean XIX sur Saint Martial fabriquée par Adémar de Chabannes, *Bulletin de Littérature ecclésiastique*, 27 (1926), pp. 117–139.

SALTER, L., Les faux d'Adémar de Chabannes: Prétendues décisions sur Saint Martial au concile de Bourges du 1er Novembre 1031, *Bulletin de Littérature Ecclésiastique*, 27 (1926), pp. 145–160.

SALTER, L., Un cas de mythomanie historique bien documenté: Ademár de Chabannes (988–1034), *Bulletin de Littérature Ecclésiastique*, 32 (1931), pp. 149–165.

TRUMBORE, J. A., Discovering the Aquitanian Church in the Corpus of Adémar of Chabannes, *Haskins Society Journal*, 19 (2008), pp. 82–99.

BELLET, CH. F. (1897), *L'ancienne vie de St. Martial et la prose rythmée* (edition of the ninth-century text).

304 BANGO TORVISO, I., Arte Románico, in *Historia del Arte de Castilla y León*, II, Valladolid: Ámbito Ediciones, 1994, p. 9.

305 Also mentioned among the objects coveted by the Aragonese prince and his ally Henry of Burgundy is the chalice's paten (LUCAS DE TUY, *Crónica de España*, Madrid, 1926, p. 385).

306 MORALES, A. de, *Viage de Ambrosio de Morales por*

orden del rey D. Phelipe II a los reynos de León, y Galicia y principado de Asturias para reconocer las Reliquias de Santos, Sepulcros Reales y Libros manuscritos de las Cathedrales y monasterios, Madrid, 1765, p. 50.

307 GRANDA, FR. T. de and MANZANO, J., *Vida de San Isidro, arzobispo de Sevilla,* Salamanca, 1732, p. 381.

308 Even in one of the most recent descriptions, produced for the catalogue for the exhibition *Wonders of Medieval Spain. Sacred Treasure and Monarchy (Maravillas de la España Medieval. Tesoro Sagrado y Monarquía)* which ran between December 2000 and February 2001, no information is given (BANGO TORVISO, I.G. (Dir.), *Maravillas de la España Medieval. Tesoro Sagrado y Monarquía. I. Estudios y Catálogo,* Valladolid, 2001, record 108, p. 335).

309 There is chronological evidence to suggest that the Valencia Chalice was dropped, causing it to lose a triangular-shaped chip which was then reattached to the original piece, which can be observed when viewing this rare treasure.

310 We refer the reader back to the chapter of this work dedicated to this aspect.

311 For the vast majority of specialists, there is no question about the age of the cup. In addition to Beltrán (BELTRÁN, A., *El Santo Cáliz de la Catedral de Valencia,* Valencia, 1960 (edition revised in 1980), p. 95), there are also the following: VIÑAYO GONZÁLEZ, A., *La Real Colegiata de San Isidoro de León,* León, 1971, p. 27.
YARZA, J., *Arte y arquitectura en España 500–1250,* Madrid, 1979, p. 210.
FRANCO MATA, Á., *El tesoro de San Isidoro y la monarquía leonesa.* Boletín del Museo Arqueológico Nacional, No. IX (1991), pp. 35–67, p. 64.
MARTÍN ANSÓN, M.L., La artesanía, La cultura del románico, siglos XI al XIII. Letras. Religiosidad. Artes.

Ciencia y vida, *Historia de España de Menendez Pidal, XI,*
Madrid: 1995, pp. 453–490, p. 470.

LASKO, P., *Arte sacro 800–1200,* Madrid, 1999, p. 264.

312 Among the most notable examples, aside from the Visigothic
votive crown of Recceswinth (seventh century, National
Archaeological Museum, Madrid), it is worth recalling
the crown of Theodelinda of Lombardy (late sixth to early
seventh century, Museum of the Cathedral of Monza),
the crown of the Virgin of the Majesty of Sainte-Foie de
Conques (tenth century), or the one belonging to the
Empress Cunigunde of Luxembourg, wife of Henry II
(eleventh century, Residenz Museum of Munich).

313 MOLINA GÓMEZ, J.A., Las coronas de donación regia del
tesoro de Guarrazar: la religiosidad de la monarquía visigoda
y el uso de modelos bizantinos, *Sacralidad y Arqueología,
Antig. Crist., XXI* (2004), pp. 459–472.

314 The image of the cross section of the Chalice of Doña Urraca
comes from an exhibition held in 1993 at the Library of
Congress in the United States, the title of which was *Scrolls
from the Dead Sea: The Ancient Library of Qumran and
Modern Scholarship,* which was made possible thanks to the
generosity of the Israel Antiquities Authority with support
from the Project Judaica Foundation, Delta Airlines and
Hilton International. Today, these objects are kept in Israel.

315 We are grateful for the help kindly given to us in this regard
by Dr Andrea Berlin, who holds the prestigious James
R. Wiseman Chair in Classical Archaeology at Boston
University.

We would also like to express our gratitude to Dr Esperanza
Martín Hernández, expert in thin-walled pottery, for her
help in seeking out chronological similarities and for her
archaeological drawing of the piece. There are numerous
pieces with typological parallels, predominately in glass,

which are kept in the Metropolitan Museum of New York (as examples see the pieces with catalogue numbers 17.194.263 and 81.10.129), the British Museum or in the Museum of Israel itself. Regarding this latter, the work of Yael Israeli makes essential reading (ISRAELI, Y., *Ancient Glass in the Israel Museum: The Eliahu Dobkin Collection and Other Gifts,* Jerusalem, 2003).

Within Israeli territory, it is common to find both glass and ceramic cups that imitate Roman forms, but which were made in local workshops. Mere copies of them, particularly from the Herodian period (first century BCE to first century CE), are often on display at the Museum of Israel. As a case in point, the ceramics from the Qumran ruins reveal this relationship in terms of the manufacture of plates, bowls, pans and cups, while still retaining their own natural simplicity and indigenous tradition.

Alongside the aforementioned publication by Dr Israeli, we also consider it apt to refer the interested reader to the following works:

ROITMAN, A. (ed.), *A Day at Qumran. The Dead Sea Sect and its Scrolls,* Shrine of the Book, 1997.

LAPP, P., *Palestinian Ceramic Chronology, 200 B.C.–A.D. 70,* New Haven, 1961.

From a strictly chronological standpoint, it is particularly interesting that, through means of dating such as the historical sources themselves, carbon dating or examining the coins found at Qumran, it is possible to establish the approximate dates of the first century CE, with the 66–70 CE period of the Jewish revolt as a cut-off point.

316 There are some notable artefacts in the Metropolitan Museum of Art in New York, which date from between the first century BCE and the first century CE, such as the cup donated by Henry G. Marquand in 1881, which is stored in the Museum's

collection under the catalogue number 81.10.129.

317 SENECA, *De Beneficiis*, VII, 9.

318 Made in a type of agate called sardonyx, it is dated within the period from the first to fourth centuries CE, although it was subject to modifications, such as additions in silver and bronze based on the French style in the early nineteenth century. At some time subsequent to its manufacture, a precise decoration of vines was added, which is suggestive of a later use within the Christian liturgy. Having lost its two original handles, they were replaced at the beginning of the nineteenth century to emulate a Roman lamp. Its first known owner was Anatole N. Demidoff, first prince of San Donato (1812–1870), and it was acquired in 1915 by J. Pierpont Morgan and, after a brief stop-off with Workart Est. (Vaduz, Liechtenstein) in 1977, they reached the collection of the National Gallery of Canada later that same year through W. Appolloni, where it is still exhibited today under the catalogue reference 1872.

319 National Gallery of Art, Widener Collection, nº 1942.9.277.

320 The sardonyx cup is decorated with a silver-gilt mounting adorned with filigree, precious stones, pearls, glass and other elements which share some similarities, on the upper part, with other medieval chalices of a similar age.

321 This is how Erwin Panofsky sees it in his study on Suger and the Abbey of Saint-Denis (PANOFSKY, E., *Abbot Suger on the Abbey Church of Saint-Denis and Its Art Treasures*, Princeton, 1979, p. 55).

We find the last hypothesis particularly interesting, because it would place a luxury Roman object in the hands of a wealthy Hebrew, destined to become a chalice thanks to the dedication of the Abbot Suger at a similar time to the production of the one belonging to Doña Urraca in León.

322 *Le trésor de Saint-Denis (catalogue)*, Paris, 1991, nº 28, repr.

175; VERDIER, P., The Chalice of Abbot Suger, *Studies in the History of Art*, 24 (1990), pp. 9–29.

323 Historiska Museet, catalogue number 1.

324 This city, known as Qift by Muslims and as Gebtu by ancient Egyptians, was the subject of excavations by W. M. Flinders Petrie, to whom a large part of the discoveries held in various museums worldwide is owed. Highly recommended due to its contemporaneous nature is the work published by the archaeologist himself in 1896 (PETRIE, W.M.F., *Koptos*, London, 1896).

325 Pliny, in his *Historia Natural*, describes not only the heightened value of objects carved in semi-precious stones, but also the provenance of different gems, such as onyx or agate, their characteristics, best deposits for extraction and uses (PLINY THE ELDER, *Historia Natural, Book XXXVII*, XXIV, XXV, LIV).

326 Particularly noteworthy for its relationship with the commerce of semi-precious stones was the trade route with Barygaza (Bharuch, a city in Gujarat, India), as documented in the *Periplus of the Erythraean Sea*, which tells the story of a first-century trader:

'(...) 47. *The country inland from Barygaza is inhabited by numerous tribes, such as the Arattii, the Arachosii, the Gandaraei and the people of Poclais, in which is Bucephalus Alexandria. Above these is the very warlike nation of the Bactrians, who are under their own king. And Alexander, setting out from these parts, penetrated to the Ganges, leaving aside Damirica and the southern part of India; and to the present day ancient drachmae are current in Barygaza, coming from this country, bearing inscriptions in Greek letters, and the devices of those who reigned after Alexander, Apollodorus and Menander.*

48. *Inland from this place and to the east, is the city called*

Ozene, formerly a royal capital; from this place are brought down all things needed for the welfare of the country about Barygaza, and many things for our trade: agate and carnelian, Indian muslins and mallow cloth, and much ordinary cloth. Through this same region and from the upper country is brought the spikenard that comes through Poclais; that is, the Caspapyrene and Paropanisene and Cabolitic and that brought through the adjoining country of Scythia; also costus and bdellium.

49. There are imported into this market-town, wine, Italian preferred, also Laodicean and Arabian; copper, tin, and lead; coral and topaz; thin clothing and inferior sorts of all kinds; bright-colored girdles a cubit wide; storax, sweet clover, flint glass, realgar, antimony, gold and silver coin, on which there is a profit when exchanged for the money of the country; and ointment, but not very costly and not much. And for the King there are brought into those places very costly vessels of silver, singing boys, beautiful maidens for the harem, fine wines, thin clothing of the finest weaves, and the choicest ointments. There are exported from these places spikenard, costus, bdellium, ivory, agate and carnelian, lycium, cotton cloth of all kinds, silk cloth, mallow cloth, yarn, long pepper and such other things as are brought here from the various market-towns. Those bound for this market-town from Egypt make the voyage favorably about the month of July, that is Epiphi...'.

(SCHOFF, W.H. (trans. and ed.), *The Periplus of the Erythraean Sea: Travel and Trade in the Indian Ocean by a Merchant of the First Century*, London, Bombay & Calcutta, 1912).

327 Although we will in due course touch very briefly on the legend of its arrival in Spain, which has become pious tradition, since it is devoid of any basis in historical fact, we have opted to focus on the empirical facts found in sources of demonstrable authenticity.

328 A. BELTRÁN, *El Santo Cáliz*, p. 54.

329 A. BELTRÁN, *El Santo Cáliz*, p. 73.

330 In studying this aspect, as well as the history of the monastery itself up until the fifteenth century, the work by Lapeña is of interest (LAPEÑA PAÚL, A.I., *El monasterio de San Juan de la Peña en la Edad Media (desde sus orígenes hasta 1410)*, Zaragoza, 1989).

331 Archivo Histórico Nacional de España, San Juan de la Peña, leg. 444, number 257.

332 It was not without reason that he professed his faith and would do so again on renouncing his throne in favour of his daughter Petronila and her husband.

333 This is the reason that Antonio Beltrán is quick to dismiss the possibility that it is the same as the Valencian Chalice, despite the fact that, in our view, it constitutes concrete proof that a stone chalice was present in the hands of the Aragonese monarchy, and in the very same monastery that tradition refers to with respect to the Hispanic location of the Cup sent, supposedly, by St Lorenzo. The finality with which Beltrán rejects this possibility is surprising.

334 To cite other examples, it is worth mentioning the tradition whereby Hispanic lands were honoured as the place where the apostle St James conducted his preaching, or the legend, also sanctified through centuries of devotion and backed up by the Asturian, Leonese and Castilian monarchies, which cites Compostela as the place where Christ's companion was buried. Without having analysed other factors, we have to treat these sorts of accounts with due caution, even if they appear in original medieval chronicles or certified manuscripts. Measure, rigour and prudence should always prevail when we are approaching subjects where history, legend and pious tradition meet.

335 '...*desideraret et afectaret multum habere in Capella sua*

illum Calicem lapideum cum quo Dominus Noster Iesus
Christus in sua Sancta Cena sanguinem suum preciossisimum
consecravit et quem beatus Laurencius qui ipsum habuit a
Sancto Sisto existente Summo Pontifice cuius discipulus erat
ac diaconus Sancte Marie in Dominica misit et dedit cum eius
litera monasterio et conventui Santi Johannis de la Penya
sito in montaneis Jacce Regni Aragonum...' (NAVARRO
ESPINACH, G., *Las Cofradías de la Vera Cruz y de la Sangre*
de Cristo en la Corona de Aragón (siglos XIV–XVI), Anuario
de Estudios Medievales, 36/2 (2006), pp. 583–611, p. 594).
In essence, legend-cum-tradition states that it was St Peter
that brought the Chalice blessed by Christ at the Last
Supper to Rome and which, from Nero's era onwards,
remained linked to the apostle's successors up until Sixtus
II, contemporary of the Emperor Valerian (253/260). Faced
with martyrdom, the pontiff asked the Deacon Lorenzo, who
was responsible for administering the Church's property,
to distribute its wealth among the poorest and put the Holy
Chalice in a place of safety. Two days before his execution
at the stake, St Lorenzo handed the Cup over to a trusted
legionnaire along with a letter he had written, who would in
turn deliver it to his parents Saints Orencia and Paciencia,
who lived close to Huesca in Aragón, in the place where the
hermitage of Loreto is today.

From there, towards 533 and the same century as the
diocese of Huesca was confirmed, some say it remained in
the city of Huesca itself (other versions say it was kept in
various holy places) up until the arrival of the Muslims in
711, when it was carried towards the Pyrenean valleys by
the Bishop St Asciclus. After wending its way around various
places, it ended up in San Juan de La Peña, where it would
be removed by Ramiro II. From that point on legend would
be bound with history, even though the King of Aragón's

official documents do not state that the stone chalice which he sought and appropriated was the same one blessed by Christ, despite the monarch's special relationship with the Church. His religious conviction led him to abdicate the throne in favour of a monastic life, a decision he was later forced to abandon following the death of his brother Alfonso I the Battler, since he was required to provide an heir to the throne.

336 Its direct delivery took place under Juan II of Castile (1437).

337 MARTÍN LLORIS, C., *Las reliquias de la Capilla Real en la Corona de Aragón y el Santo Cáliz de la Catedral de Valencia (1396–1458),* Doctoral thesis completed in the History of Art Department of the University of Valencia, 2005.
This work was published by the same university in 2010.

338 BELTRÁN, A., *El Santo Cáliz de la Catedral de Valencia.*

339 Although the proceedings have still not been published to date, a 6 DVD recording is available, made by Magnavox Producciones. Our thanks to Felisa del Río Medina for getting hold of this.

340 MARTÍN LLORIS, C., *Las reliquias de la Capilla Real en la Corona de Aragón y el Santo Cáliz de la Catedral de Valencia,* pp. 263–264.

341 The authority of the Venerable Bede, accepted by the Church, is in this case backed up by other medieval authors, Christian and Muslim alike, who attest to the presence of Christ's Chalice in a chapel of the Holy Sepulchre of Jerusalem. Contrasting these sources with the work of Sales i Alcalá (SALES I ALCALÁ, A., *Dissertacion histórica, critica i expositive del Sagrado Caliz en que Christo Señor Nuestro consagró en la noche de la Cena, el qual se venera en la Santa Metropolitana Iglesia de Valencia,* Valencia, 1736), as Beltrán purports to do (*El Santo Cáliz*, p. 91, n. 25), seems, at best, rather presumptuous.

342 He considers these accounts in the same vein as the Chalice

of Charlemagne, the one at Reims given by St Remigio in 545, or the Holy Catino in Genoa, among others (A. BELTRÁN,, *op. cit.,* pp. 92–94).

343 BELTRÁN, A., *op. cit.,* pp. 38–39.

344 The Muslim chronicler al-Maqrizi tells us that al-Mustansir had to do away with a large part of his treasures through a public auction, to be able to pay his troops. Among them was a collection of rock crystals (KAHLE, P., Die Schätze der Fatimiden, *Zeitschrift der Deutschen Morgenländische Gesellschaft,* 89 (1935), pp. 329–362).

This information appears in: GARCÍA GIMÉNEZ, R. and VALDÉS FERNÁNDEZ, F., Acerca del origen y de la cronología de los cristales de roca llamados fatimíes: el vidrio de Badajoz y la botella de Astorga *CuPAUAM,* 23 (1996), pp. 260–276.

345 Anonymous Pilgrim of Piacenza, 22, Holy Zion (v 162).

346 PROCOPII CAESARIENSIS, *De aedificiis Dn. Iustiniani.* Liber III, *Corpus Scriptorium Historiae Byzantinae* (ed. B.G. Niebuhrii C.F.), vol. II, part III, Bonn, 1838.

347 *Itinera Hierosolymitana et descriptiones. Terrae Sanctae.* Ginebra, 1879, pp. 119, 227, 252.

348 Joseph of Arimathea, member of the Sanhedrin and, therefore, the Jewish aristocracy of the time, is described in the Gospels as a 'rich man' and 'disciple of Jesus' (Matthew), 'illustrious' (Mark), 'a good and honourable person' (Luke). John, the fourth evangelist, maintains that he was linked with Jesus, although he does remind us that this connection was clandestine in nature for fear of the Jewish authorities. In truth, we know little more about him, except that he asked the Romans for Christ's body in order to give it a proper burial in its own tomb. This suggests that he had an unusually close relationship with the Messiah, and a preeminent position within the Hebraic hierarchy of the

time, as well as being on good terms with Pontius Pilate. A legend can be traced which begins by tentatively positing that the Last Supper took place at his house, which would mean that the vessels used at the meal were his, one of which was of course the Cup of Blessing. Others claim that he used the Chalice to collect Christ's blood, either on the cross itself or during his burial.

The myth does not end here since, for the bearer of the Grail to be connected to Britain, he had to flee Jerusalem for Avalon or Glastonbury, with close companions. There he founded the first church devoted to Mary, where from then on the priests conducted the holy offices of the Eucharist using the Chalice. Tradition has it that King Arthur and his wife Guinevere were buried in Glastonbury, linking the Grail's resting place with the history of the Knights of the Round Table. It is in fact believed that Joseph of Arimathea, first custodian of the sacred cup, created a dynasty of guardians which would include such characters as the famous Fisher King, also known as Anfortas in the myths of the Grail. He is undoubtedly a creation based on the historical monarch Alfonso VI the Emperor, son of Ferdinand I, King of León and the first recipient of the Chalice of Jerusalem.

349 In 2001 Justin Griffin published his book entitled: *The Holy Grail: The Legend, the History, the Evidence,* published by McFarland & Co, within which the interested reader will find numerous references to the Nanteos Cup. If you find your curiosity is still not satisfied, you would do well to turn to the following work:
MORGAN, G., *Nanteos. A Welsh House and its Families,* Gwasg Gomer, 2001.

350 This series of claims can be found in his work *The Chalice of Magdalene. The Search for the Cup that held the Blood of*

Christ, Rochester, 1995.

That same year this book was published by Edhasa under the Spanish title *El Cáliz de María Magdalena*.

351 This information was construed on the basis of the other extant objects found alongside it, which were, like the chalice, hurriedly hidden under a boulder.

352 WALLACE, P.F. and O'FLOINN, R. (eds), *Treasures of the National Museum of Ireland: Irish Antiquities*, Dublin, 2002.

353 Catalogue number 1874.99.

354 BARBER, R., *The Holy Grail: Imagination and Belief*, Cambridge, 2004, p. 168.

355 HUYGENS, R.B.C., *Willemi Tyrensis Archiepiscopi Chronicon*, Turnholt, 1986.

356 ERASMI, S., *Interpretamentum Gemmarum*, Erfurti et Lipsiae, 1736.

357 Treasury Museum, Cattedrale di San Lorenzo.

358 News of this was published in the newspaper *El País*, 8 April 1985.

359 In 1564, the Emperor Ferdinand I himself stipulated that his property belonged not to a member of the dynasty, but rather to the House of Austria.

360 BRADFORD, E., *The Great Betrayal. Constantinople, 1204*, London, 1975.

More recently, on the same subject:

PHILLIPS, J., *The Fourth Crusade and the Sack of Constantinople*, New York, 2004.

361 The *Achatschale* can be found on display at the Kunsthistorisches Museum, Vienna.

Bibliography

AGUILAR, M.I., Rethinking the Judean Past: Questions of History and a Social Archaeology of Memory in the First Book of the Maccabees, *Biblical Theology Bulletin*, 30, No. 2 (2000).

AKRAM, A.I., *The Sword of Allah: Khalid bin al-Waleed – His Life and Campaigns*, Oxford, 2004.

AL-MAQQARI, Abu-l-Abbas, *Nafh al-Tib min gusn al-Andalus wal- ratib, wa dikr wisirahu Lisan al-Din ibn al-Jatib.* 10 books in 5 vols, El Cairo, 1959.

AL-MAQRIZI, *Itti`at al-Hunafa bi-l-ajbar al-Amirat al-Fatimiyyin al Jirafa*, vol. II, Cairo, 1973.

AL-MUQADDASI, M., *Ahsan at-Taqasim fi Ma`rifat il-Aqalim*, Leiden, 1906.

AL-SANTARINI, A. Y ABBAS, I., *Al-Dajira fi mahasin ahl ahl-Yazira*, Tunis, 1989.

APPLEBAUM, S., *Judaea in Hellenistic and Roman Times: Historical and Archaeological Essays*, Leiden, 1989.

ARCE, A. (ed. and trans.), *Itinerario de la Virgen Egeria (381-384)*, Madrid, 1996.

ARCO GARAY, R. del, *Sepulcros de la Casa Real de Castilla*, Madrid, 1954.

ARNOULD, C., Les arcs romains de Jérusalem. Architecture, décor et urbanisme, *Novum Testamentum et Orbis Antiquus*, 35 (1997), pp. 9–147.

L'espace urbain d'Aelia Capitolina (Jérusalem): Rupture ou continuité?, *Histoire urbaine* 2005/2 – No. 13 (2005), pp. 85–100.

AYÁN CALVO, J.J., *Didaché*, Madrid, 1992.

AZUAR RUIZ, R., *Denia islámica. Arqueología y poblamiento*, Alicante, 1989.

La Taifa de Denia en el comercio mediterráneo del siglo XI, *Anales de la Universidad de Alicante. Historia medieval*, No. 9 (1992–1993), pp. 39–52.

BAGATTI, B., *Excavations in Nazareth*, vol. I: *From the Beginning till the XII Century*, Jerusalem, 1969.

BANGO TORVISO, I. G. (Dir.), *Maravillas de la España medieval. Tesoro sagrado y monarquía. I. Estudios y Catálogo*, Valladolid, 2001.

BAR, D., Aelia Capitolina and the Location of the Camp of the Tenth Legion, *Palestine Exploration Quarterly*, 130 (1998), pp. 8–19.

BARAULT-BERCASTEL, A.H. de., *Historia de la Iglesia*, v. XIV, Valencia, 1831.

BARBER, R., *The Holy Grail: Imagination and Belief.*, Cambridge, 2004.

BARKAI, R., *El enemigo en el espejo. Cristianos y musulmanes en la España medieval*, Madrid, 2007.

BAUMGARTEN, J. M., *The Purification Rituals in DJD 7*, in DIMANT, D. and RAPPAPPORT, U., *The Dead Sea Scrolls: Forty Years of Research*, Leiden-Jerusalem, 2002, pp. 199–209.

THE VENERABLE BEDE, *Historia eclesiástica del pueblo de los anglos*, Madrid, 2013.

BELAYCHE, N., Dimmenticare . . . Gerusalemme. Les paganismes à Aelia Capitolina du IIe au IVe siècle de notre ère, *Revue des Etudes Juives*, 1 58/3–4 (1999), pp. 287–348.

BELTRÁN, A., *El Santo Cáliz de la Catedral de Valencia*, Valencia, 1960 (edition revised in 1980).

BERLÍN, A. M., Archaeological Sources for the History of Palestine: Between Large Forces: Palestine in the Hellenistic Period, *The Biblical Archaeologist*, 60, No.1 (1997), pp. 2–51.

BIRLEY, A., *Hadrian. The Restless Emperor*, London, 1997.

BISHKO, C. J., The Liturgical Context of Fernando I's Last Days According to the So-Called *Historia silense*, in *Hispania Sacra. Miscelánea en memoria de Dom Mario Férotin, 1915–1964*, XVII–XVIII (1965), p. 47–59.

BLANCO LOZANO, P., *Colección diplomática de Fernando I (1037–1065)*, León, 1987.

BLÁZQUEZ, J.M., *Adriano*, Barcelona, 2008.

BOLOIX GALLARDO, B., La taifa de Toledo en el siglo XI: aproximación a sus límites y extensión territorial, *Tulaytula: Revista de la Asociación de Amigos del Toledo Islámico*, 8 (2001), pp. 23–57.

BORG, M., The Currency of the Term 'Zealot', *Journal of Theological Studies*, 22 (1973), pp. 504–512.

BOSCH VILÁ, J., *Historia de Sevilla. La Sevilla islámica 712–1248.*, Seville, 1984.

BRADFORD, E., *The Great Betrayal. Constantinople,* 1204, London, 1975.

BRANDON, S.G.F., *Jesus and the Zealots: A Study of the Political Factor in Primitive Christianity*, Manchester, 1967.

CAHEN, C., *El Islam. Desde los orígenes hasta el comienzo del Impero Otomano*, Madrid, 2002.

CALDWELL, S.H., Queen Sancha's 'Persuasion': A Regenerated León Symbolized in San Isidoro's Pantheon and its Treasures, in S. D. ROSS, *The Gift of Self: Shattering Emptiness, Betrayal,*Binghamton, 2000, p. 1–48.

CARRIEDO TEJEDO, M., Una reina sin corona en 959–976. La infant Elvira, hija de Ramiro II, *Tierras de León*, XLIX–113 (2001), pp. 118–137.

CASSIUS DIO, *Historia romana. Obra completa*, Madrid, 2004.

CASTIGNOLI, P., *Piacenza e i pellegrinaggi lungo la Via Francigena*, Piacenza, 1999.

CERRADA JIMÉNEZ, A.I., *Tres generaciones de mujeres en el poder: Urraca de Zamora, Urraca de Castilla, Teresa de Portugal y doña Sancha,* en SEGURA GRAIÑO, C. and CERRADA JIMÉNEZ, A.I. (ed.), *Las mujeres y el poder: representaciones prácticas de vida,* Madrid, 2000, pp. 99–106.

CHARLESWORTH, J., *Jesus within Judaism: New Light from Exciting Archaeological Excavation,* New York, 1988.

CORRAL, J.L., *Historia de Zaragoza. Zaragoza musulmana (714–1118),* Zaragoza, 1998.

CORTESE, D. and CALDERINI, S., *Women and the Fatimids in de World of Islam,* Edinburgh, 2006.

D'ABADAL, R. and GALTIER MARTÍ, F., *El condado independiente de Ribagorza,* Zaragoza, 1981.

DASXURANCI, M., *The History of the Caucasian Albanians,* II, 51, London, 1961.

DONNER, H., Die Palästinabeschreibung des epiphanius monachus hagiopolita, *Zeitschrift des Deutschen Palästina-Vereins,* 87 (1971), pp. 45-92.

DRAPER, J., Ritual Process and Ritual Symbol in Didache 7-10, *Vigiliae Christianae,* 54, nº 2 (2000), pp. 121-158.

ELIAV, Y. Z., The Urban Layout of Aelia Capitolina: A New View from the Perspective of the Temple Mount, in P. SCHAER, *The Bar Kokhba War Reconsidered,* Tübingen, 2003.

ERASMI, S., *Interpretamentum gemmarum, erfurti et lipsiae,* 1736.

ESCHENBACH, W. von, *Parzival,* Madrid, 1999.

ESHEL, H., The Date of the Founding of Aelia Capitolina. *The Dead Sea Scrolls, Fifty Years after Their Discovery,* Jerusalem, 2000, pp. 637–643.

ESPARCIANO, E., Vida de Adriano, in *Biógrafos y panegiristas latinos,* Madrid, 1969.

EUSEBIUS OF CAESAREA, *Historia eclesiástica,* Madrid, 2001.

FALQUE, E., *Lucas Tudensis, chronicon mundi, Corpus Christianorum continuatio mediaevalis LXXIV,* Turnhout, 2003.

FERNÁNDEZ DEL POZO, J.M., *Alfonso V (999–1028) y*

Vermudo III (1028–1037), Burgos, 1999.

FERNÁNDEZ LADREDA, C. and REDÓN HUICI, F., *La arqueta de Leyre y otras esculturas medievales de Navarra,* Pamplona, 1983.

FINNEGAN, J., *The Archeology of the New Testament,* Princeton, 1978.

FLAVIUS JOSEPHUS, *Antiquities of the Jews.*

FRANCO MATA, Á., El tesoro de San Isidoro y la monarquía leonesa, *Boletín del Museo Arqueológico Nacional,* No. IX (1991), pp. 35-67.

GALVÁN FREILE, F. and TORRES SEVILLA, M., La condesa doña Sancha. Una nueva aproximación a su figura, *Medievalismo,* 5 (1995), pp. 9–29.

GAMBRA GUTIÉRREZ, A. *Alfonso VI, cancillería, curia e imperio,* 2 vols., León, 1997 and 1998.

GARCÍA GIMÉNEZ, R. and VALDÉS FERNÁNDEZ, F., Acerca del origen y de la cronología de los cristales de roca llamados fatimíes: el vidrio de Badajoz y la botella de Astorga *CuPAUAM,* 23 (1996), pp. 260–276.

GEVA, H., Jerusalem. The Roman Period. *The New Encyclopedia of Archaeological Excavations in the Holy Land,* II, Jerusalem, 1993, pp. 758–767.

GEYER, P., Antonini Placentini itinerarium, in *Itineraria et alia geographica,* Turnhout, 1965, pp. 127–174.

GIBSON, S. and TAYLOR, J.E., *Beneath the Church of the Holy Sepulchre: The Archaeology and Early History of the Traditional Golgotha,* London, 1994.

GIGANTE, M. (ed.), *Sophronius Anacreontica,* Rome, 1957.

GIL, M., *A History of Palestine, 634–1099,* Cambridge, 1997.

GOODMAN, M., *The Ruling Class of Judea: the Origins of the Jewish Revolt against Rome, A. D. 66–70,* Cambridge, 1987.

GRANDA, Fr T. de and MANZANO, J., *Vida de San Isidro, arzobispo de Sevilla,* Salamanca, 1732.

GRANT, M., *The Jews in the Roman World*, New York, 1998.

GRIFFIN, J., *The Holy Grail: The Legend, the History, the Evidence*, Jefferson, 2001.

HAYWARD, R. C.T., *Targums and the Transmission of Scripture into Judaism and Christianity*, Leiden, 2010.

HENGEL, M., *The Zealots: Investigations into the Jewish Freedom Movement in the Period from Herod I until 70 A. D.*, London, 2010.

HENRIET, P., Deo votas. L'Infantado et la fonction des infantes dans la Castille et le León des Xe–XIIe siècles, in HENRIET, P.; LEGRAS, A.M. (ed.), *Au cloître et dans le monde: Femmes, hommes et sociétés (IXe–XVe siècles), Mélanges en l'honneur de Paulette L'Hermite-Leclercq* (Cultures et Civilisations médiévales No. 23), Paris, 2000, pp. 189-203.

HERBERT, S., *Tel Anafa I. Final Report on Ten Years of Excavation at a Hellenistic and Roman Settlement in Northern Israel*, Ann Arbor, 1994.

HESSE, B. and WAPNISH, P., Can Pig Remains Be Used for Ethnic Diagnosis in the Ancient Near East?, in SILBERMAN, N. A. and SMALL, D. (eds), *The Archaeology of Israel: Constructing the Past, Interpreting the Present*, Sheffield, 1997, pp. 238–270.

HOEHNER, H. W., *Herod Antipas: A Contemporary of Jesus Christ*, Cambridge, 1980.

HOLDER, M., *History of the Jewish People*, New York, 2000.

HORSLEY, R. A., *Archaeology, History and Society in Galilee: The Social Context of Jesus and the Rabbis*, Valley Forge, 1996.

HORSLEY, R. and HANSON, J., *Bandits, Prophets and Messiahs: Popular Movements in the Time of Jesus*, Minneapolis, 1985.

HOWARD, L., ROSENTHAL, M., *The Feasts of the Lord God's Prophetic Calendar from Calvary to the Kingdom*, Nashville, 1997.

HOYLAND, R., *Seeing Islam as Others Saw It*, Princeton, 1996.

HUYGENS, R.B.C., *Willemi Tyrensis Archiepiscopi Chronicon*, Turnholt, 1986.

IBÁÑEZ IBÁÑEZ, J. and MENDOZA RUIZ, F., *Melitón de*

Sardes. Homilía sobre la Pascua. Pamplona, 1975, pp. 204–207.

IBN AL QALANISI, *Dhail* or *Mudhayyal Ta'rikh Dimashq,* Damascus, 1983.

IBN BASSAM AL-SANTARINI, *Al-Dajira fi Mazzini ahl al-yazira,* 8 vols, Tripoli, 1989.

ISRAELI, Y., *Ancient Glass in the Israel Museum: The Eliahu Dobkin Collection and Other Gifts,* Jerusalem, 2003.

Itinera Hierosolymitana et descriptiones. Terrae Sanctae, Geneva, 1879.

JANDORA, J. W., Developments in Islamic Warfare: The Early Conquests, *Studia Islamica,* 64 (1986), pp. 101–113.

JOHNSON, M.P., *World English Bible,* 2014.

KAHLE, P., Die schätze der fatimiden, *Zeitschrift der deutschen morgenländische Gesellschaft,* 89 (1935), pp. 32–362.

KATZ, S.T. (ed.), *The Cambridge History of Judaism. The Late Roman-Rabbinic Period,* vol. 4, Cambridge, 2006.

KEPPIE, L., Legiones Britanniae. Legiones II Augusta, VI Victrix, IX Hispana, XX Valeria Victrix, in WOLFF, C. and LE BOHEC, Y., *Les légions de Rome sous le Haut-Empire,* Lyon, 2000, pp. 25–37.

KINDLER, A., Was Aelia Capitolina Founded Before or After the Outbreak of the Bar Kokhba War? A Numismatic Evidence, *Israel Numismatic Journal,* 14 (2000–2002), pp. 176–179.

KNOBLET, J., *Herod the Great,* Lanham, 2005.

LANGE, N. de, *El Judaísmo,* Madrid, 2006.

LAPEÑA PAÚL, A. I., *El monasterio de San Juan de la Peña en la Edad Media (desde sus orígenes hasta 1410),* Zaragoza, 1989.

LAPP, P., *Palestinian Ceramic Chronology, 200 B.C.–A.D. 70,* New Haven, 1961.

LASKO, P., *Arte sacro 800–1200,* Madrid, 1999.

Le Trésor de Saint-Denis (catálogo), Paris, 1991.

LEVINE, L.I., *Judaism and Hellenism in Antiquity: Conflict or Confluence,* Massachusetts, 1998.

LLORCA VIVES, C.B., *Historia de la Iglesia católica. I: Edad Antigua: la Iglesia en el mundo grecorromano*, Madrid, 1990.

LOCK, H. O., *The Conquerors of Palestine through Forty Centuries*, New York, 2010.

LOFFREDA, S., *La Ceramica di Macheronte e dell' Herodion (90 a.C.– 135 d. C)*, Jerusalem, 1996.

LOFFREDA, S., *Holy Land Pottery at the time of Jesus. Early Roman Period 63 B.C.–70 A.D.*, Jerusalem, 2003.

LUCAS DE TUY, *Crónica de España*, Madrid, 1926.

MAGEN, Y., Jerusalem as a Center of the Stone Vessel Industry During the Second Temple Period, en GEVA, H. (ed.), *Ancient Jerusalem Revealed*, Jerusalem, 1994, pp. 244–256.

MAIER, J., *Storia del Giudaismo nell antichità*, Brescia, 1992.

MARTIN, G., Le testament d Elvire. (Tábara, 1099), *e-Spania, Revue interdisciplinaire d'études hispaniques médiévales et modernes*, 5 (2008).

MARTIN, G., La Historia Legionensis (llamada Silensis) como memoria identitaria de un reino y como autobiografía, *e-Spania, Revue interdisciplinaire d'études hispaniques médiévales et modernes*, 14 (2012), pp. 1–22.

MARTIN, T., Hacia una clarificación del infantazgo en tiempos de la reina Urraca y su hija la infanta Sancha (ca. 1107–1159, *e-Spania. Revue interdisciplinaire d'études hispaniques médiévales et modernes*, 5 (2008).

MARTÍN ANSÓN, M.L., La artesanía, La cultura del románico, siglos XI al XIII. Letras. Religiosidad. Artes. Ciencia y vida, *Historia de España de Menéndez Pidal, XI*, Madrid: 1995, pp. 453–490.

MARTÍN DUQUE, Á., Definición de espacios y fronteras en los reinos de Asturias-León y Pamplona hasta el siglo XI, *Los espacios de poder en la España Medieval. XII Semana de Estudios Medievales de Nájera*, Logroño, 2002, pp. 315–339.

MARTÍN DUQUE, Á., *Sancho III el Mayor de Pamplona. El rey*

y su reino (1004–1035), Pamplona, 2007.

MARTÍN LLORIS, C., *Las reliquias de la Capilla Real en la Corona de Aragón y el Santo Cáliz de la Catedral de Valencia (1396–1458)*, Valencia, 2010.

MARTINET, S., Elinand, évêque de Laon méconnu (1052–1098), *Fédération des Sociétés d'Histoire et d'Archéologie de L'Aisne. Mémoires*, vol. XXXVI, Saint-Quentin, 1991.

MARTOS QUESADA, J., Los reinos de Taifas en el siglo XI, in CARRASCO, A.I., MARTOS, J. and SOUTO, J.A., *Al-Andalus*, Madrid, 2009, pp. 147–272.

MEEHAN, D. (ed. and trans.), *Adomnan's De locis sanctis*, Dublin, 1983.

MENÉNDEZ PIDAL, R., *La España del Cid*, vol. 1, (repr.), Madrid, 1969.

MESHORER, Y., *The Coinage of Aelia Capitolina*, Jerusalem, 1989.

MÍNGUEZ FERNÁNDEZ, J.M., *Alfonso VI: poder, expansión y reorganización interior*, Hondarribia, 2000.

MITRE, E., *Ortodoxia y herejía: Entre la Antigüedad y el Medievo*, Madrid, 2003.

MOLINA GÓMEZ, J.A., Las coronas de donación regia del tesoro de Guarrazar: la religiosidad de la monarquía visigoda y el uso de modelos bizantinos, *Sacralidad y Arqueología, Antig. Crist.*, XXI (2004), pp. 459–472.

MONTES PERAL, L.Á., *Tras las huellas de Jesús: seguimiento y discipulado en Jesús, los Evangelios y el 'Evangelio de dichos Q'*, Madrid, 2006.

MORALES, A. DE, *Viage de Ambrosio de Morales por orden del rey Phelippe II a los Reynos de León y Galicia y principado de Asturias para reconocer las reliquias de santos, sepulcros reales y libros manuscritos de las cathedrales y monasterios*, Madrid, 1765.

MORERI, L., *El gran diccionario histórico o miscelánea curiosa de la historia sagrada y profana*, vol. V, Paris, 1753.

MORGAN, G., *Nanteos. A Welsh House and Its Families*, Gwasg Gomer, 2001.

MORILLO CERDÁN, Á. and GARCÍA MARCOS, V., Nuevos testimonios acerca de las legiones VI Victrix y X Gemina en la region septentrional de la Península Ibérica, in WOLFF, C. and LE BOHEC, Y., *Les légions de Rome sous le Haut-Empire*, Lyon, 2000, pp. 589–607.

MURPHY O'CONNOR, J., *The Holy Land, An Oxford Archaeological Guide from Earliest Times to 1700*, Oxford, 1998.

NAVARRO ESPINACH, G., Las Cofradías de la Vera Cruz y de la Sangre de Cristo en la Corona de Aragón (siglos XIV–XVI), *Anuario de Estudios Medievales*, 36/2 (2006), pp. 583–611.

NETZER, E., *The Architecture of Herod, the Great Builder*, Tübingen, 2006.

NEWMAN, H. and LUDLAM, R.M., *Proximity to Power and Jewish Sectarian Groups of the Ancient Period: a Review of Lifestyle, Value and Halakhah in the Pharisees, Sadducees, Essenes and Qumran*, Leiden, 2006.

NICOLLE, D., *Yarmuk 636 A.D.: The Muslim Conquest of Syria*, Oxford, 1994.

The Great Islamic Conquests AD 632–750, Oxford, 2009.

NÚÑEZ CONTRERAS, L., Colección diplomática de Vermudo III, rey de León, *Historia, instituciones, documentos*, 4 (1977), pp. 381–514.

ORR, J., *Les oeuvres de Guiot de Provins, poète lyrique et satirique*, Manchester: University Press, 1915.

PALAO VICENTE, J.J., *Legio VII Gemina (Pia) Felix. Estudio de una legión romana*, Salamanca, 2006.

PALMER, A., *The Seventh Century in the West-Syrian Chronicles*, Liverpool, 1993.

PANOFSKY, E., *Abbot Suger on the Abbey Church of Saint-Denis and Its Art Treasures*, Princeton, 1979.

PAUL, A., Las Biblias Arameas: los Tárgumes, *Inter-testamento*:

26–33, Estella, 1983.

PÉREZ DE URBEL, J. and GONZÁLEZ RUIZ ZORRILLA, A. (trans. and ed.), *Historia silense,* Madrid, 1959.

PÉREZ GONZÁLEZ, M. (trans.), *Crónica del Emperador Alfonso VII,* León, 1997.

PETRIE, W. M. F., *Koptos,* London, 1896.

PHILIPPS, G., *The Chalice of Magdalene. The Search for the Cup that Held the Blood of Christ,* Rochester, 1995.

PHILIPPS, J., *The Fourth Crusade and the Sack of Constantinople,* New York, 2004.

PLINY THE ELDER, *Historia Natural,* Madrid, 2007.

PRINGLE, D., *The Churches of the Crusader Kingdom of Jerusalem:* vol. 3, *The City of Jerusalem,* Cambridge, 2007.

PROCOPII CAESARIENSIS, *De aedificiis Dn. Iustiniani. Liber III, Corpus Scriptorum Historiae Byzantinae* (ed. B.G. Niebuhrii C.F.), vol. II, part III, Bonn, 1838.

REAL, E., Perceval de Chrétien de Troyes. El nacimiento de un mito, in RAPOSO FERNÁNDEZ, B. (ed.) and ANDRESEN, K., FERRER MORA, H., GUTIÉRREZ KOSTER, I. and KASPER, F. (eds.), *Parzival. Reescritura y transformación,* Valencia, 2000, pp. 11–34.

REED, J.L., *Archaeology and the Galilean Jesus. A Re-examination of the Evidence,* Harrisburg, 2000.

REICH, R., Archaeological Evidence of the Jewish Population at Hasmonean Gezer, *I.E.J.* No. 31 (1981), pp. 48–52.

REILLY, B.F., The Chancery of Alfonso VII of León-Castilla: The Period 1116–1135 Reconsidered, *Speculum,* 51-2 (1976), pp. 243–261.

RESINA, J. R., *La búsqueda del Grial,* Barcelona, 1988

RICHARDSON, P., *Herod: King of the Jews and Friend of the Romans,* Edinburgh, 1999.

RIGHETTI, M., *Manual de Historia Litúrgica,* vol. I, Madrid, 1955.

RIUS-CAMPS, J., *De Jerusalén a Antioquía. Génesis de la Iglesia Cristiana. Comentario lingüístico y exegético a Hch* 1-12, Córdoba, 1989.

ROCCA, S., *Herod's Judaea: A Mediterranean State in the Classical World*, Tübingen, 2008.

RODRÍGUEZ FERNÁNDEZ, J., *Ramiro II, rey de León,* Burgos, 1998.

RODRÍGUEZ GONZÁLEZ, J.J., *Historia de las legiones romanas* (2 vols), Madrid, 2003.

ROITMAN, A. (ed.), *A Day at Qumran. The Dead Sea Sect and Its Scrolls,* Shrine of the Book, 1997.

RONART, S. and RONART, N., Maqrizi, in *Concise Encyclopaedia of Arabic Civilisation. The Arab East,* New York, 1985.

RUBIERA MATA, M.J., *La Taifa de Denia,* Alicante, 1985.

SAFRAI, S. and STERN, M. (eds). *The Jewish People in the First Century,* 2 vols, Assen, 1974–1976).

SAFRAI, Z., The Roman Army in the Galilee, in LEVINE, L.I. (ed.), *The Galilee in Late Antiquity,* New York, 1992, pp. 103–114.

SALAZAR ACHA, J., Una hija desconocida de Sancho el Mayor reina de León, *Primer Congreso General de Historia de Navarra,* vol. 2. *Comunicaciones,* Pamplona, 1988, pp. 183–192.

SALES I ALCALÁ, A., *Dissertacion histórica, critica i expositiva del Sagrado Caliz en que Christo Señor Nuestro consagró en la noche de la Cena, el cual se venera en la Santa Metropolitana Iglesia de Valencia,* Valencia, 1736.

SÁNCHEZ CANDEIRA, A., *Castilla y León en el siglo XI: estudio del Reinado de Fernando I,* Madrid, 1999.

SANDERS, E.P., *Judaism: Practice and Belief 63 B.C.E.–66 C.E.,* Philadelphia, 1992.

SCHÄFER, P., *The Bar Kokhba War Reconsidered: New Perspectives on the Second Jewish Revolt Against Rome,* Mohr Siebeck, 2003.

SCHICK, R., *The Christian Communities of Palestine from*

Byzantine to Islamic Rule. A Historical and Archaeological Study, Princeton, 1995.

SCHOFF, W.H. (trans. and ed.), *The Periplus of the Erythraean Sea: Travel and Trade in the Indian Ocean by a Merchant of the First Century,* London, Bombay & Calcutta, 1912.

SCHÜRER, E., *Historia del pueblo judío en tiempos de Jesús,* vol. II. *Instituciones políticas y religiosas,* Madrid, 1985.

SEAGER, R., *Pompey the Great: A Political Biography,* Oxford, 2002.

SÉNAC, P., *La frontière et les hommes, VIIIe–XIIe siècle: le peuplement musulman au nord de l'Èbre et les débuts de la reconquête aragonaise,* Paris, 2000.

STEGEMANN, H., *Los esenios, Qumram, Juan el Bautista y Jesús,* Madrid, 1996.

STERN, M., Judaea and her Neighbors in the Days of Alexander Jannaeus, in LEVINE, L., *The Jerusalem Cathedra* 1, Jerusalem, 1981, pp. 22–46.

STORME, A., L'Église de la Circoncision d'après les fouilles et les études récentes, *Australian Journal of Biblical Archaeology* (available at *http://www.biblicalarchaeology.org.uk*).

TEUBNER, B.G. (ed.), *Itinerarium Burdigalense,* Stuttgart, 1990.

THEODORET DE CYR, *Histoire ecclésiastique,* 2 vols, Paris, 2006 and 2009.

TORRES SEVILLA, M., Una intervención leonesa en el Califato de Córdoba. A propósito de la identificación del conde Ibn Mama Duna al-Qumis, *Estudios Humanísticos,* 18 (1996), pp. 239–249.

Cruzados y peregrinos leoneses y castellanos en Tierra Santa (ss. XI–XII), *Medievalismo,* 9 (1999), pp. 63–82.

La monarquía leonesa, en *La Historia de León,* vol. II,. *Edad Media,* León, 1999, pp. 105–137.

Los aliados cristianos de Almanzor: las redes familiares como base del sistema clientelar amirí, *Cuando las horas primeras. En el milenario de la batalla de Calatañazor. Colección 'Monografías*

Universitarias', 13 (2004), pp. 89–114.

TURK, A., *El Reino de Zaragoza en el siglo XI de Cristo (V de la Hégira)*, Madrid, 1978.

VALLEJO GIRVÉS, M., Miedo bizantino: las conquistas de Jerusalén y la llegada del Islam, in *Milenio: Miedo y religión. IV Simposio Internacional de la SECR, Sociedad Española de Ciencias de las Religiones*, La Laguna, 3–6 de febrero de 2000 (consulta online: www.ull.es/congresos/conmirel/VALLEJO. htm).

VÁZQUEZ ATOCHERO, A., *Badajoz árabe, el reino aftasí*, Badajoz, 2004.

VERDIER, P., The Chalice of Abbot Suger, *Studies in the History of Art*, 24 (1990), pp. 9–29.

VERMEER, G.F.M., *Observations sur le vocabulaire du pèlerinage chez Egérie et chez Antonin de Plaisesance*, Nijmegen, 1965.

VIGUERA MOLINS, M.J., *Los Reinos de Taifas y las invasiones magrebíes (Al-Andalus del XI al XIII)*, Madrid, 1992.

VIÑAYO GONZÁLEZ, A., La llegada de San Isidoro a León, *Archivos Leoneses*, 17 (1963), pp. 65–112, and 18, (1964), pp. 303–343.

La Real Colegiata de San Isidoro de León, León, 1971.

L'Ancien royaume de León roman, Paris, 1972.

Reinas e Infantas de León, abadesas y monjas del monasterio de San Pelayo y de San Isidoro, *Semana de historia del monacato cántabro-Astur-leonés*, Oviedo, 1982, pp. 123–135.

Fernando I, el Magno (1035–1065), Burgos, 1999.

VINCENT, H. and ABEL, F.M., *Jérusalem. Recherches de topographie, d'archéologie et d'histoire. II. Jérusalem nouvelle*, Paris, 1914.

Vita Lietberti Episcopi cameracensis auctore Radulfo Monacho S. Sepulchri Cameracensis., Hannover, 1934.

WALLACE, P.F., O'FLOINN, R. (eds), *Treasures of the National Museum of Ireland: Irish Antiquities*, Dublin, 2002.

WALTER, E., *Byzantium and the Early Islamic Conquests*, Cambridge, 1995.

WASSERSTEIN, D.J., *The emergence of Taifa Kingdom of Toledo, Al-qantara*, 21 *Fasc.* 1 (2000), pp. 17–56.

WEITZMAN, S., Forced Circumcision and the Shifting Role of Gentiles in Hasmonean Ideology, *The Harvard Ideological Review*, XCII, 1 (1999), pp. 37–59.

WILKINSON, J., *Jerusalem Pilgrims before the Crusades*, Oxford, 2002.

WRIGHT, B., Jewish Ritual Baths —Interpreting the Digs and the Texts: Some Issues in the Social History of Second Temple Judaism, in SILBERMAN, N.A. and SMALL, D., *The Archaeology of Israel: Constructing the Past, Interpreting the Present*, Sheffield, 1997, pp. 190–214.

YADIN, Y., BALLESTEROS GAIBROIS, M. and TORRE, V. DE LA, *Masada: la fortaleza de Herodes y el último bastión de los zelotes*, Madrid, 1992.

YARZA, J., *Arte y arquitectura en España 500–1250*, Madrid, 1979.

Picture Acknowledgements

King Arthur battles the Saxons
(from the *Rochefoucauld Grail*):

Photo by Fine Art
Images/Heritage Images/
Getty Images

All maps, city plans and floor
plans:

Reino de Cordelia
(maps and family trees
in English translation
adapted by David
Woodroffe)

Reconstruction of the entrance to
the Basilica of the Holy Sepulchre:
Ortega/Torres

The Holy Sepulchre complex
according to Arculf and Adomnan:
Ortega/Torres

Reconstruction of the Courtyard
of the Rotunda:
Ortega/Torres

Coin and Fatimid dynasty:
Reino de Cordelia

Leonese monarchy family tree:
Reino de Cordelia

Royal Vaults of San Isidoro:
Ortega/Torres

Last Supper painting:
Ortega/Torres

Christ Pantocrator:
Ortega/Torres

Crucifixion of the Lord:
Ortega/Torres

View of the upper cup of the
Chalice of Doña Urraca:
Ortega/Torres

Otto III's Crown:	Ortega/Torres
Detail of the Chalice of Doña Urraca:	Ortega/Torres
Qumran pottery:	Ortega/Torres
Drawing of Roman pottery - Ritterling Hofheim Form 8:	Ortega/Torres
Drawing of the Chalice of Doña Urraca:	Esperanza Martín
Roman agate cup:	Paul Getty Museum (Digital image courtesy of Getty's Open Content Program)
Agate cup:	Crescent Gallery, Tokyo
Nielloed silver casket:	Ortega/Torres
Cleric Jacinto (Hyacinth) parchment:	Ortega/Torres/León Cathedral archive
Casket of Sadaqa:	Ortega/Torres
The Chalice of Doña Urraca:	Ortega/Torres
Detail and upper view of the Chalice of Doña Urraca:	Ortega/Torres
Parchments:	Ortega/Torres

Index

A

H